DIVIDED THEY FELL

THE DEMISE OF THE DEMOCRATIC PARTY, 1964–1996

RONALD RADOSH

THE FREE PRESS

New York   London   Toronto   Sydney   Singapore

THE FREE PRESS
A Division of Simon & Schuster Inc.
1230 Avenue of the Americas
New York, NY 10020

Manufactured in the United States of America

10 9 8 7 6 5 4 3 2 1

Library of Congress Cataloging-in-Publication Data

Radosh, Ronald.
    Divided they fell : the demise of the Democratic Party, 1964–1996
/ Ronald Radosh.
        p.   cm.
    Includes bibliographical references and index.
    ISBN 0-684-82810-3
    1. Democratic Party (U.S.)   2. United States—Politics and
government—1945–1989.   3. United States—Politics and
government—1989–   I. Title.
JK2316.R327   1996
324.2736—dc20   96–18047
                                                                      CIP

For my wife, Allis, and in memory of my mother, Ida Radosh

CONTENTS

Introduction   ix

1. Atlantic City 1964: The First Fault Line in the
   New Deal Coalition   1

2. The New Politics Convention   27

3. Vietnam: The Great Wedge   51

4. McCarthy and the Quixotic Campaign   75

5. The Chicago Convention: The New Left Strikes Back   107

6. McGovernism and the Captured Party   133

7. The Wilderness Years: From Carter to Reagan-Bush   183

8. The Clinton Contradiction: The Campaign
   and the Presidency   211

References   241
Bibliography   269
Acknowledgments   277
Index   281

INTRODUCTION

As I write, Bill Clinton is gearing up for the 1996 campaign. He may or may not be reelected; I would not presume to say he can't win. The electorate is particularly volatile, and demagoguery and cynicism on the part of both major political parties is likely to make many voters believe that aspects of the Republican Revolution, as it has been called, are dangerous and unwarranted. It is not hard, after all, to scare many Americans into believing that cutbacks in existing social programs means that their grandmother might end up on the street.

Nonetheless, it is my contention that Bill Clinton's party, the Democratic Party, which for most of the 20th Century was defined by Franklin D. Roosevelt and the New Deal liberal-labor coalition, is finished. That coalition dominated American political life from the late 1930s through the 1950s. It reflected the unity behind the national Democratic Party of Northern liberals, the labor movement, and white Southern Democrats who, although they consistently opposed civil rights for black Americans, supported the national economic programs of the New Deal era. It was the strength of that liberal-labor coalition, in particular, that gave FDR his landslide victory in 1936 and that kept Harry S Truman in the White House in 1948.

There have been many efforts to resurrect this coalition, especially as the nation moved toward the Right and liberals saw the social programs of the 1930s fade into oblivion and unpopularity. But as well-meaning as these efforts are, the economic and social basis for that coalition no longer exists. One result, as I show in this book, is the steady erosion of the Democratic Party's political base, and its change from a majority to a minority party. It is time, therefore, for a political history of the Democratic Party's fall from grace; one that reveals and explains the reasons for its slow decline.

The focus of this book is on the events of those critical years in America from 1968 through 1972, when the war in Vietnam and the counterculture began to change the face of the nation, and when the domestic discord and division were bound to have political implications. It was during those years that the Democratic Party began its leftward shift, and when those who hoped for major social and economic change worked to have the Democrats respond to new interest groups, those which composed the "New Politics" movement that soon dominated the ranks of Democratic Party activists. As a result, the old Democratic Party ceased to exist. The Left, which at first boycotted working with the Democratic Party, moved *en masse* into its ranks. They essentially took it over, and as one young historian has accurately written, "dismantled its traditional hierarchy, disenfranchised professional politicians, and turned the party apparatus over to young parvenus."[1]

Not only did the party adopt the mantle of the antiwar move-

Introduction

ment, the social programs it advocated identified the party with the rise of crime, the influence of drugs, the decline in moral standards, and the breakup of the traditional family structure. The Democrats, after all, could have adopted a socially conservative position. But after 1968, the Democrats stood in the public's eye for a new kind of liberalism, one that spelled permissiveness and moral nihilism, and that ignored and ridiculed the conservative desires of white ethnic working-class Americans who once voted Democratic as a matter of ritual. Once the Democrats were seen as supportive of both exotic lifestyles and revolutionary rhetoric, it was only a matter of time before former working-class Democrats would be driven straight into the waiting arms of conservative Republicans.

This writer is in agreement with the judgment of Thomas B. Edsall and Mary D. Edsall, who have written:

> Vietnam and the antiwar protests were essential to the decline of support for the then dominant wing of the Democratic party, a wing controlled by the old guard of organized labor, the last of the urban machine leaders, and by such political figures as Vice President Hubert H. Humphrey and the Democratic Senator Henry Jackson of Washington. It was, however, the fusion of *race* with an expanding rights revolution and with the new liberal agenda, and the fusion, in turn, of race and rights with the public perception of the Democratic party, and the fusion of the Democratic Party with the issues of high taxes and a coercive, redistributive government, that created the central force splintering the presidential coalition behind the Democratic party throughout the next two decades, long after Vietnam and the counterculture had faded into the background.[2]

What I attempt to show in this book is precisely how this pattern took place. The narrative begins with the yet untold story of the 1964 Democratic Party convention, in which as a result of the fight over seating of the Mississippi Freedom Democrats many Democrats began to assert that no progress could be made unless white liberals subordinated themselves to the agenda of black radicals. This attitude, not quite open at first, came to a head with the New Politics Convention in 1967, in which many Democrats sympathetic to the antiwar cause abandoned all reason, and thoroughly supporting the program of extremist black radicals, decided to leave the ranks of the Democratic Party altogether.

Their departure would, much to the eventual dismay of old-line Democrats, be rather short-lived. With the escalation of the war in Vietnam, the New Politics groups soon saw activity within the Democratic Party as the best chance for achieving political success. A group of antiwar Democrats contended for supremacy and sought the party's nomination in 1968. They worked hard for either Eugene McCarthy or Robert Kennedy. Their quest to gain their party's nomination failed. But as a result, their efforts spelled the final rupture of the labor-liberal coalition, whose trade union component tended to support the war and favored support of the national party's old liberal policies. When Hubert Humphrey had finally won the position he sought for years, the antiwar group turned against him with a vengeance, and seeking to teach the old Democratic establishment a lesson, in effect guaranteed the election of Richard M. Nixon.

With the 1972 campaign, and the eventual leadership of the Democratic Party falling into the hands of George McGovern, the triumph of the New Politics group was apparent. George McGovern did more to harm the future interests of his party than simply create an impression that it was soft on defense. Under his helm, the Democrats began to actively seek major support from new constituency groups they defined as oppressed: women, blacks, Hispanics, young people, and gays. The new rules for the party developed by the commission chaired by McGovern identified ethnic and racial groups with ideas and ideologies, and thought by their actions they were opening up and broadening the base of the party. What they did, instead, was to diminish its breadth and give more power to extremely liberal activists who were unrepresentative of the party's membership at large. It is here that the "social issues," so central to the 1980s and 1990s, first came into play. As McGovern fought a bitter contest for the nomination with his arch rival, Senator Henry "Scoop" Jackson of Washington, the two poles of the Democratic Party were starkly revealed for the first time. The defeat of Scoop Jackson showed that the Center had eroded, and that the social and economic policies of the party's left wing were now the accepted doctrine of the Democratic leadership.

The story ends with the trajectory of the Democratic Party from the wilderness of the Reagan-Bush years to the return to power of the Democrats with Bill Clinton's election in 1992. Clinton had a chance to create a new and restored Democratic Party, one that returned to the traditions of its old mainstream days and chartered policies that would guide the nation into the new realities of the postindustrial and post–Cold War world. Although he ran a campaign that touched on the themes most people had long forgotten that Democrats could espouse, by the time he was elected, Clinton acted like most of the left-liberal activists in his party. Always considerate of the need to keep the support of core constituency groups, as well as the liberal Congressional Democrats, Clinton found himself bending to their agenda, perhaps against his own instinctive centrism.

As one who remains a registered Democrat, albeit one who is on the center-right of that party, I am saddened by my own story. But by reflecting on events, and what caused us to move to where we are, we can hopefully be guided more wisely in the future. Whether it is too late for the Democrats is up to readers to decide.

1

ATLANTIC CITY 1964

The First Fault Line in the New Deal Coalition

Americans of the 1990s, unless they have long memories and direct experiences of the battleground of the civil rights movement, cannot remember what the Deep South, particularly Mississippi, was like for blacks in the early postwar epoch. The region was completely segregated, and black citizens lived in a virtual state of terror, wary that the slightest infraction could lead to loss of livelihood, and perhaps even one's life. A white Mississippi historian, who taught at the state's university, had categorized it as a "closed society."

The Democratic Party there mirrored its political reality. The regular Democratic organization controlled the legislative, executive, and judicial branches of government. All the forty-nine state senators, and all but one of the one-hundred twenty-two congressmen were Democrats. And the state legislature regularly enforced segregation and discrimination against its black population. The Negro vote was highly restricted; conventions were held in segregated facilities, and the party was devoted to what the Freedom Democrats called "racism and suppression and oppression of minority expressions."[1] It is here, in Mississippi, that our story begins, for it was the civil rights movement that launched the Democratic Party on a trajectory that ended in disaster. From a much-needed end to Jim Crow exclusions which had created a whites-only party in the Southern states, Democrats would move on to a disastrous overreaction and takeover by guilty white liberals and race-conscious black militants. From an understandable opposition to the Vietnam War, to an embrace of the enemy, the Democratic Party's story as told in these pages is a tragedy of overreaching. The intentions of the early generation of activists were noble, their cause—especially that of civil rights—was necessary and just. But the momentum of the struggle would lead them to extreme positions, and within a few decades, remove them from the mainstream concerns of Americans that they once reflected.

Missisippi, as *Washington Post* journalist Juan Williams so graphically put it, "led the nation in beatings, lynching, and mysterious disappearances. Only 5 percent of black Mississippians [who made up 45 percent of the state's population] were registered to vote, the lowest rate in the United States. With majorities in many counties, blacks might well have controlled local politics through the ballot box. But segregationists were not about to let blacks vote; many would sooner kill them."[2] It was only a matter of time before the nascent Southern freedom movement would turn toward politics, and to the question of the vote. The goal of the movement became the formation of a new multiracial party. Given the hostility of regular Democrats, it is almost surprising that the movement would even bother with the party; their only hope was a separate party that could challenge and perhaps replace the regulars.

A product of the 1964 Freedom Summer, the Mississippi Free Democratic Party (MFDP) as it came to be known, first met with sixty-eight delegates representing some 80,000 rural black voters who had signed onto its ranks. They were prepared for battle, ready to take over the state's delegation to the 1964 national convention. The regular, white, racist state party planned to oppose and condemn the Civil Rights Act of 1964, as well as the platform of the national party. The Freedom Democrats, on the other hand, were pledged to support the convention's expected choice of Lyndon B. Johnson as presidential candidate; the Mississippi Democrats, by contrast, were widely expected to bolt the ticket, and vote for conservative Republican Barry Goldwater.

The events that transpired before and during the Atlantic City convention had ramifications that went well beyond the history of the civil rights movement. Out of the fight that ensued around the seating of the Freedom Democrats grew the birth of the New Left, and its early stand of hostility and opposition to both the Democratic Party and its erstwhile New Deal era allies—the labor movement, white Northern liberals, Socialists and radicals, and other minority groups. Together, this coalition had given steam to the later New Deal, and was largely responsible for the large electoral landslide achieved by Franklin Delano Roosevelt in the 1936 election. For the first time, that tight coalition would begin to rip asunder, as young new radicals sided with black militants against it.

Jeane Kirkpatrick, then a Humphrey Democrat, remembers the 1964 convention as "the last happy Democratic Convention," since she saw the party as united "on the basis of traditional New Deal–Fair Deal principles . . . but which was moving creatively in the direction of being much more inclusive . . . on civil rights." The struggle between the old guard and the challengers, she recalled, led to compromise, and to members of the Democratic Party feeling "pretty good about the party."[3] Others, especially militants in the civil rights movement, have hostile and negative memories. To the radicals little was accomplished, and the true lesson to be learned was that of the need to organize on the left fringe of the party.

Heading into Atlantic City, it was already clear that Lyndon B. Johnson would not have easy sailing. The civil rights movement was in full swing, and up in arms over a recent bombing of a Birmingham church by Southern white racists, in which six young schoolgirls were killed. LBJ had sought to put together black and white southerners, business and labor, intellectuals and traditionalists, who would work together for a liberal agenda from which all would benefit. But the civil rights movement's agenda, which he had endorsed, and which resulted in the legislative victory of the Civil Rights Act of 1964 and the Voting Rights Act of 1965, seemed endangered as moderate leaders were replaced by brash young militants, such as Stokely Carmichael of the Student Nonviolent Coordinating Committee (SNCC), who called for "black power" rather than integration.

At first, there were some hopeful signs that a new coalition would combine the militants' energy with the realism of the old labor-liberal Democratic Party coalition. At a meeting of liberal Democrats in Washington, SNCC chief Bob Moses spoke with Joseph Rauh, head of the capital's Democratic Party, a vice president of Americans for Democratic Action, and general counsel to the United Automobile Workers. Joe Rauh by that time was the dean of old liberal activists, a man whose credentials were cut in the 1948 fight to get a civil rights platform into the Democratic convention. An anti-Communist of the Democratic Left, Rauh had also led the fight to ostracize the left-wing followers of Henry A. Wallace from the Democratic Party, and to brand them with the Communist brush. He was involved with virtually every major liberal and civil rights organization, as well as the trade union movement. Rauh was also in the forefront of those trying to make the Democratic Party a standard bearer of the moderate Left. And although he vigorously opposed the Communists, he believed in the civil liberties of all Americans. As a result, Rauh came to prominence when he served as playwright Lillian Hellman's counsel when she appeared as a reluctant witness before the House Committee on Un-American Activities. It was not a surprise when the young SNCC activists, knowing of his role in the past, approached Rauh and asked him to help them in their quest. Rauh immediately agreed to support the Freedom Democrats and promised Moses that "if there's anybody at the Democratic convention challenging the seating of the outlaw Miss Dems, I'll make sure that the challengers are seated."[4]

LBJ, however sympathetic he was to civil rights for black Americans, had to contend with keeping the Southern Democrats in tow; he felt compelled to try to avoid their threatened defection to Goldwater. Therefore, Johnson opposed the Freedom Democrats. As Rauh later put it, "you had the whole Democratic political machine, the president, the whole White House, and the whole labor movement, all trying to stop a few little Mississippi Negroes and me from making a little stink at the Democratic convention."[5] Joe Rauh never capitulated to White House pressure, and despite many charges that he did just that, he fought a tough and unrelenting fight to seat the Freedom Democrats.[6]

Vice President Humphrey put pressure on Rauh and those working for the MFDP to avert their challenge to the regulars. But Rauh resisted Humphrey's pleas. Indeed, Rauh was first called by UAW president Walter Reuther, who held great power over his legal counsel. Reuther let Rauh know that the president was very upset and this might cost Hubert the vice presidency. Johnson, in effect, was trying to blackmail the liberals. If they persisted in fighting for MFDP representation, he threatened to take the second spot away from one of their own, the old fighting liberal from Minnesota. Rauh responded that it was better to be in the fight for representation than out, and Reuther retorted that he, Rauh, would be to blame if Humphrey were bounced off the ticket. Max Kampelman, then a major advisor to the senator, called Rauh to confirm that Johnson was most upset when he saw Rauh on television threatening a floor fight at the convention on the issue.

Kampelman, according to Rauh, then went even further. Another Humphrey advisor, Jim Rowe, had told Kampelman that he and the president thought it might be a good moment to have it out "with the Negroes, and if there were demonstrations to go ahead and make some arrests and show that the Democratic Party was the party of law and order." In the meantime, Johnson phoned Reuther repeatedly, to let him know that the vice presidential spot going to Humphrey rested entirely on the issue of the MFDP challenge.[7] It was then that Joe Rauh sought to use SNCC's flirtation with Communist lawyers to pressure the Johnson Administration. Talking with Democratic boss Ken O'Donnell in July, Rauh told him there would be a floor fight whether they supported one or not, and he argued that it would be best that it was led "by thoughtful people with the best interest of the [Democratic] Party at heart rather than by the Lawyers Guild crowd," the legal arm of the Communist Party to which SNCC had gone for help. Using that pitch, Rauh tried to convince O'Donnell that it was in the President's interest to ditch the regular Mississippi Democrats who in any case were not pledged to support him in the campaign. It was after this talk, on July 24, that Rauh saw Humphrey. LBJ was worried, Humphrey said, but he advised Rauh that it was better that he be involved in the effort than not. Although they discussed the Administration compromise proposal that both delegations be seated, by July 28 the White House made it known that they wanted only the regular Mississippi Democrats to have the convention seats. Bayard Rustin, Martin Luther King's trusted lieutenant, was worried. He told Rauh that the white liberals had to make a good showing at this convention or life would become intolerable for those Negroes who believed in cooperation with the white liberals. Thus Rustin hoped that Johnson and Humphrey would in the end "see the wisdom of letting us have the battle."[8]

The state convention of the MFDP on August 6 had been held in Jackson, with more than 2,500 in attendance. A delegation of sixty-four blacks and four whites was chosen to attend. The leadership included Aaron Henry, Fannie Lou Hamer, Victoria Gray, Ed King, and Annie Devine. Returning to Washington, Rauh recalled that the "White House suddenly realized that we had a strategy that was pretty hard to beat." Humphrey was on the phone with Rauh right away, telling him: "Joe, just give me something to tell the president." Rauh recalled answering, "Why don't you tell him I'm a dirty bastard and completely uncontrollable?" To which the senator replied, "Well, the president wouldn't like that." Rauh then told Humphrey he would have to tell Johnson himself, as he decided to move "ahead with the fight."[9]

Johnson, however, had to deal with the immense national publicity given to the Freedom Democrats. In particular, television viewers throughout America were galvanized by the testimony given to the convention's Credentials Committee by a local MFDP organizer, a rural sharecropper named Fannie Lou

Hamer. Hamer had told of how she was brutally beaten for try-ing to exercise her right to vote, and in the North, the sympathy of most Democrats was with the MFDP. Therefore Johnson sought to have Humphrey try to reach a favorable compromise. Humphrey, in turn, gave the task over to his young aide, Walter Mondale, who was then Attorney General of Minnesota. As Mondale saw it, the MFDP was seeking an "open door in terms of preventing a future lily-white segregated delegation," and a victory for them that entitled kicking all white delegates out would not have established a "rule of law for civil rights," and would pit black against white with one losing and the other win-ning. That course, he thought, offered "no hope for a healthy po-litical party."[10]

Therefore, at the president's urging, Humphrey and Mondale sought a compromise. In the 1964 convention, white Mississippi regulars would be seated if they swore loyalty to the ticket chosen at the convention, alongside two MFDP delegates, Aaron Henry and Ed King. Rather than represent the state, they would be del-egates "at large." In the future, the Mississippi party and other southern Democratic groups would have to pledge to integrate all delegations to future conventions. Immediately most white Mississippi delegates objected, and eventually they stormed out of the Atlantic City convention, refusing to pledge allegiance to a party that allowed any black representation. But the black MFDP members would also not compromise; they demanded all the Mississippi seats as the only legal Democratic body present.

The administration had tried to exert heavy pressure for com-promise. A black California supporter of the MFDP was told that her husband would not get a scheduled judgeship if she con-tinued to back them, and the Secretary of the Army told the Canal Zone delegate that he would lose his job if he did not get on board.[11] On August 23, a caucus of black delegates was held to discuss the proposed compromise. MFDP delegates expressed fury when some black leaders, such as Rustin, favored acceptance. Annie Devine yelled that "we have been treated like beasts in Mississippi. They shot us down like animals. We risk our lives coming up here . . . politics must be corrupt if we don't care none about people down there."[12]

The anger was understandable, even admirable. But as a form of politics, it made little sense. Those blacks forged in the movement, like Bayard Rustin, understood that a black minority needed the support and backing of whites in a coalition, one that alone would afford them the strength to achieve future victory. First, a new compromise was put forth by Congresswoman Edith Green of Oregon, who issued a simple proposal to seat all the Mississippi delegates who took a loyalty oath, in which they would pledge to support the party's ticket. The whites and blacks would then share the delegation's sixty-eight votes equally, regardless of whether they were mainstream Southern Democrats or MFDP members. Rauh was supportive, but the proposal failed to satisfy the all-white Mississippi regulars.

As for Rauh, he kept putting off a decision on how he would vote, and kept on working for the proclaimed goal of full recognition for the MFDP. Testifying before the Credentials Committee, for example, he told the Democratic parliamentarians that the only question, since the MFDP was pledged to support and work for LBJ, was whether the Democrats would stand "for the oppressor or for the oppressed." Mississippi, Rauh emphasized, was a "dictatorship as bad as that in any totalitarian country of the world."[13]

In retrospect, it is clear that the valiant generals of the MFDP went too far. Acceptance of the administration compromise did not require opposition to new civil rights legislation or to an end to segregation in the state of Mississippi. It is also clear that, contrary to most historians' claims, leaders like Rauh and Rustin did not vote for compromise because they gave in to pressure from either the administration or the United Automobile Workers. Rauh, for example, stresses that Humphrey never once sought to get Rauh to bend because of the chance he might not get the nomination. "It's the kind of integrity that makes people stick with Humphrey even when he's wrong," Rauh noted.[14] Indeed, Rauh points out that when he at first met with Robert Moses and Martin Luther King, Jr., the Sunday evening before the August 26th meeting, Robert Moses, the leader of SNCC, had himself been willing to accept the compromise offer of two delegates. "It wasn't until Tuesday night that he turned on everybody and called them racist for thinking it was a victory." Indeed, Reuther was truthful when he told Rauh that because the white Mississippi delegation wouldn't take a loyalty oath to the ticket, they would end up being excluded anyway from the 1964 convention. "They're going to give you a pledge that they never seat lily-white delegations again," Reuther pleaded. "So you've won this . . . tremendous victory."[15]

Reuther was right, but Rauh, who was representing the Freedom Democrats, was caught between both camps. Confusion arose when after a meeting held with Martin Luther King, Jr., Ed King, Robert Moses, and Reuther, the White House released a statement saying the MFDP had accepted their compromise offer. Rauh immediately called a press conference to respond, and told the media that the MFDP had in fact not voted. As Rauh recalled, the atmosphere was akin to a lynch mob. One hundred people were screaming "Vote, Vote" while he was talking, and Rauh had to ask them to shut up. "It was like a machine in there," he told Juan Williams, "and it . . . mowed me down." The Credentials Committee of the convention, however, accepted the compromise before the MFDP had a chance to make its position known. At that very moment, Bob Moses and other MFDP leaders sat with Vice President Hubert Humphrey in a hotel room, and watched Mondale and Rauh on TV. "Bob Moses lost his cool," Rauh recalled after Moses had seen him later that day. "It . . . was like hitting him with a whip . . . [He felt] everyone had ratted on him . . . So that evening when we were on the news, I said we would continue to fight but I also said this is a great victory which will end up with a new Democratic Party." Most MFDP delegates, and especially the young SNCC militants, saw it as proof that the system was a corrupt blockade, holding them back.[16]

On August 26, a critical MFDP meeting was held, during which Rauh, supposedly under pressure of losing his UAW job as well as not wanting to jeopardize Humphrey's chance to attain the vice presidency, spoke up on behalf of the compromise. Rauh, King, and Rustin endorsed the compromise, while MFDP militants opposed it. Fannie Lou Hamer, in her earthy streetwise voice, opined: "We didn't come all this way for no two seats!" One historian attributes the stance of Rauh, Rustin, and King to economic and political pressure coming from Reuther, who warned Rauh and King that the Southern Christian Leadership Conference which King led (SCLC) would not receive another cent from the UAW, which had already given them close to $200,000, unless they supported LBJ's compromise. Rustin, by this account, also advanced his support because of his "own ties to liberal leaders like Walter Reuther."[17]

"You could cut through the tension" at that meeting, MFDP and SNCC activist Charles Sherrod would recall for the television series, "Eyes on the Prize." "People were touchy and on edge. It had been a long fight."[18] According to his recollection, James Forman, one of the most radical SNCC leaders, was aghast as he sat at the black church in Atlantic City where the meeting was held, to hear the long group of eminent leaders from the civil rights and labor movements, as well as political leaders, speak on behalf of compromise. Most upsetting, he wrote, was to find Rustin, the mentor to Moses, SNCC activist Courtland Cox and others, working with the labor-liberal coalition and urging that nothing be done to prevent Humphrey from obtaining the vice-presidential nomination. "The whole liberal-labor syndrome," Forman put it, saw the possible election of Humphrey as their finest hour, "the crowning glory to years of sellout, compromise, and so-called coalition." The labor movement's "darling," Forman wrote, would not find his chances crushed by "upstarts from Mississippi."[19]

Forman reserved his greatest hatred for the role played in Atlanta by Bayard Rustin. Claiming that Courtland Cox and Bob Moses had invited him for the purpose of trying to convince Martin Luther King to support the MFDP, the man who had been a mentor to Carmichael and others gave the MFDP delegates a lesson in coalition politics. "There is a difference between protest and politics," he pointed out. "The former is based on morality and the latter is based on reality and compromise. If you are going to engage in politics than you must give up protest. . . . You must be willing to compromise, to win victories and go home and come back and win some more." Informing his friends who had waged such a valiant struggle that they were now in a new arena—that of politics—Rustin told them that they had to think of their "friends in labor," such as Reuther, who had supported them in so many ways. To reject the compromise, Rustin argued, meant that they would be saying they wanted to go it alone, and they would find they would then not be able to get the help they needed in years to come. Arguing that the Humphrey compromise could be construed as a "symbolic victory," Rustin urged the delegates to focus on greater victories to be won in the future. The response from a white SNCC worker was immediate: "You're a traitor, Bayard, a traitor," screamed Mendy Samstein, a white Jewish SNCC worker from Atlanta.[20]

Next on the rostrum was King. Where would the man who had emerged as virtual leader of the Freedom Movement cast his vote? King, like Rustin, stressed that delegates could not travel alone on the path to freedom. Despite the existence of segregationists within the Democratic Party, King told them it was "the best we have and we must work to make it better." Refusing to counsel them to accept or reject the administration compromise, King told them Hubert Humphrey had assured him that "there would be a new day in Mississippi if you accept this proposal."[21] James Farmer of the Congress of Racial Equality (CORE), who wavered between King and Rustin's political position and sympathy with the MFDP activists, argued that the MFDP was neither a protest movement nor a political party, and he pledged to back them in whatever choice they made.

As for Forman, he pulled out all the stops on the other side. Seconding Moses' argument that one had to bring morality into politics for it to be worthwhile, Forman argued that the MFDP represented the people, and the Democratic Party in the South represented only white racists who ruled illegitimately, in violation of the U.S. Constitution. Their concern was not that of LBJ, but that of challenging the "racism in the Democratic Party." This argument—a victory of symbolism over substance—prevailed. The meeting's vote against the compromise demonstrated a fateful fact for the Democrats: Moralism easily outruns politics. From Forman's perspective, the delegates were simply rejecting what he called the "crumbs offered them," and he saw Atlantic City as a metaphor for the relation of activists to the Establishment—activists who knew the impossibility of the federal government ever changing the situation in the South. The message was clear. Those who started as "idealistic reformers" had to become "full-time revolutionaries."[22]

The final treachery, according to Forman, occurred at a meeting of the National Council of Churches held in New York on September 18, after the Democratic convention. Forman saw it as an attempt "to undermine or neutralize SNCC by the liberal-labor Establishment and its brokers."[23] At that meeting, SNCC representative Mendy Samstein took detailed notes. As well as SNCC representatives Bob Moses and James Forman, the assembled group included James Farmer, Jack Greenberg of the NAACP legal department, the liberal former student leader Allard Lowenstein, Joe Rauh, King's lieutenant Andrew Young, and leaders from the National Council of Churches. Samstein's notes indicate a fight between those who saw themselves as revolutionaries, and those who saw themselves as working on behalf of a political coalition for change. Thus Young argued for uniting the moral power of Fannie Lou Hamer with the political power of the moderate head of the NAACP, Roy Wilkins, CORE's James Farmer, and King, a move that would generate national momentum for the right to vote in Mississippi. This was hardly selling out to the established party—but it *was* a strategy that stressed working within the system of voting registration and partisan organization building. Rauh called for a push on behalf of federal registrars to enforce the civil rights of black voters; a measure that required passage of the proposed Voting Rights Act which depended on the president's support. While NAACP activists questioned SNCC's approach and its members' alienation from Rustin and other moderates, SNCC workers responded that they stood with "the people" and particularly those of the "lowest economic situation." To SNCC, those who were poor in the black South could ostensibly not favor the political path favored by the moderates, who by nature opposed social revolution.

Atlantic City 1964

Rauh in particular raised another point; as Samstein remembered it, he said: "I would like to drive out the Lawyer's Guild. I think it is immoral to take help from Communists," a sentiment with which Allard Lowenstein agreed. Calling for representative democracy, not the "participatory" democracy favored by the New Left, Lowenstein argued that questions surrounding Lawyer's Guild participation had to be decided by vote of a truly broad-based coalition, the Council of Federated Organizations, or COFO—which was seen by Forman as a rejection of militance. But after the meeting, in the wake of SNCC's hostility, Rauh was replaced as SNCC attorney by Arthur Kinoy, William Kunstler, and Morty Stavis, all pro-Communist members of the Guild. A new link thus joined the white Old Left and the new SNCC black militants, a link that would further work to destroy the realism, cooperation, and honest hopes of Democratic opponents of racism in the Democratic Party.[24]

The fight between the two Mississippi camps and the division between Rauh, Reuther, King, and Rustin with the MFDP and SNCC activists foreshadowed future splits within the Democratic Party over Vietnam. A terrible new pattern was established: Radicals at the church meeting had argued that traditional mainstream Democrats were beyond the pale. Others in SNCC began to talk of seizing and demanding power, even at the cost of rioting and shedding of blood. Charles Sherrod, an SNCC activist, castigated compromisers. As he and others saw it, those in power were guilty of racism. To have accepted compromise, Sherrod argued, would have told blacks across America "that we share the power, and that is a lie!" As a country of racists, Sherrod claimed, America demanded "naked confrontation."[25]

Yet another divisive issue would arise that would further tear apart the tenuous coalition between white Democratic liberals and more radical young black activists—the issue of Communism. Since the outbreak of the civil rights movement in the South, white racist political leaders like Mississippi's Senator James Eastland had used the brush of Communism to taint the movement. Communist penetration of the civil rights movement, therefore, was more than sensitive. Indeed, Joe Rauh was himself aware that some of the most militant leaders had secret Communist ties. It was back on March 22 of 1964 that Rauh had first met with two Southern black activists, Milly Jeffrey and Ella Baker, the latter known as the "grandmother of SNCC." They had told him of their plans to challenge the Mississippi delegation at the Atlantic City convention, and Rauh agreed to help in the effort. But privately, he reflected that he "didn't care for the idea of having Miss Baker, as I had little doubt about her Communist affiliations, but there was nothing I could do to stop it."[26] Rauh's fears were well taken. He would find that Ella Baker led the effort to castigate white liberals and their record, and regularly condemned Hubert Humphrey as well as himself to the MFDP delegates.[27]

The issue of Communist penetration of the civil rights movement was to become more than sensitive. It was inevitable that white racists from the South would seek to brand the new black militants as Communist, in order to forestall change in their region of the country. Months after the MFDP challenge had been resolved, Representative Colmer sent Speaker John McCormack a "Fact Sheet on the Mississippi 'Contest,'" which asserted that the "revolutionary character of the Mississippi Freedom Democratic Party and many of its leaders has been pointed out by national columnists Evans and Novak [and] *Newsweek* . . . and has not been denied. Some of its leaders quote Marx, some Mao, some Castro, some the late French Algerian author and intellectual Albert Camus, some author James Baldwin. . . .

Some by act, appearance, and word show themselves to be simply anarchists."28

The very real issue of Communist influence on the Democratic Party (via SNCC) became confused by transparent red-baiting. It was one thing for Congressman Colmer to yell Communism, and to confuse Communist propaganda with the arguments of a Camus. It was another matter, however, when a fiery old liberal like Joe Rauh expressed concern. The militants of SNCC had already alienated many old liberals during Freedom Summer when the organization refused to exclude Communists from participating in its activities. Forman and Stokely Carmichael, a West Indian-born SNCC leader who would later emerge as the main spokesman for "black power" within SNCC, both used the argument that they could not take a "defensive" stand on Communism: Whatever group or organization offered to help them was acceptable, and the militants would simply not pay credence to the idea that Communists had their own private agenda that they would seek to implement by tying in with legitimate civil rights groups. Hoping that the issue would go away, SNCC at first opted only for having no political test for membership. But in 1964, Allard Lowenstein and NAACP counsel Jack Greenberg moved to end support for the Summer Project, unless SNCC refused to accept legal aid from members of the National Lawyers Guild. SNCC did not listen, and Lowenstein, who had first suggested the massive summer voter registration, quietly withdrew his own support.29

The Communist taint took on steam after Atlantic City. Many white volunteers from the North in Freedom Summer were Communists or Red diaper babies, and their literature was widely available at southern movement headquarters. Evans and Novak wrote that SNCC leader Moses was "dangerously oblivious to the Communist menace to the rights movement."[30] In February of 1965, the strongest salvo was levied by Senator James Eastland of Mississippi, perhaps the most racist and firm segregationist in the U.S. Senate—but not, like Colmer, a man who played loosely with his facts. Many MFDP supporters, Eastland charged, including SNCC members, had Communist or pro-Communist backgrounds. Eastland charged in particular that Moses had sought to avoid the draft, that James Forman had supported a call for blacks to take arms in self-defense made by an activist named Robert F. Williams, who would eventually seek sanctuary in Communist Cuba in 1961; that SNCC's research director had given a speech opposed to J. Edgar Hoover's FBI, and that SNCC activist and Southwest Georgia staff member Joni Rabinowitz was the daughter of leftwing counsel Victor Rabinowitz, who was legal representative of Fidel Castro's Cuba. In addition, Eastland pointed accurately to the National Lawyers Guild affiliation of many SNCC and MFDP counsel, including George Crockett of Michigan, whom Eastland identified as counsel to Michigan Communists. Others, including Benjamin Smith of New Orleans, had visited Cuba and praised Fidel Castro. Another Northern supporter, Jesse Gray of Harlem, was a tenant organizer who openly admitted to previous Communist Party membership. Gray, Eastland had noted, had just obtained a $2,500 gift for the MFDP, donated from the trust fund of Cora Weiss, daughter of Samuel Rubin of Fabergé, and a later source of funds for the radical Washington think tank, the Institute for Policy Studies(IPS)[31]

Eastland's remarks gained credibility when *Newsweek* reported that anxiety about SNCC being infiltrated by Communists was "less easy to dismiss" than similar charges against mainstream civil rights groups. Referring to SNCC activists as "dangerously innocent," the magazine's editors admitted that the members were contemptuous of any "organized ideology." Nevertheless, they warned, "for all their hip enthusiasm, the bleak history of Communist efforts to subvert good causes is against them. Time and time again, liberal movements have had to banish Communists from their midst or take the bitter consequences."[32] The response of SNCC workers was similar to that taken by Students for a Democratic Society (SDS)—the main organization of white young New Leftists. To charges of Communist infiltration, John Lewis, then the SNCC chairman and later a congressman from Georgia, simply responded that it was part of an effort to discredit their work for civil rights. Conceding that Communists might be in their organization, he argued that they would accept anyone who would work in Mississippi for freedom.[33]

Most historians have probably agreed with the contemporary judgment offered by the dean of Southern historians, Yale University's C. Vann Woodward, who wrote that SNCC was part of a "spontaneous Left," whose hearts were "in Mississippi or Harlem, not in Moscow or Peking, but [who] often profess a profound alienation from American society, refuse to ally themselves with labor, liberals, and church groups, reject established civil rights leaders, and despair of established institutions."[34] Woodward may have been generally correct, but the insistence by SNCC leaders that they accept the help of the National Lawyers Guild, to the exclusion of mainstream civil rights counsel, marked a willingness to turn directly for help to the pro-Communist Left.

But in Atlantic City on August 6, the MFDP delegates listened to a major speech by Ella Baker, the elderly civil rights activist who had sought out the young SNCC radicals and become their major advisor. But Baker, whose courage and commitment to civil rights was second to none, was also close to the American Communist Party, and was a staff member of the Southern Conference Education Fund (SCEF), a well-known Communist-front group. It was Baker's influence in particular that led SNCC activists to seek out groups like the National Lawyers Guild. In her keynote address to the MFDP delegates, Baker castigated liberals who attacked Communists as red-baiters. Talking to the MFDP delegates on the very eve of the convention fight, Baker had insisted that the movement adopt a policy of anti-anti-Communism. Joe Rauh recalled that Baker's speech was so stridently Red that it could have been lifted from an editorial in the Communist party paper, the *Daily Worker*.[35]

A few months after the defeat, Rauh, still close to his convention opponent Hubert Humphrey, further elaborated on what led to the breakup of the old labor-liberal coalition. "Quite shrewdly and not at all unexpectedly," Rauh wrote to the vice president-elect, "the domestic Communists have made a real attempt to infiltrate the Mississippi civil rights movement." And, Rauh continued, "Communist influence was, of course, evident at the convention in Atlantic City."[36]

The danger, Rauh noted, was broader than Communist Party influence on the MFDP. Rauh explained what motivated him not to give in to Humphrey and easily accept the offered compromise: As a compromiser, he correctly believed that he would be ousted as counsel by SNCC, and the Southern freedom movement would then be taken over "to the detriment of the civil rights movement" by the Lawyers Guild. Sadly, Rauh reported this had come to pass, and the Guild had supplanted "the NAACP lawyers in Mississippi as lawyers for the Council of Federated Organizations," which was practically the entire civil rights movement in the South. In addition, the Communist-front SCEF people played an influential role in both the MFDP and COFO, and now even Bob Moses "appears to have gone the whole way now, having just issued an appeal for funds for the

National Guardian," a pro-Communist newsweekly published in New York.

Rauh, who is of course widely regarded as a responsible defender of civil liberties and who was a key opponent of McCarthyism in the 1950s, informed Humphrey that it was not a new problem, it had "been building up for some time." He had been told two or three years back that James Forman, the SNCC director who played a key role at Atlantic City and who ran COFO in Mississippi, "was a member of the Communist Party." Indeed, Rauh went so far as to second the observations of the South's most hated racist senator, James Eastland of Mississippi. The 1965 speech Eastland had given on the Senate floor on Communist activities in his state, Rauh wrote, "was not an inflammatory speech, but rather a factual report obviously prepared by knowledgeable people." Seven out of eight protest incidents in the state, Rauh told Humprhey, "involved Communists."

Rauh's judgment might seem shocking. But reading Eastland's speech today, as it appears in the *Congressional Record,* one is struck by its accuracy and the care with which it had been prepared. Because of the uses to which Eastland hoped to put this knowledge, it took great courage for Rauh to acknowledge the basic validity of Eastland's information about Communist penetration. It would have been easy to simply ignore Eastland's charges, since the racial motivation for his making them was so evident. But the senator's speech was a careful and documented account of Communist attempts to make inroads into the civil rights movement.

Rauh, however, departed from Eastland and the McCarthyites on his prescription for how to deal with the problem. He emphasized that the "vast bulk of the people working in these organizations are obviously non-Communist idealists." They were merely from a new generation that was unaware of the historic role played by Communists and who refused to see that any problem existed. Every attack by J. Edgar Hoover on Reds made them "more determined to stick with their leadership."

Along with the Communist issue, Rauh complained that COFO and the MFDP contained a "wholly understandable Negro nationalism and a considerable amount of bohemianism among the white civil rights workers," all of which fed the same "end of extremism as does the Communist infiltration." The result, Rauh claimed, was deleterious to civil rights, since it had "disaffected a substantial segment of the indigenous Mississippi Negro population."

The result, Rauh wrote Humphrey, was that mainstream groups were moving away from support of legitimate MFDP efforts on behalf of Mississippi blacks. Rauh noted that Roy Wilkins thought the NAACP should withdraw its COFO affiliation; that even King was cautious, since he was aware that COFO leaders attacked him "privately at every turn." It was a movement syndrome, Rauh noted, that "none of the civil rights groups can afford to appear less militant than the others . . . as a result the situation drags on and deteriorates."

Rauh stressed that Mississippi's appeal for democracy to young people of America is valid, and it was "quite wonderful to watch this idealistic outpouring." But he warned against the leadership of both COFO and the MFDP, which had become "the greatest boon to the left wing on the campuses of the nation in our generation." Foreshadowing what would happen a few years hence on Vietnam, Rauh noted that Moses was a hero to young people, and when he spoke on campuses and denounced United States action in the Congo, he was "worth a great deal to the Communist movement." Rauh, however, proceeded to offer constructive suggestions for dealing with the problem—not McCarthyite solutions. Yelling Communism, he warned, would not affect the struggle. The Mississippi situation itself was "worth divisions to Peking and pages of advertisements to the domestic Communist movement."

Finally, Rauh warned that in the long run, "only the right to vote can change the face of Mississippi." Only 6 percent of the state's black population was then registered. Moreover, he stressed, existing civil rights legislation was woefully inadequate. The sole answer was "federal registrars who register and vote Negroes," and protection for those who dared to vote. A congressional mandate, he was sure, was warranted and legal. As for those who said further laws were not needed and not feasible, Rauh emphasized that Mississippi had caught the nation's attention, and the right to vote for blacks was long overdue. The president, he was sure, was dedicated to it, and all other measures had failed. In making the case for dramatic new action for voting rights, Rauh was presenting a subliminal message: The fight against Communist infiltration of the movement had to be combined with strong and dramatic civil rights measures.

Rauh was right. In 1965, the Voting Rights Act would pass into law, and mark the beginning of the Southern blacks' equal democratic participation. Within a decade, the face of Mississippi would be dramatically changed. Those who swore that no progress could be made through the system, or that working within the Democratic Party was an impossibility, would be proven wrong.

Yet, for the New Left—from 1964 through 1972—Johnson's Atlantic City compromise would be used again and again as an argument on behalf of the revolutionary perspective. That single event soured blacks and New Left supporters from the old labor-liberal coalition. As far as the Left was concerned, the liberal-labor group was forever marked as an accomplice to racism and as a supporter of a corrupt and bankrupt American political system.

Privately, at least, some of the early New Left were more supportive of Rauh and his efforts. Arthur Waskow, one of the founders of IPS, wrote Rauh that he was "filled with admiration for the effective way in which you presented [the MFDP's] case and fought for their seating." Waskow, however, tried to explain to Rauh why the militants felt they could not have done as he did, and accept the compromise. Acceptance, he wrote Rauh, "would have damaged their own constituency back home," since the only real power they held was that of saying no "at the right time." Nevertheless, Waskow expressed his feeling that the "offer itself was a major victory."[37] Similarly, noted author Tristram Coffin wrote that while the MFDP was not seated, "no one [had] expected it . . . [still] Negroes from Mississippi were given a status no one had dreamed of."[38] Even Marc Raskin, an IPS founder who was much given to radical rhetoric, acknowledged that Rauh had helped make the Democratic Party "much more democratic in future years."[39]

Rauh always understood that the fight had been successful, and that accepting the compromise would not have been a catastrophe. Writing to one correspondent in 1965, he noted that the MFDP had achieved a success "far beyond anything that could reasonably have been anticipated a month or two earlier." For one, he argued, their work had led directly to the Voting Rights Act, had driven the racist regular delegations from the convention, and given Mississippi blacks new legitimacy as well as partial recognition.[40]

But instead of capitalizing on this victory, black militants argued that the events transpiring at Atlantic City proved that the entire political system had to be brought down. Stokely

Carmichael, reflecting on the MFDP fight, wrote that it revealed not only that America's conscience was unreliable, but that Negroes in Mississippi and elsewhere "could not rely on their so-called allies."[41] And the MFDP's chairman Lawrence Guyout, and its Washington representative, a white radical named Mike Thelwell, made the comparison between the false consciousness of American blacks in the South and that of Russian peasants before the October Revolution. Like those peasants, American blacks held a "simplistic faith somewhat akin to that of the Russian peasants under the Czars. Caught in the direst kind of oppression and deprivation, the peasants would moan, 'If only the Czar knew how we suffer. He is good and would give us justice. If only he knew.' The fact was," they wrote, referring to Lyndon B. Johnson, "that he knew only too well."[42]

By the time of the 1966 elections, the local Mississippi black population had clearly decided that the hope for change in their segregationist state lay within the national Democrats and not with the MFDP veterans. The attempt to build an independent black movement had come to naught. County branches of the MFDP disappeared, and the Lowndes County Freedom Organization, dubbed the Black Panthers because of their electoral symbol, was badly defeated in November county elections. In Mississippi, 150,000 blacks had already registered and had been joined by 200,000 in Alabama. Politicians who once joined the popular racist bandwagons quickly changed their tune, and sought the new black vote. White candidates who repudiated segregation replaced the Bilbo-Eastland old-style racists. Moreover, the Johnson administration used federal programs such as Head Start and VISTA to give jobs to former civil rights activists, including those of the MFDP. In one such example, 3,000 civil rights veterans were put on the payroll of the Child Development Group in Mississippi. To the New Left, of course, these were tokens, even dangerous ones, since they led movement people to attach themselves to the liberal wing of the Democratic Party.[43]

The Atlantic City compromise and the subsequent progress of civil rights within the Democratic Party marked the beginning of the shift toward black nationalism, espousal of armed rebellion, and revolutionary posturing by black radicals. And the white New Left, led by Students for a Democratic Society, "an amalgam of avowedly radical, mostly college-educated foes of racism, sexism, nuclear weapons, and the war in Vietnam," as historian Robert Weisbrot writes, "offered a hardy network of white support for black militants." Tom Hayden, who had written SDS's famed "Port Huron" statement, favored the SNCC goal of "participatory democracy" as well as their call for revolution. Mario Savio of Berkeley, who had led that institution's Free Speech movement in 1964, offered "earnest, even imploring, overtures for unity." Indeed, as young whites began to attack the "system" as the force behind the war in Vietnam, "unconditional solidarity with black activists increasingly became a badge of white leftist commitment."[44]

From that moment on, black militants from Stokely Carmichael to Eldridge Cleaver, Huey Newton and the Black Panther Party, allied with the white young New Left, concentrated on opposition to the United States in Vietnam, support of the "movement" and preparation for "revolution," and total opposition to the existing system. In political terms, this meant unrelenting opposition to working within the Democratic Party. Sympathetic but more mainstream liberals increasingly were forced to choose between the militants and the Democratic Party. Soon, at the Chicago-based "New Politics" convention in 1967, the radicals and proponents of the liberal mainstream would reach a head-on collision.

2

THE NEW POLITICS
CONVENTION

By 1967, a number of major events in the world had affected activists of the Left. These involved the dramatic growth of the civil rights movement after Freedom Summer, the continuing escalation of the war in Vietnam by the Johnson administration, and the Six-Day War against Israel in June of 1967. Seemingly separate events, they would intertwine with and affect the social movements that operated in and around the orbit of the Democratic Party.

Involved closely and emotionally with all three movements was Marty Peretz, a Bronx-born former Brandeis University student who, through a second marriage to the wealthy Anne Farnsworth, heiress to the Singer Sewing Machine company fortune, became a benefactor to both the civil rights and emerging peace movements. Peretz, recently out of graduate school and teaching at Harvard, was typical of those Jewish activists who found themselves on the left wing of the Democratic Party—furious with Lyndon Johnson for his commitment to intervention in Vietnam, and hopeful of creating a new America pledged to civil rights and peace.

Peretz had begun his public activity in the early sixties. With his close friend, political philosopher Michael Walzer, Peretz formed an Emergency Public Integration Committee, and led the picketing of Woolworth's in downtown Boston, in protest of the national chain's segregationist policies in the South. This event was one of the first mass activities of the nascent civil rights coalition throughout the nation. As Vietnam escalated and touched the consciousness of student activists, Peretz responded with the rest of his generation. But because of the gift of his wealth, he and his wife became major funders of both movements. Funding both Martin Luther King's Southern Christian Leadership Conference and the militant Student Nonviolent Coordinating Committee, Peretz came to know King and his aide Andrew Young, as well as young radicals like James Forman and Stokely Carmichael.

In 1966, Peretz convened a small group of activists at his Truro summer home in Cape Cod, Massachusetts. The purpose, as one journalist has written, was to "discuss bringing peace activists and civil rights activists together to influence and perhaps make inroads into the Democratic Party."[1] It may have been the first time that those on the New Left sought to find out how and if they could move within the circles of the Democratic Party. Working with national peace activists like Dr. Benjamin Spock and Yale chaplain William Sloane Coffin, Peretz desired to build a multiracial coalition that could transform the Democratic Party into a mass left-wing party in the European tradition. It was Peretz's hope that if the Democrats did not listen, their forces could form a new political party, a third-party ticket that would nominate Martin Luther King, with Benjamin Spock as his running mate, in 1968. As America's best-known pediatrician, whose book on baby care had virtually been the bible for most mothers in the 1940s, Spock's new commitment to the peace movement gave the cause added luster. Hence his willingness to run on a national third party with King made the proposed campaign a virtual dream ticket which, as its advocates saw it, would bring together the two most potent forces for change in America, and forever transform American politics.

That meeting was soon transformed into planning sessions for a conference on the New Politics, to be held in Chicago in 1967, and to be funded primarily by Peretz. Preparatory meetings took place that next summer, once again at his Cape Cod home. Peretz recalled that, late at night, he was awakened by the sound of some of the activists camping out on his living room floor singing anti-Semitic doggerel about Jewish landlords exploiting the black poor. The episode led to a confrontation with Jim Forman, who told Peretz that Jews who owned stores in Harlem owed blacks reparations. Forman's personal views were compounded by a growing hostility toward Israel that was emerging in SNCC, and the argument that American blacks had a natural solidarity with the Palestinian and Arab enemies of Israel.

SNCC's position created another crack in the civil rights coalition, after a period of participation in and support for the black freedom struggle by liberal urban Jews. The precipitating event for the rupture was the Six-Day War. On May 15, 1967, Egypt mobilized its troops. Two days later, President Gamal Abdel Nasser demanded that the U.N. withdraw from the Sinai and the Strait of Tiran. On May 22, he had announced a blockade of the Gulf of Aqaba, which cut off the Israeli port of Eilat. More than 100,000 troops were then massed on Egypt's borders with Israel.

Radio Cairo called for "total war," and "extermination of the Zionist existence." Jordan put its troops under Egyptian command on May 30, as did Iraq. Syria mobilized on the Golan Heights. By the start of June, Israel was surrounded on all sides. It appeared to the world that Israel was doomed, as France cut off arms shipments, and the U.N. acceded to Nasser's demands. But on June 5, Israel attacked the Arab countries, and in less than a week emerged victorious. For most Jews, as the noted Rabbi Abraham Joshua Heschel had written, "many of us felt that our own lives were in the balance," that "all of Jewish history was at stake." Heschel had been in the forefront of those who favored active support of the civil rights movement, spurring on Jews in its early days to become involved. Yet, witnessing the reaction of the world to the attempt of the Arab nations to destroy Israel, Heschel commented that "the world that was silent while six million died was silent again . . . the isolation was dreadful. . . . I had not known how deeply Jewish I was."[2] Israel's victory, accomplished against all odds, gave heart to America's Jews. No longer would they be victims. They could fight back and defend their land and their people with integrity and pride.

Meeting in the midst of the Six-Day War, SNCC's Central Committee asked its staff to prepare a report on the Israeli-Arab conflict. By that time, a militant advocate of black power, H. Rap Brown, had been elected new SNCC chairman, and in May the organization had proclaimed itself a "Human Rights Organization" that had as its purpose the encouragement and support of "liberation struggles against colonialism, racism, and economic exploitation." As their leadership now saw things, the struggle against racism at home was part of the worldwide struggle against imperialism, and hence the focus on civil rights for black Americans within the United States alone was inadequate to their larger goals. Requesting nongovernmental organizational status before the U.N. Economic and Security Council, Jim Forman was made head of SNCC's International Affairs Commission.

The SNCC report was prepared by Ethel Minor, a former member of Elijah Muhammad's Nation of Islam, who had been particularly close to Palestinian students at college. It was an odd choice for an author of the "objective critique of the facts" which the SNCC leadership purportedly asked for. Actually, Forman and the others all expected and wanted a pro-Palestinian document, but Forman, coming from New York, was well aware of the pressure the organization would face once their conclusions were made public. Minor's article, appearing in the *SNCC Newsletter*, created a storm. Listing what she called thirty-two "documented facts" about the Palestinian-Israeli problem, she attributed the first Arab-Israeli War to a just effort by Palestinians to regain the land taken from them by the Jews. "Zionists conquered the Arab homes and land," she wrote, "through terror, force, and massacres." The article was compounded by the presence of a clearly anti-Semitic cartoon, composed by SNCC artist Koffi Bailey. It showed Moshe Dayan with dollar signs on his epaulets, which reminded Marty Peretz of the Nazi propaganda prepared by the notorious anti-Semite, Julius Streicher. Another photo showed Zionists shooting Arabs lined up against a wall. The caption accompanying the photo read: "This is the Gaza Strip, Palestine, not Dachau, Germany."[3]

Those in SNCC who favored stepping back did so for only tactical reasons. Jim Forman later wrote that SNCC should support the Arab cause "regardless of how ragged the formation of our position," because no version of their analysis would "have satisfied the Zionists and many Jews."[4] In this regard, at least, he was correct. Peretz in particular was more than upset. Peretz immediately brought the SNCC pamphlet to his closest friends in the movement. Much to his consternation, he found them ambivalent and waffling. "You have to understand," one friend told him. "The movement is young. The movement is feeling its oats."[5]

It seemed, at that moment, that concern for Israel and its security was felt only by American Jews. Most of the broad liberal community cared first and foremost about the the American commitment in Vietnam. By 1967, the escalation of the Vietnam War had attained massive proportions. No political candidate had emerged to challenge the war policy of the administration, and radical activists were intent on proving that the Democratic Party itself was a corrupt institution tied intrinsically to the war machine. Particularly disheartening to reformers was the increased federal budget spent on waging the war in Vietnam. Spending had already reached a peacetime total of $55 billion in 1965. By 1968, it had soared past $80 billion. That meant much less funding available for Johnson's heralded Great Society reforms, which the New Left had attacked from the start as too modest in scope. An estimated $322,000 per American citizen was being spent on Vietnam; the War on Poverty, in contrast, received $53 for each poor person in the nation. Michael Harrington, the Socialist leader whose work had first inspired John F. Kennedy to pursue an attack on poverty, commented that with such a limited commitment, the war was actually more of a skirmish. The movement soon echoed a simple cry: "Guns or Butter!"

The administration's commitment to Vietnam seemed firmer than ever. By 1967, the number of U.S. combat troops in Vietnam climbed to 485,000. The air war in particular grew in intensity. Said Brigadier General William DePuy: "The solution in Vietnam is more bombs, more shells, more napalm . . . till the other side cracks and gives up." Coming back from a meeting at

the White House, Assistant Secretary of Defense John Mc-
Naughton noted that the United States was "proceeding on the
assumption that the way to eradicate the Vietcong is to destroy
all the village structures, defoliate all the jungles, and then cover
the entire surface of South Vietnam with asphalt." To the New
Left, that kind of attitude typified the arrogant and self-serving
haughtiness of an empire in decline. When Secretary of Defense
Robert McNamara announced in May of 1967 that the air war
was killing 1,000 Vietnamese noncombatants per week, it suggested to the antiwar forces that not only did the United States
not belong in Vietnam, but that the war it was waging was also
immoral. None of this moved the administration to reconsider
its policies. In a speech on September 29, LBJ declared that "the
security—indeed, the survival, of this American nation" was at
stake in Southeast Asia.

What the antiwar New Left had hoped for had finally taken
place. The moment had arrived when Martin Luther King, Jr.,
already considered by many Americans to be the nation's conscience, decided that he could no longer keep silent about Vietnam. In February of 1967, King spoke out in a speech delivered
in Los Angeles, in which he stated that the Johnson policy had
made America "morally and politically isolated," and that the
United States had become an "arch antirevolutionary" nation,
which showed no sympathy for the "oppressed of the world."
America, he said, faced a series of triple evils: "racism, extreme
materialism, and militarism."

King's shift to a Vietnam focus culminated in two appearances
in New York City in April. The first was at the famed Riverside
Church, long the repository of the social gospel tradition. King
gave a major and lengthy antiwar speech before important liberal
and antiwar leaders. "This madness must cease," King declared.

In his anguished voice, King poured out what he claimed was the unity of effort on behalf of civil rights at home and opposition to the war in Vietnam abroad:

> I speak as a child of God and brother to the suffering poor of Vietnam. I speak for those whose land is being laid waste, whose homes are being destroyed, whose culture is being subverted. I speak for the poor of America who are paying the double price of smashed hopes at home and death and corruption in Vietnam. I speak as a citizen of the world, for the world stands aghast at the path we have taken. . . . The great initiative in this war is ours. The initiative to stop it must be ours.[6]

To the assembled activists, King said that he could never raise his voice against the violence in the ghettos if he remained silent, and in a rhetorical display of anti-Americanism rare for the minister, King referred to "the greatest purveyor of violence in the world today—my own government." Arguing that Lyndon Johnson's goal was probably to occupy Vietnam as an American colony, King called upon the President to declare a unilateral ceasefire, end all bombing, negotiate with the Vietcong, and set a date for withdrawal of American troops.

Later that week, 125,000 New Yorkers marched in a downpour to a block adjacent to the United Nations, where they heard Martin Luther King, Jr., once again turn his attention to Vietnam, this time in a march sponsored by the Vietnam Mobilization Committee, which also had put Stokely Carmichael on the speaker's podium and which included many marchers waving Vietcong flags. It was one thing to turn against the war; yet another to decide to speak at a Left-led and militant antiwar demonstration in New York City. As King's biographer David Garrow has written, King's association with Carmichael and the VMC was opposed not only by the other mainstream Negro leaders—Roy

Wilkins of the NAACP and Whitney Young of the Urban League—but also by many of his own top advisors including the left-wing former Communist Stanley Levison, and the social democrat Bayard Rustin.

As these men saw it, too great an association by King with the antiwar movement, particularly with pro-Communist extremists, would interfere with King's role as the leading proponent of civil rights in America. It would also assure that his contact and influence with the White House would be entirely cut off. Even strong antiwar liberal Democrats, and the old Socialist leader Norman Thomas, who had wanted King to come out against the war, opposed his taking part, lest King "end up associated with any number of colorful fringe elements."[7]

King's response was telling. Opposition to the war, he argued, was gaining a large constituency. Many white liberals now saw the war, and not civil rights, as the most pressing problem facing America. Before committing to the New York appearances, King came in contact with two prominent liberal Democrats close to Robert F. Kennedy, William and Jean Vanden Heuvel. They discussed what strategy to pursue on both domestic and foreign policy. In a follow-up letter, King's SCLC associate Andrew Young suggested that the forces coalesce into a "pincer movement." Young noted that "with you working from within the structure of politics and economics and us working on the outside we can move the country along more quickly." Young suggested that they call when they desired King or the SCLC to act on the issue of Vietnam when Senator Kennedy had to be reticent, since that would prove "no problem for Dr. King."[8]

King, Garrow reports, decided to turn actively against the war after he read and pored over a photo essay appearing in *Ramparts* magazine, which had evocative photos of maimed Vietnamese children. The civil rights leader told the *New York Times* that racism and militarism were interrelated, and it was out of a moral commitment to human dignity and the worth of an individual personality that he took his stand against U.S. policy in Vietnam.[9] When King asked the SCLC board to come out strongly against the war, however, they resisted. Strong dissension from Aaron Henry and Little Rock minister Roland Smith tabled the proposal. Older allies from the civil rights mainstream were more than upset by King's New York speeches. Roy Wilkins and Whitney Young dissociated themselves publicly, and A. Philip Randolph and Bayard Rustin refused to comment, privately making known their disagreement. In addition, King was bitterly attacked in editorials in both the liberal *Washington Post* and *New York Times*, which decried linking up the civil rights and antiwar movements. Others were even more harsh, accusing King of serving Hanoi's ends, thereby weakening confidence in his vision and leadership.[10]

It was at the April 18 march and rally to the United Nations that supporters of King first made the suggestion that he possibly run as a third-party presidential candidate. Speaking after King, William F. Pepper of the National Conference for New Politics (NCNP), which had scheduled a convention in Chicago, proposed that King consider running for president in 1968, as a mechanism for increasing opposition to the war. But King firmly made it clear that he held no political ambition. Instead, he joined with Joe Rauh to initiate the founding of "Negotiation Now!," a moderate mainstream peace group, which sought to obtain one million signatures calling for initiation of Vietnam peace talks.

Trying to stand between moderates and radicals, civil rights activists and antiwar militants, King agreed to present a major speech at Marty Peretz's New Politics conference. By the time of the conference, many attending, particularly white radicals from

Berkeley and New York, promoted a King-Spock ticket in '68, despite King's refusal to run. The growing militancy and radicalism of King's speeches had only encouraged them, particularly since King had begun to talk of the need to radically restructure the system, and even to hint that he was leaning toward socialism. But King worried about the conference, both because of these King-Spock supporters and because of the dangers of too close a tie to left-wing extremists. He appeared, nevertheless, only to find his worst fears materialized.

From the very start, the meeting was rife with built-in contradictions. Just as young black militants became intoxicated with the vision of taking power into their own hands, white New Leftists began to argue that subordination to the black struggle was the only path toward revolution in America. Blacks at home became the substitute proletariat—an internal Third World wherein lay the last chance for structural change. Sympathy for the plight of blacks forced to live in a segregated society led many young white radicals away from working to realize the potential of the American dream, and into adopting a stance of kowtowing to the most mindless, extreme, and morally intransigent among the black movement. Therein lay the future danger that awaited the Democratic Party as a whole—the demands of its most radical black constituents would come to dominate its ranks, just as opposition to the war in Vietnam and a call for a negotiated settlement led many in its ranks to shift toward a pro-Vietcong position.

The Conference for a New Politics, held at the posh Palmer House grand ballroom, brought together black radicals and white New Leftists with white moderates and leaders of the older moderate civil rights movement. As Martin Luther King delivered his opening address—calling for creation of a new coalition of conscience based on nonviolence—young Chicago black militants marched outside the ballroom, chanting: "Kill Whitey! Kill Whitey!" The 2,100 odd delegates were in for a long-remembered charade of revolutionary politics.

The event was widely covered by the media, but as SANE's Political Action Director Sanford Gottlieb put it, most reports failed "to convey the spirit, the emotion, the dynamics, and the flavor." Gottlieb regarded himself as a typical antinuclear activist, a mainstream liberal whose chief concern was to move the world toward a nonnuclear deterrence. The Sane Nuclear Policy Committee—the leading moderate antinuclear group, tried to be responsible, although it was widely known that key chapters were heavily controlled by members of the American Communist Party. Describing himself as a radical liberal, Gottlieb shared the "New Left's criticisms of American society but almost none of their conclusions about how to change it." What he hoped to gain at Chicago was creation of a "serious, responsible radical Left," which would benefit the United States "by offering the country some new perspectives and by moving the political spectrum slightly leftward." Looking about at the assembled multitude, he immediately expressed doubt that "such a Left could be established by the potpourri of invited groups." Before long, Gottlieb found that most of the 2,117 delegates representing three-hundred seventy-two different groups were radicals who "rejected working through the established institutions of American society." Instead of liberals, he reported that the meeting was filled with "white middle-class radicals with guilt feelings about Negroes."[11]

In his report on the convention, executive committee member and IPS founder Arthur I. Waskow, a young historian who had studied at the University of Wisconsin, explained that the convention "was built on the assumption that there was one movement, with many parts." Therefore the steering committee had proposed that community groups engaged in "New Politics" works should have as many votes as they had active members. The assumption was that the majority of votes cast would then "reflect the political realities of the American Left." Waskow and the delegates were in for a rude shock. Instead of one movement, they found that there were two different movements, "one black and one white." With more white delegates than blacks, a majority of whites could in theory bind the black minority "to a given course of action against their will."[12]

Since the black delegates were not about to submit to this, they quickly announced formation of a separate Black Caucus, composed of members of SNCC, CORE, the SCLC, the Socialist Workers Party, the Communist Party of the United States, and assorted black militants. The group chose as its spokesman an unknown Panama-born social worker, Carlos Russell of Brooklyn, New York. Instead of developing a strategy to defeat Lyndon Johnson and bring the Vietnam War to an end, the assembled delegates, as *Nation* magazine reporter put it, "transformed their convention into a kind of 20th century morality play on race relations." The Black Caucus quickly created an atmosphere of intimidation around itself. "Meeting continuously in secrecy," Richard Blumenthal wrote, "with shaven-head bodyguards posted at the doors, shifting from one building and one room to another, staring fiercely at whites as they walked past them in the hallways, and taunting them as they solicited contributions for 'our black brothers in the jails.'"[13]

The Black Caucus began by demanding its own meeting room and its own arrangements, necessary to guard the truth that their own ranks were deeply divided between moderates interested in political action and civil rights legislation, and radicals committed to a black-led revolution. It was decided that members of the Black Caucus would be beholden only to the caucus, and not to

the entire convention. Deadlocked at first between black delegates who wanted to participate in the convention, and those
who did not, the competing black groups finally agreed on a
strategy, as Waskow put it, of discharging "their energy upon the
white convention."

They devised what Waskow called "the toughest criteria" they
could; if the whites accepted the test, they would stay. If they refused, the Black Caucus would leave the convention. The test
comprised a thirteen-point program drawn up by the Black Caucus—a document, as Walter Goodman reported in the *New York
Times Magazine*, that called for 50 percent black representation
on all committees; condemnation of "the imperialist Zionist
war;" efforts to humanize "the savage and beastlike character that
runs rampant through America, as exemplified by George Lincoln Rockwells [a self-proclaimed American Nazi leader] and
Lyndon Baines Johnsons;" [sic] and support for all the resolutions passed at a Newark, New Jersey, Black Power conference,
which, Goodman wrote, "so far as a generous sampling of opinion could determine, nobody in the Palmer House that Saturday
had read." The Black Caucus demanded acceptance by the entire
convention by 1 p.m.—a scant few hours after release of the thirteen points.

The points, of course, were all highly charged and controversial. The introduction spoke of a "United States system that is
committed to the practice of genocide, social degradation, and
the denial of political and cultural self-determination of black
people." Rejecting reform, it demanded "revolutionary change,"
not the cosmetic inclusion of blacks taking place at the New Politics meeting. Aside from the points already mentioned, the
Black Caucus demanded "total and unquestionable support to all
national people's liberation wars," including those in the Middle
East and Latin America. Demanding that whites unshackle their

minds from old stereotypes, it called for "immediate reparations" by white America for the "exploitation of black people." The resolutions also called for creation of an armed all-black militia, the right of blacks to revolt, and a dialogue about partitioning the United States into two separate nations, one black and one white.

Upon presentation of these demands, a white delegate from New Haven rose to urge endorsement, arguing that the resolution's black sponsors were correct to stress the white race's "own responsibility for centuries of oppression." Astonishingly, by a three-to-one margin, the white delegates voted to accept all of the black resolutions. Septima Clark of Alabama said that the points were designed to "test the social barometer of the delegates," and they had passed the test with flying colors. The assembled liberals, as Waskow reported, had "voted to castrate themselves as organizers ... because they accepted the responsibility and guilt of American racism." The castration metaphor seemed to be widespread. One Jewish delegate, obviously trying to ward off his taking offense at the anti-Zionist resolution, told one caucus: "After four-hundred years of slavery, it is right that whites should be castrated!"[14]

Pleased with their performance and subservience to the black radicals, the white delegates gave themselves an ovation after the vote was taken. But the black militants immediately upped the ante. They now asked for half of the convention votes, necessary, they said, to establish trust. That too passed, by a two-to-one margin, which meant that one-third of the delegates at the convention now controlled the meeting. Bert Gaskoff, a white delegate from Ann Arbor, Michigan, explained: "We are just a little tail on the end of the very powerful black panther, and I want to be on that tail—if they'll let me." Whites, he continued, "must trust the blacks the way you trust children." Realizing his faux pas, Gaskoff added: "I don't mean to say it like that ... these are very sophisticated people and they've taught the whites a hell of a lot."[15]

Black militants were jubilant. Jim Forman, once again, set the tone. Continuing his attack on the old social-democratic New Deal coalition, Forman seized the microphone, surrounded by men wearing dashikis. Declaring himself the convention's "dictator," Forman screamed: "Black people have been oppressed the longest. We wage our own war of liberation as we see fit. Absolutely no one has the right to dictate our forms.... Anyone who doesn't like it can go to hell!" To Forman, the black dispossessed had to provide "leadership to the New Politics. If this doesn't happen, the liberal-labor treachery will recur." SNCC, he argued, had been the "victims of the liberal-labor circle lies ... their misleading of the masses of people in this country." No longer, he stated, would "we allow black militants to assemble in the presence of these double-crossing, liberal-labor coalition exponents, both Negro and white, without raising our voice in protest."[16]

Hearing these words, and realizing the gulf between himself and those he admired, Marty Peretz walked out of the conference. Other whites reacted differently. Waskow, rationalizing their support, tried to explain that the Black Caucus had inserted the anti-Israel plank "not for any worked-out ideological reasons, but to establish solidarity with SNCC and prevent the political isolation of SNCC in a period of great danger of violence to our police repression of its members."[17] He continued to explain that even if whites, especially Jews, felt the point was anathema, they did not vote on the basis of their own agreement or disagreement, but solely on the basis of trying to prove they rejected white racism. Of course, the attitude Waskow favored was itself a paternalistic vestige of the old racism, although few liberal whites could see that at the time.

All attempts at compromise had been rejected. When *Ramparts* editor Robert Scheer, who had waged a tough race to gain the Democratic congressional spot in the Berkeley, California Democratic primary, suggested modifying the Israel resolution, he was shouted down. Scheer favored asking Israel to withdraw to her pre-June borders, in exchange for a commitment from the Arab states to respect them. "What right has the white man got amending the black man's resolution?" yelled a black voice from the floor. Arguing fiercely with a black delegate, a white radical stormed away, proclaiming that "Goyim do not understand Zionism!" Other whites proudly accepted the flagellation. "I'm not going to quibble over words," one white girl told Walter Goodman, "while Negroes are dying in the streets of Newark and Detroit."[18]

According to Waskow, it was mainly white liberals—not radicals—who wallowed in guilt and meekly went along with the black militants. In his eyes, liberals accepted the guilt for racism, while white radicals felt no guilt, because they were busy organizing in white communities for antiracist action. Waskow was one of the few who understood that to meekly accept black demands without thought was a "patronizing gesture." His own favored compromise, which he was never able to publicly raise on the floor, was that the white delegates make their own statement couching the same demands as the black's thirteen points in language acceptable in white communities. How that would be any less patronizing, Waskow never explained. Waskow felt that the thirteen points had been accepted by the whites "because 1,000 liberals thought they could become radicals by castrating themselves." Objecting to his arithmetic, Gottlieb more accurately commented that "there weren't 1,000 liberals at the convention;" but rather, "1,000 conflicted white middle-class radicals."[19]

Reading over Gottlieb's and Waskow's reports and notes on the convention, as well as the press coverage, it is quite clear that Gottlieb was nearer the truth: Most of the whites in attendance certainly did not consider themselves liberals. As Walter Goodman perceptively noted, the dominant mood of the whites in attendance was to show that they "were of a different breed from liberal Democrats, who play up to blacks only to manipulate them." Noting that when Forman appeared to speak, after Waskow, Scheer, Paul Booth, and Marty Peretz had walked out, "the remaining whites fairly tingled with pleasure under the whiplash of his demagogy." The Black Caucus "want to be trusted," cochairman Simon Casady said, "[and]we have to show them that we trust them."[20]

The result, Goodman wrote, was the victory pronouncement from Carlos Russell. Proclaiming that they had shown the world that "black people can fight," Russell took over the meeting "on behalf of a group which represented, at best, a sixth of the convention's constituency and had no noticeable program beyond the humiliation of their white comrades."[21] One of the striking things about the meeting was the active participation and involvement of American Communists who, true to their theory that blacks composed an independent American nation, became the chief spokesmen for the Black Caucus and its demand for 50 percent of the vote. Given the close ties between some SNCC leaders and the Communists, their participation was not surprising, but it was highly effective. According to Goodman, what they really hoped for was to gain black support for a third-party ticket, which they could use to break out of political isolation.

And this, aside from the black-white issue, was the key divisive fight of the convention. The question was whether or not to approve a call for a permanent new third party, a third ticket of

King-Spock for the 1968 race, or simply to endorse local organizing on a variety of "progressive" issues. The choice soon narrowed to a third ticket versus local efforts. As Waskow saw it, the third ticket was "supported by peacenik liberals who wanted to defeat Johnson," as well as New Politics groups that had support and a base and welcomed a campaign. Radicals, who wanted to change America and not just defeat Johnson, opposed the concept. With the convention split at the seams, the NCNP chose a combination of localism and political action: The delegates agreed to support local tickets in those states where the New Politics movement had some strength, but not at the expense of a broad commitment to local organizing, which would simultaneously continue.

Most of the delegates agreed that, as Gottlieb wrote, "the 'system' must be changed and that local organizing is the key to changing it"; the difference was over whether or not electoral politics was a valid organizing tool. When the final vote was taken, local organizing received 13,519 votes and a third ticket 13,517. The closeness of the final vote is what led to the compromise solution, which satisfied neither side. Gottlieb noted that in the internal politicking, "the Communist Party and its youth allies in the DuBois clubs were visibly working for a third ticket ... no doubt seeing its big chance to regain some influence on the Left."

What all this meant for moderates was, in retrospect, the main question. At the time, Gottlieb believed that if one could get the militant blacks to see that pressure to end the Vietnam War would lead to funds for America's internal needs, then what he called "coalitions based on mutual self-interest" could be built. The problem with the NCNP convention, according to Gottleib, was that the frustration felt by moderates against the war pushed them toward actions initiated by radicals with whom they actually shared little in common.

As for working through the Democratic Party, those who favored that option had simply walked out. Andrew Young, who would become mayor of Atlanta in the 1980s, had worked with Peretz in setting up the meeting. Young left in anger at the antics displayed by the Black Caucus militants. "These cats don't know the country has taken a swing to the right," Young told Peretz, "I wish the violence and riots had political significance," Young said, referring to those who saw the ghetto eruptions of the decade as rebellion, "but they don't."[22] Although there was ample opportunity for Democrats to pressure the administration through politics, "the convention delegates were so hostile to the two major parties and so oriented toward long-range radical perspectives," Gottlieb perceptively put it, "that there was ... no discussion of the seven Senate doves who [were] up for reelection in 1968," nor was there any "programmatic discussion of Vietnam."[23] The name of Robert Kennedy, already an opponent of the war, got bigger boos from the delegates than that of Lyndon Johnson. When Ted Weiss, a future congressman from New York's left-wing Upper West Side, and then a member of New York's City Council, got up to suggest that one should work through the Democratic Party to defeat LBJ, he was condemned for endorsing the "lesser evil" alternative.[24]

Strangely, the moderate Gottlieb revealed that his disenchantment was on the tactical level. Peace movement moderates, he argued, could have sought to regain their lost identity at the NCNP. Instead, they subordinated themselves to fiery radicals, who wanted to change the American social structure first, and who had no concrete program for the transformation they ostensibly sought. The levers of existing institutions, said Gottlieb, had to be used, however imperfect they might be. The radicals might well have asked whether the Vietnamese people and the American Negroes would agree with the timetable being suggested at the Palmer House. But rather than reject working with extremists, Gottlieb favored parallel action when their interests overlapped. Church members, he noted, could more easily discuss Vietnam with fellow parishioners than could members of the Maoist Progressive Labor Party. And while white radicals might be able to interpret the problem of the ghettos, their main task should be to end the Vietnam War—whether by advocating unilateral withdrawal or by urging a political settlement. Gottlieb saw all tasks as complementary, and brushed over the substantive differences.

Was the NCNP a viable vehicle for the Left? Gottlieb was pessimistic on this question, since he noted that most of the white young delegates saw America's dispossessed as the key to social change, and wanted to ignore the middle-class and electoral politics. Yet he observed accurately that while the NCNP may have failed, "the kind of people who participated in the Chicago convention will remain a part of the American scene for a long while." Believing in nonexclusion and working to change America with anyone on the far Left, they were a new coalition composed of anarchists, New Left advocates of decentralization, and various sects of the Old Left: Communists, Trotskyists, Maoists, and Black Power advocates. What the liberals had to do, Gottlieb said, was to engage these forces in dialogue, in order to achieve understanding of common interests.[25]

Waskow, caught between the liberals and the New Left, was even more hopeful. Pointing to the compromise solution—in which the NCNP seemed to endorse both local organizing and a national ticket in which localities had managed to put their choice on the ballot, Waskow saw the last day of the convention as one of "reconciliation, triumph, and final reeducation." Liberals were "toughened and radicalized," he wrote, and the Black Caucus and white Radical Caucus had managed to "build ongoing groups" where originally there had only been "hazy acquaintances." Thus, he believed, the mystical movement had come out stronger from the whole event. Organizationally, their antics had produced what he accurately called a "bad PR image," but he had great hopes that each side, acting on its own, could raise money and gain members more easily anyway.[26]

Others were not as sanguine. Walter Goodman saw the main point as "an argument for a kind of apartheid, with the goals of civil rights and integration being written off as stale promises of phony liberals." The worst was over, Waskow told him. "Now ... black and white radicals will work together in a man-to-man way." Waskow, Goodman revealed, was ignoring one new issue: sexism. He "found no humor in the pair of earnest girls who approached him with the suggestion that 51 percent of the convention's votes be given to women to make up for their centuries of inequality."[27]

The correspondent for *Nation* found the outcome less heartening. Richard Blumenthal thought that the NCNP leaders came off like regular politicians, papering over differences with vague statements about solidarity and brotherhood, instead of putting forth coalitions for action based on real interests. The tests they put forth were purely emotional, not political, centering on the spirit of resolutions rather than on their actual function or worthiness. Forecasting the movement's doom, Blumenthal commented that the convention "demonstrated that a New Poltics based on abstract tests of inner motive may be even more corrupting than the old politics—and ludicrous without power."[28]

When the meeting was over, the New Politics imbroglio had produced little of substance. The media reported it as a futile exercise in self-flagellation. Few realized that a new habit within the Left had been born, and would recur, that of willing subordination by white liberals and radicals to the demands and programmatic initiatives of radical blacks. And a second pattern that emerged would prove equally damaging. The white Left, frustrated at its inability to interfere effectively with the waging of the Vietnam War, had concluded that any participation within the two major parties was little more than a sellout of principle. The two alternatives they debated were those of local organizing outside the electoral sphere, or a third ticket that would challenge the major parties' presidential slates. Those moderates who preferred to operate within the existing political structures walked out in disgust and dismay. This was a great blow to the Democratic Party.

The radicals' next step would be more limited and practical, but also damaging to the Democrats, when they would call for major demonstrations at the party's 1968 convention in Chicago. But first, the liberal-radical community would split over a new development—the emergence of antiwar candidates working within the Democratic Party structure. Some would move into the ranks of the youth brigade working to advance the candidacy of Senator Eugene McCarthy of Minnesota; others would move to support Senator Robert F. Kennedy of New York, whose appeal, they thought, was greater to the public.

Those liberals who moved to support antiwar candidates in the Democratic Party were mobilized by a young independent liberal from New York named Allard Lowenstein. A one-man crusade who toured the nation's campuses, his overriding goal, as he put it, was to "dump Johnson." Eventually, with the Mc-Carthy and then Kennedy candidacies, Lowenstein's strategy would pay off. It was to be the start of what came to be called "the New Politics group" within the Democratic Party. By 1972 and the candidacy of George McGovern, the New Politics group not only emerged triumphant, but even united the divergent liberal and radical forces.

3

VIETNAM

The Great Wedge

Lyndon B. Johnson's election, Arthur M. Schlesinger, Jr., told liberals gathered at the convention of Americans for Democratic Action, offered the nation "the greatest opportunity for constructive liberalism in a generation."[1] But that opportunity, despite seemingly optimistic conditions, was not to be. Instead, the Johnson years would become the subject of mourning over lost opportunities, or the beginning of bitter memories of unrealized dreams. The one simple answer that surrounds all explanations for the tragic failure of the Johnson administration and LBJ's Great Society program, is one event—the war in Vietnam. The war, the shrewd British observer Godfrey Hodgson wrote, "became the organizing principle around which all the doubts and disillusionments of the years of crisis since 1963, and all the deeper discontents hidden under the glossy surface of the confident years, coalesced into one great rebellion."[2]

Vietnam was to drive a major wedge in the cracks of the liberal-labor New Deal and Fair Deal coalition. It was perhaps foolhardy to think that with war raging in Southeast Asia the old 1940s liberal order would be able to remain standing. Nevertheless, its old stalwarts tried their best. The fight that tore them apart took place first within the ranks of the old liberal left's key postwar organization, the Americans for Democratic Action. The leading players included the young and charismatic activist from New York, Allard Lowenstein; the principled chief counsel for the United Automobile Workers, Joe Rauh; and eventually, a new group of Democrats who would take up the cudgels to challenge Lyndon B. Johnson—Eugene McCarthy, Robert F. Kennedy, and George McGovern. The end result would be the triumph of the New Politics, and the collapse and decline of the old Democratic Party.

From the liberals' vantage point, it seemed that the only future for the Democrats was to seize the momentum by moving into the forefront of the burgeoning antiwar movement. That meant forthright condemnation of LBJ for his waging of the war. The more the president rejected their counsel, the more it seemed that the Democrats had but one choice: rejection of Johnson and a step toward further radicalization—to join those outside the ranks of the party who favored unilateral withdrawal from Vietnam and censure of the Democrats for their foreign intervention. Each escalation of the U.S. role in Southeast Asia, then, would push essentially moderate Democrats into the hands of left-wing radicals, with the effect of finally making it appear that the Democratic Party had become not the force of the American Center, but an extremist group that had betrayed its old and established roots.

Originally, the commitment of some fifty thousand troops to Vietnam in 1965 brooked little opposition. Young radicals in the Students for a Democratic Society (SDS) had sponsored a March on Washington, which brought some 25,000 young people to the nation's capital in protest. The media had all but ignored this early noninterventionism, and mainstream liberals, while wary of the effort, did not feel called upon to oppose the president's actions. Even radicals like Bayard Rustin and Irving Howe counseled their followers not to participate in the march, less they give aid and comfort to those who were actually supporting North Vietnamese Communism. Opposition centered not on the war, but on whether it was wise to pursue a policy of bombing in the North. Protest against the war, insofar as it could be said to even exist, took place only at the very fringes of American society. The Washington rally, one historian has written, "clearly reflected the radicals' victory."[3]

Escalation of the war, however, increased the voracity and the amount of protest politics. How could the nation refuse to intervene to prevent violence in the South against black Americans seeking freedom, and at the same time insist upon sending troops to far-off Vietnam to protect the freedom of South Vietnamese? Student radicals began to depict the president as a murderer of Vietnamese women and children. No longer concerned with keeping together a broad coalition of the labor-liberal Left—a coalition which had inspired trade unionists, civil rights leaders, churchmen, and intellectuals with the Democratic Party, the emerging New Left argued that the time had come to shift from politics to protest. The enemy, SDS leader Carl Oglesby had proclaimed in a speech given at a later march on Washington sponsored by the SANE Nuclear Policy Committee (which came to symbolize the position taken by SDS), was the "liberal Left," and its ideology was what he called "corporate liberalism." The term, a politicization of an intellectual approach formulated by the editors of *Studies on the Left*, a radical student journal at the University of Wisconsin, was meant to reveal that the liberalism prevailing in America was synthetic; liberal in guise, it actually revealed beneath its core the systemic domination of the nation by its corporate elites. To those involved in radical politics, this intellectual concept meant something much more practical: The enemy was no longer the old Republican right wing of the 1940s—the Taftite antilabor and isolationist wing of the Republican Party—but rather, it was the soul of modern liberalism— the liberals who dominated the center of the Democratic Party— and who had brought the nation to intervention in Vietnam.

Escalation, of course, was turning others to criticism besides far Left students. In April of 1966, J. William Fulbright, chairman of the Senate Foreign Relations Committee and the senior senator from Arkansas, accused the United States of displaying an "arrogance of power," and of "not living up to its capacity as a "civilized example for the world." Fulbright, who had voted with the majority in the Senate for the 1964 Gulf of Tonkin Resolution, (which gave the president unlimited powers to respond to North Vietnamese acts of aggression), became the most well known and outspoken critic of the administration's policy in Vietnam. By the time of the president's 1967 State of the Union message, the Vietnam War was consuming $10.5 billion of the federal budget, while the War on Poverty, a major Great Society program, received only $1.6 billion of the same federal budget.

It was in this context that a new group of activists arose to wage a head-on assault on the old Vital Center. Primary among them was a young man in his mid-twenties, the charismatic activist named Allard Lowenstein. Lowenstein, as his biographer William Chafe has pointed out, had grown up in the liberal milieu of New York City, where he was virtually raised in the Democratic Left. Always anxious to break new ground, Lowenstein chose to attend the southern University of North Carolina at Chapel Hill, a campus where he would stand out as one of the few Jewish students. It was there, as a protégé of the university's liberal president, that Lowenstein revealed his magnetic personality and his hyperkinetic behavior. He would work around the clock, stay up all night engaged in political bull sessions that would mesmerize his fellow students, and dedicate himself to gathering support in particular for work on behalf of civil rights. Later in his career, Lowenstein would criss-cross the country, stopping at one campus after another, becoming a virtual one-man pied piper of political activism. He would assume a leadership role in the National Student Association, and would gather international fame when on a trip to southwest Africa, he helped a dissident young black activist escape the country in order to testify before the United Nations. In the early 1960s, Lowenstein became a leader of the student support movement for civil rights. Freedom Summer in 1964, in which thousands of white students volunteered to work in Mississippi registering black citizens to vote, was Lowenstein's dream and his doing. Now, as Vietnam threatened to undo the dream of a Great Society, Lowenstein turned his attention to opposing the war in Vietnam, and to getting the Democratic Party to depose Lyndon B. Johnson as its leader and presidential candidate.

Lowenstein was to become best known as organizer of what came to be called the "dump Johnson" movement; a strategy that concentrated on personalizing the war as the president's and focused on getting a new candidate, rather than on chastising the United States for imperial ambition. Lowenstein, then, was no young radical. Indeed, his criticism of administration policy was made within the existing mainstream consensus. In one of his first speeches to students about the war, delivered sometime in

1965, Lowenstein called the claim that "this war is being fought for democracy" to be a deception. The regime in Saigon was authoritarian, he explained, "without popular support or social conscience." The very regime propped up by the United States was not offering freedom or reform to its own people; the claim that they suffered aggression from the North was an "insult to human intelligence." Like others in the emerging antiwar movement, Lowenstein saw the conflict as a civil war, in which legitimate nationalism had become intertwined by both sides, "by Communists terrorizing village chiefs and the CIA enabling the repression of the Diem regime."[4]

Most upsetting to Lowenstein, who prided himself on being a liberal, was that his own nation was appropriating "the vocabulary of liberalism to justify the politics of reaction." Especially painful, he thought, were the policies espoused by Vice President Hubert Humphrey, whom Lowenstein thought spoke out of both sides of his mouth. But unlike the New Left, Lowenstein was clear about one thing: "Opposing U.S. policy," he said, "we hold no brief for the other side. *We know how ugly totalitarianism, whether of left or right, can be.*" (author's emphasis) Indeed, he argued that hard-line Communists wanted a protracted war. The only answer was to hold truly free elections in which all political tendencies could participate. The United States had to be ready to negotiate with Ho Chi Minh's forces, arrange a cease fire, and abide by the results of the elections. But, he emphasized, so did Ho Chi Minh.[5]

Vice President Humphrey was caught in between; probably sympathetic to Lowenstein and his views but forced by his position to endorse and support the policy of the president he served. Speaking before the Americans for Democratic Action in 1966, the Vice President explained the issue as toleration of aggression. The National Liberation Front (NLF) did not have popular support, Humphrey believed, and not one opposition figure in South Vietnam supported it; neither had they "called for a coalition government with the Vietcong since Ho Chi Minh's abortive 'popular front' efforts in 1946 and 1947." Humphrey, who gained his own understanding of popular fronts from the Communist efforts to undermine him in Minnesota in 1946, noted that he did not have to tell old Cold War liberals "how the Communists operate, how the demand for 'coalition' is a staging point in . . . slicing up the non-Communists." But while no one in the ADA might have to be informed about that, Humphrey seemed unaware that to the new young rebels, such arguments were antiquated and unnecessary red-baiting. They thought one had to understand and accept the other side as a legitimate force. Humphrey's correct understanding that the NLF was simply a "front for Hanoi" was, of course, historically accurate, as was his claim that they were a "vehicle for the seizure of power in South Vietnam." But the New Left wanted the Vietcong to gain that very power, and saw any resistance to their attempts to be immoral. Asking what might have happened had the United States not intervened with "timely aid" in Greece after World War II, Humphrey pointed out the obvious: nonintervention would have meant a Communist victory. To determine their own future, people needed elections and not to have their future secured by a disciplined minority movement which practiced guerrilla warfare.[6]

Lowenstein, himself a dedicated anti-Communist, agreed with much of what Humphrey said. But he, economist John Kenneth Galbraith, Arthur M. Schlesinger, Jr., and others were moving quickly toward the Left. Lowenstein's circle of correspondents, in fact, were more concerned that it would be the Republicans who would lead the United States out of Vietnam, given Johnson's commitment to involvement and escalation. "We aren't alone,"

one friend wrote, "in predicting . . . a nice big juicy S.E. Asia land war. . . . We figure our only hope rests with the Republicans. The bastards have got to do an about-face in midstream and assume a dove-like posture to counter the Democrats in the coming elections."[7]

At the same time, Lowenstein was deeply concerned that the antiwar movement would be co-opted by anti-American New Leftists, whose sympathies were with the Vietcong, and who secretly—and often not so secretly—favored Vietcong victory and saw themselves as the cutting edge within "the belly of the beast" for the revolutionary forces at home. One New Leftist who had heard Lowenstein speak at her campus, complained to him that he had "warned about the SDS," and she had ignored what he said. At Chapel Hill, she argued, the student radicals had a solid leadership, with a lazy and inarticulate cadre with "energy, but no thought." Although his correspondent tried to sympathize with the distinctions he made among opponents of the war, she was "still enough of the child of thirties' libs [i.e., Communists or Socialists] to think that the guys on my side must be good."[8]

Lowenstein was opposed to the war, but his opposition was clearly not that of the student Left or the adult radicals and revolutionaries. He was opposed, he tried to make clear in a 1967 speech, to either "precipitate withdrawal, or on the other hand, massive escalation." The two options facing America were those of extensive and extended bombing of North Vietnam, expanded search-and-destroy missions by American ground troops, and an increased U.S. presence. The object of such an escalation would be to force Hanoi to surrender and to exterminate the Vietcong. Their goal, on the other hand, should be to keep *"South Vietnam a pro-Western, viable, non-Communist state."* (author's emphasis) Unlike so many of the emerging "peace" movements, Lowenstein understood that freedom was tied to the fortunes of the West, and that if it went Communist, the South Vietnamese would have lost something basic and precious. The problem, as he saw it, was that an open-ended war would consume both sides, and there would be no prospect for an American military triumph, since "we cannot win a total American victory."

Thus the object to gain, Lowenstein tried to persuade his followers, was to "press for a negotiated settlement of the war"; one that would build upon political realities and end the killing on both sides. Such an outcome, he hoped, could be welcomed by all sides, although it clearly meant a compromise in terms of America's optimal desires. Primary among these was to gain representation in negotiations for all elements to the conflict, including those of the indigenous enemy, by which he meant the Vietcong, or National Liberation Front operating within South Vietnam. The Vietcong had to be a full partner in negotiations, Lowenstein proposed, and the United States had to acknowledge a political role for it in a postwar South Vietnam. Such a role demanded internationally supervised free elections, and guarantees by all foreign powers for Vietnam's neutrality in international relations.[9]

Lowenstein was therefore clearly not proposing what others in the antiwar movement would soon demand: agreement in advance for a coalition government in South Vietnam which included the NLF. A seemingly sensible plan, but critics were correct to point out that such an arrangement was perfectly contrived to guarantee Communist victory via the salami tactics perfected by the post–World War II Communists in Eastern Europe. Coalition governments, in effect, had come to mean the tactic by which a minority of Communists quickly arranged to take over the seat of government, with the subsequent purge, arrest, and executions of non-Communists originally part of the coalition. As such, Lowenstein's views were actually closer to those of Vice President Humphrey. Writing in *Pageant* magazine in 1966, Humphrey had stated that the war was "the effort of a liberal, forward-looking United States to use its strength to limit destructive and expansionist ambitions." As liberals, the vice president wrote, "we cannot close our eyes to Communist aggression. For if Marxist seeds are sown with impunity, the world will reap a bitter harvest." Like Lowenstein, Humphrey hoped that as of 1967, Vietnam could be concluded with a political solution and a negotiated settlement.[10]

Lowenstein agreed with Humphrey and the old liberals but felt that a land war in Vietnam would only lead to debacle, and further away from the goal both he and the old liberals shared. As soon as the president began to escalate, moreover, Lowenstein feared that Johnson was so personally committed to military escalation that all reason would be abandoned. His views coincided with an emerging split within the oldest liberal pressure group, the ADA. Toward the end of the year, ADA member Don Fraser had called the war the "single greatest threat to world security." According to Fraser, LBJ's policies had turned a minor civil conflict into a "major test of wills," with Americans now serving as front-line combatants. Bombing was at a level higher than raids on Germany during the Second World War, so that Vietnam had increased "in scope, size, and barbarity."

According to Fraser, it was neither "necessary nor desirable for us to seek to win the war." It was far better to seek a compromise settlement that would allow the "Vietnamese to determine their own destiny." Fraser, of course, begged the question of whether the North Vietnamese would agree to such a solution. What he assumed was that a solution could never be gained by the "force of American guns," although withdrawal, as Lowenstein understood, would definitely allow the North Vietnamese to gain such an end through *their* guns. Fraser's call was simple: an end to the bombing, de-escalation of the ground war, and negotiations directly with the NLF. That, he thought, would "offer the adversary some incentive to lay down his arms and negotiate." Fraser was already moving toward the direction favored by the revolutionary Left. The main job, he argued, was to give the NLF a major role in the life of South Vietnam, "either as part of a coalition government or as a recognized political party in free elections in South Vietnam." What he refused to consider was whether those were mutually exclusive options. In free elections, the NLF might very well have lost, just as did the Sandinistas in Nicaragua in 1989. But given a governmental role in a coalition without elections, they would be handed the very mechanism through which they could seize power.[11]

The war was precipitating a crisis within the old liberal community. Nowhere did this come to the surface more than within ADA, which had just agreed to elect Lowenstein to a vice presidency, a move seen as cementing the organization's ties to youth. "The question ADA had to confront in 1967," writes the organization's historian, "was how to translate its growing frustration with the war into political action."[12] What soon emerged was a split between ADA's older liberal wing—the group associated with both Truman Democrats from the forties and the Congress of Industrial Organizations leadership—and younger elements sympathetic to both the New Politics movement and the New Left.

As ADA gathered for its annual convention in April 1967, these issues came to a head. It was clear that the members would go on record in opposition to the Vietnam War. The real question was how far, and in what manner. Would they merely question the policy, or turn on the Johnson administration? Would they support working with the administration to reach a settlement, trusting the president to implement whatever policies he believed would lead toward that end? Or would they, as Lowenstein and others hoped, break with LBJ and tell liberals to find and support a new candidate?

At first, the convention's choice of John Kenneth Galbraith as chairman was neutral and acceptable to all sides. Critical of the war, Galbraith was felt to not be in favor of a total break with the administration. Indeed, in his speech to the convention, he carefully avoided overt criticism of LBJ and his policies. John P. Roche, an old liberal who fully supported the president, was so pleased that he informed Johnson that Galbraith was actually a "restraining force within ADA."[13] Roche's enthusiasm was to prove misplaced. The thrust of the resolution passed at the convention was to turn ADA toward the Left, and to pull moderates like Galbraith along with the tide. The four-hundred delegates meeting at the Shoreham Hotel in Washington passed resolutions expressing their "disenchantment and dismay over many aspects of administration policy in Vietnam." The blame for escalation was laid at LBJ's door, and the president was condemned for increasing the scale of the war "in size, scope, and barbarity," the words taken directly from oppositionist Fraser. ADA called for an end to the bombing of North Vietnam, a truce, and (the key point) recognition by the United States of the Communist guerrillas, the National Liberation Front.

Debate on political issues was vivid. Rauh and Lowenstein both praised Republicans who were speaking out in opposition to the war in liberal terms. Their praise was meant to warn the administration that if it did not shift course, some liberal Democrats would find themselves able to cast a dissenting vote by supporting Republicans. Gus Tyler tried in vain to take a more moderate path. Tyler favored praising the administration's legislative programs, and urged a settlement of the war. What was important, he argued, was to retain the labor-liberal coalition. A "strong statement of anger, protest, and frustration against the president on Vietnam," he said, would "mislead the liberal community."[14]

For the time being, ADA deferred the question, and took no position on the looming issue of whom to support in the 1968 presidential elections. They did utter an ominous phrase about being pledged "to no man and no party," but in practice, the liberals had always been and would have to be, until the 1970s and the birth of neoconservatism, in the camp of the Democrats. ADA also gave its backing to the pressure group called Negotiations Now!, an antiwar action group composed of Democrats and peace activists who sought to force the president's supporters to back a negotiated settlement instead of a military victory. A moderate force within the peace movement, the Negotiations Now! group was supported by a few moderate labor leaders and Social Democrats, who in contrast to militants who demanded unilateral U.S. withdrawal from Vietnam, combined a call for negotiations with political support to LBJ and his goal of a Great Society.

ADA's compromise was short-lived. The next month, at the meeting of their national board, forty of the body's one-hundred forty-three members passed an extreme resolution, pledging to back the candidate of either party in 1968, as long as that candidate offered hope "for restraint in the conduct of the war in Vietnam." Vietnam, in other words, was now to be the sole test of the liberals' support of the ticket in the forthcoming electoral contest. The vote infuriated Tyler and his supporters, who sought to have the decision overturned.

From Tyler's perspective, liberals simply could not abandon support of the Johnson administration, since in his eyes, LBJ had done more for liberal legislation than any president since FDR. Regretting a shift by liberals from economics to morality and culture, Tyler argued that as in the thirties, a good percentage of the nation was still ill-clothed, ill-housed and ill-fed. One-quarter of Americans still suffered deprivation, he argued, as many as had suffered in the Depression. But now, with the standard of living on the increase, the poor expected more—"bigger pensions, hospitalization, free medicine"; and blacks, no longer subservient, also "expected more and they explode" when they don't get it.[15]

To stay focused on economics, Tyler argued, ADA had to dissociate itself from the resolution introduced by Fraser. Otherwise, he thought, it would remove itself "from liberal politics in America, and that would "make a coalition of labor and liberal elements impossible." It was also regrettable that ADA was limiting its choices so narrowly, a step which would leave them "obliged to back a reactionary Republican isolationist against a liberal Democrat, because the former promises peace." ADA, Tyler insisted, was committing itself to "monomania" that would isolate it "from the mainstream of American politics, and from the vast body of liberal voters in America," including those who had backed ADA from its inception.[16] Vietnam, Tyler said, should not become the exclusive concern of liberals who were already divided at a moment when both the ghettos and the Middle East were about to blow up. Union leaders were already breaking ranks with ADA, The resolution was passed by a small group of people "dressed up" to appear as one-hundred forty-three, and Tyler was adamant that their effort would not push Johnson to the peace table.[17]

By June, Tyler had got signatures for his position from John P. Roche, Charles Cogen of the United Federation of Teachers, Victor Reuther of the United Auto Workers, Joseph Bierne of the Communications Workers, Louis Stulberg and David Dubinsky of the ILGWU, churchman Paul Seabury, civil rights leader Bayard Rustin, and economist Leon Keyserling. All of them vigorously opposed the ADA resolution passed at the board's May 1967 meeting. This body, however, reflected the leftmost part of the labor-liberal coalition, those in the labor movement whose perspective was Social-Democratic, and whose politics had evolved out of support for Franklin D. Roosevelt and the CIO during the New Deal era.

Now that Lyndon Johnson was in office, liberal intellectuals who once were part of the coalition with labor began to view things differently. They did not buy Tyler's argument that ADA would be isolated not only from the mainstream, but from elements with which they once were influential. Indeed, it was clear that they could not care less about their relations with the remnants of the once-strong organized labor movement. Now, they thought, liberals had to appeal to youth. Thus James Loeb wrote Tyler that the old coalition could not persist forever. Moreover, he pointed out, "youth was part of that [newer] coalition," and he and Tyler were no longer youth.[18] The real question, opined Arthur Schlesinger, was whether they would have more influence "if the administration can assume it has ADA in its pocket." Writing to Tyler, Schlesinger said any other policy would forfeit ADA's claim to independence.[19]

John Kenneth Galbraith, himself one of the old liberal intellectuals, also saw the issues differently than those who had emerged from the trade union movement. "We must . . . correct some errors of liberalism which have damaged us," he wrote a friend. The single greatest error, Galbraith thought, was to "concentrate on domestic matters and leave foreign policy to the experts . . . [to have] imagined that we could be liberal at home and conservative abroad."[20]

If liberals concentrated on one issue alone, Tyler retorted, they would be dead politically. "Apparently," he wrote historian Schlesinger, "you believe that so long as we are deeply involved in

Vietnam we *can* not or *will* not do the right thing about civil rights, war on poverty." But Tyler believed that the United States could fight in Vietnam and have the economic wherewithal to "do the necessary job on the domestic front." The problem was simply political will to do the job; by concentrating on Vietnam, liberals were abandoning their task before they even waged a fight. "It may well be," he concluded, "that there are some who are so preoccupied with the Vietnam matter that they have no time or energy left to do the fighting on the domestic issues." Speaking for himself, Tyler assured Schlesinger he was devoting his own energy to poverty, civil rights, and the minimum wage such "that I resent being told there is only one issue; namely, Vietnam." Twitting Schlesinger, whom he not too subtly was accusing of having abandoned his own position on liberalism, he argued that ADA should be a "'vital center'—between both these elements;" the far Left and the moderate Right.[21] Tyler was on solid ground. Most liberal social policy, from the prolabor regulations of the First World War to the spurt of unionism during the Second World War, had come about because of, not despite, foreign wars.

Galbraith, Schlesinger, and Lowenstein had, in effect, split the liberal coalition at the seams. Senator Paul Douglas, whose roots in politics came from the same old Socialist movement of Debs and Thomas as Tyler, was livid about any move against LBJ. His own membership in ADA, he wrote Galbraith, was conditional upon a firm "non-Communist, anti-Communist, anti-totalitarian pledge as a requirement for membership." Now, under the influence of a new Left, Douglas feared that ADA was growing weak on the issue of "resistance to aggressive communism in Southeast Asia." Its very strength, he warned, was in its understanding that Communism was a danger to liberal democratic society. While that danger had not diminished, ADA's "steadfast-

ness in this regard has been mistakenly eroded." That had occurred, he thought, because of the "nature and impetuousness of
youth" as well as an "irrational" attraction on young people's part
to Third World revolutions. As he saw it, ADA, by condemning
Johnson, had capitulated to this very irrationality, and he had "a
strong feeling of revulsion." It seemed, he thought, that liberals
might even "go Republican on the peace issue alone."[22]

In a turnabout that confirmed his own earlier fears, Allard
Lowenstein came to the fatal conclusion that the liberal movement simply could not give its support to the Johnson administration in 1968, even if that meant a Republican would gain the
presidency. Brash, young, and ever so opinionated, Lowenstein
viewed LBJ as the one obstacle and the one enemy of those committed to a more rational foreign policy. Once Lowenstein was
on the ADA Board, moderates who had supported his nomination found much to be disappointed about. Almost immediately,
the upstart clashed with Tyler.

Events in 1967 only served to up the ante. Each escalation of
the war led to a radicalization of the peace movement. Black un-
rest, the explosion of the ghettos, and the growing cry of "black
power" led men like Tyler and Rustin to favor attention to domestic racism and social programs to deal with it. But to Lowenstein and others, the war was now the single determining issue. If
not for Vietnam, dissenters were arguing, there would have been
money to spend on social programs that would have prevented
the bitter explosions in Watts, Detroit, and Newark. That logic
did not sit well with the older and more traditional liberals. "I
suppose the temptation to tie our social problems to the war in
Vietnam is virtually irresistible," presidential advisor John P.
Roche wrote in June. "I fully expect cranberry growers to blame
any bad crop on the war."[23] Under Tyler and Roche's influence,
the ADA Executive Committee issued a resolution in July that

attacked the conservative coalition in Congress, and which purposely failed to mention Vietnam.

Schlesinger tried to downplay the split within ADA, and the May National Board resolution. It only meant, he argued, that the group would support the candidate best suited to avoiding a third World War. That candidate, Schlesinger wrote to ADA members, "could not be a reactionary or an isolationist." Schlesinger did realize that the dispute was whether Vietnam was just another topic, such as minimum wage laws, or the "most important of the day," and that if liberals kept treating it as just "one among many issues, it will lose any hope of keeping the support of the independent liberals and the young." But he concluded that an antiwar resolution actually "creates the possibility of liberal politics in America," while unconditional support of the administration "strengthens those who tell LBJ he doesn't have to worry about liberals; they have nowhere else to go." Influence is to be gained, he retorted to Tyler, by "indicating independence," while Tyler's path pointed to "liberal bankruptcy."[24]

For columnist James A. Wechsler, editor of the *New York Post*, the new discord revealed an "unparalleled" conflict, one that even transcended that between the anti-Stalinist liberals and fellow-travelers in the late 1940s. Division, it seemed, was the "grievous price" at home for Vietnam; perhaps a foreshadowing of "the strife that will divide the liberal-labor coalition" if Johnson continues to escalate in Vietnam.[25] Gus Tyler responded at once and tried to defend the group as a whole. He agreed that a one-issue movement would be finished, and that the problem was that the Left in ADA saw Vietnam as "the ONLY issue." But his only goal, Tyler claimed, was to stop making Vietnam the single concern of liberals, not to silence protest against the war. "To call this a conspiracy of 'White House loyalists' is similar to the charge that ghetto riots are manufactured by Communist agents." Should liberals, he asked, be mute on all issues but Vietnam?[26]

The issue finally broke out fully at the September 1967 ADA National Board meeting. There, Allard Lowenstein worked to gain ADA support for a dump-Johnson resolution. The leader of the campus ADA chapter, the young Harvard student Elliott Abrams, worked feverishly to support Lowenstein's effort. He backed a resolution which read that "since Vietnam, race, and poverty are the moral tests of this generation, it is equally plain that moral Americans cannot support Lyndon Johnson. He must be rejected in the most practical way—electing delegates to the Democratic national convention pledged to oppose his nomination in 1968." Tyler countered with his own resolution, which said that ADA should not be involved in any such effort, should work for Vietnam negotiations, and argued that Johnson and his administration could not be judged solely on Vietnam, but on the "wide range of liberal domestic legislation" the president favored.[27]

Standing between Lowenstein and Tyler was Joe Rauh, the old liberal stalwart, not only an ADA vice president, but chief counsel to the United Automobile Workers. Deeply opposed to the war, Rauh also wanted to hold the liberal-labor coalition together. He proposed a compromise he thought both sides could live with. The group would elect peace delegates to the '68 convention, which would oppose the war but at the same time would *support* Johnson's nomination as presidential candidate of the Democratic Party. For the pro-Johnson and prowar faction, it spelled a strategic retreat that was good for their own policy.

Rauh thought that Lowenstein's effort would destroy "the liberal-labor-Negro coalition that had elected every liberal president and made possible every liberal advance since the 1930s."[28] Believing in normalcy, Rauh wanted work carried out through "responsible" figures in the Democratic Party and through the political process, a process he believed would slowly reveal the true breadth and strength of the antiwar movement.

Rauh was particularly worried that the forthcoming New Politics conference would set in motion a movement on behalf of a third party in 1968. If they succeeded in getting Martin Luther King to run on a new ticket, Rauh thought a lot of Negro voters would be added to the million whites who would vote a protest ticket. But even then, they could not get more than 2 million votes; "an infinitesimal fraction of the peace feeling in America." Indeed, Republicans might become so heartened, Rauh argued, that they "may delude themselves in believing that the third party will siphon off enough Democratic votes to make victory possible even with their most favored candidate—Richard Nixon;" a step that would *end all chance of the Republicans nominating a moderate candidate offering some hope for peace.* (Rauh's emphasis)

Rauh, then, was motivated by a desire to bring out the peace forces not just within the Democratic ranks, but also within the Republican Party. Still, his heart was with the Democrats. Robert Kennedy, he thought, might even enter the New Hampshire primary opposing the draft and working for LBJ. Any "dump Johnson" movement, he predicted, would hurt the peace forces, since no responsible Democrat would enter a drive against a sitting Democratic president. The only way to maximize the peace strength would be to work for a peace plank in the 1968 platform. The goal would be to "maximize the political pressure upon the Democratic administration to end the war." Citing the past, Rauh stressed that *every Democratic National Convention has a large degree of built-in liberalism.* Thus influential delegates sought to help the Mississippi Freedom Democrats in 1964; and many who opposed the war would now do the same for such a platform fight. Rauh looked forward to a massive convention fight, ignoring the reality that an administration taking a different course would simply ignore such sentiment, and that delegates pledged to endorse such an administration regardless of its view were boxing shadows.

Rauh hoped that would be a "restraining influence" on the administration, thinking that LBJ would pause before escalating the war in Vietnam if he was aware of fights going on in all state parties. And many who opposed the war, Rauh thought, would only speak up if there was no threat of a dump-Johnson movement. Rauh also worried that organized labor—a force strongly committed to LBJ, as well as to his Vietnam policy—would be further antagonized by the hostility to the president. But ultimately, since Johnson was the very president pursuing a war policy, Rauh's plan was impractical.

Some said LBJ would not follow a peace plank if it passed; after all, he did much of what many feared Goldwater would have done if he had been elected in 1964. But with a determined party, he could not disregard their wishes. A peace fight, moreover, would make that issue the major one "at an otherwise dull convention." Rauh thus saw the proposal as one with more advantages than any other suggestions that had been offered; it would "stimulate discussion and comment among people who want to bring the Vietnam war to an honorable compromise solution rather than to escalate for 'victory.' "[29]

Lowenstein feared that Rauh's proposed path was insufficiently tough. Rauh was overestimating the effectiveness of the Negotiations Now! coalition, he told the ADA board, as well as national popular revulsion against LBJ's escalation of the war.[30] Roche, however, reported to Johnson that he thought the majority of ADA would stand with the moderates or with the president. There were only "twenty on the nut fringe," he wrote Johnson, referring to Lowenstein, "forty in Rauh's center lump, and thirty with me." Schlesinger, he sarcastically told the president, was "cooing like a dove in the Rauh caucus," and Lowenstein was "left a querulous, bitching, pleading casualty." Thus he predicted an indecisive outcome in a fight between "the peace nuts and the Rauh entourage."[31]

To Rauh, as to Tyler, a crack-up of the old liberal coalition was as important to avoid as negotiating an end to the divisive war in Vietnam. "A polarization of the left of center would only strengthen the far Right and the radical Left," he wrote to Tyler. Indeed, Rauh tried to argue that it was to the president's own interest that the main forces of liberalism not collapse during his administration. "Our differences," he stressed, "have to do with strategy and tactics, not with principles. None of us is 'soft on Communism.'" The issue at hand was whether they had to win every battle, and Rauh suggested that perhaps they had to accept a "strategic retreat" this time around, on Vietnam. "Overcommitment," Rauh argued, "can mean losing the war itself."[32]

The whole point of a peace caucus at the 1968 convention, Rauh explained, was to find an alternative to the dump-Johnson movement put together by Lowenstein, although, he wrote a friend, if Kennedy or McCarthy or George McGovern were to become all-out candidates, he would have to support them. As for backing McCarthy against LBJ, he had done so "more in sorrow than anger." As Rauh saw things, Johnson had done "some magnificent things in the early days and we must always be mindful of them." Agreeing that the president had "lost his way" on Vietnam, Rauh favored disagreement among liberals who supported a common domestic agenda, "without tearing up everything else for which they have always worked together." America was being torn apart by "division and hostility," and as a patriot, Rauh clearly was not happy with the rupture of the body politic. His hope was that McCarthy could "make some dent" in the leftward end of the political spectrum, and by making peace part of the political process, undermine the more extreme Left.[33] Rauh was also opposed to what he called the "control of the McCarthy campaign by the 'dump-Johnson' people." He himself had tried to get McCarthy to run before the convention, and the job was to get "responsible" people into the McCarthy campaign in the various states. It was imperative that he get ADA, "not [Henry] Wallace or New Left types" active, Rauh stressed, and that McCarthy personally "put more fire" into his campaign. Nevertheless, Rauh understood well that McCarthy had given them a political mechanism for acting against the war, and they had to back him "as an act of faith."[34] Having started out in opposition to a race against the incumbent Democratic president, Rauh, not wanting to break with those who were waging the fight to extricate the United States from Vietnam, abruptly had reversed himself, and now accepted the efforts of those seeking another candidate.

Rauh's tortured trajectory itself shows how the die was already cast. The Democratic Party was rapidly moving leftward—a shift that would become evident in the years after the 1968 convention. The issue that men like Joe Rauh, Gus Tyler, Arthur Schlesinger, and other liberal Democrats confronted was the key one for the present as well as the future health of their party— how could it maintain its center during a war that had become unpopular with one group of its constituency, the important liberal political activists? Rauh especially had tried. He sought unsuccessfully to support compromise solutions that would have the liberals still supporting an LBJ ticket, but working to get the Democratic Party to oppose the war. That solution pleased neither side in the debate. By the time it was over, Rauh himself had shifted to supporting Gene McCarthy's quixotic attempt to challenge the incumbent in the primary campaigns.

Once people like Rauh had decided to establish opposition to the war in Vietnam as their major focus, it had to be but a short time before they would decide to break with the labor-liberal coalition, membership in which demanded that the war not come between the main goal of voting in an administration that was liberal in its domestic policy. By accepting the argument of the Left—that any administration could not be liberal at home and support foreign war abroad—they had no choice but to quickly move to the Left. Their decision would come to haunt their party for decades.

4

McCARTHY AND THE
QUIXOTIC CAMPAIGN

The split in the liberal community had hardened beyond repair. The young New Left had opted out of the mainstream, while the old liberal mainstream, anxious to prove its credentials and credibility to the young, continued to shift toward the Left. The strategy was a no-win situation. The more they moved, the harder the New Left pushed. To its erstwhile and tough leaders, the kind of compromise envisioned by moderate ADA leaders was hardly sufficient. For that matter, neither was the challenge offered to Lyndon Johnson by the candidacy of Eugene McCarthy.

No one reflected the hardened New Left better than the charming president of Students for a Democratic Society, Carl Oglesby. A thirty-year-old man often quoted by the media and cited as an individual who stood on the cutting edge of radical dissent, Oglesby was an articulate and smart college graduate, a self-proclaimed novelist and playright who gave up a successful career in military-related research, and a family life to boot, to assume the mantle as SDS's main spokesman in its heyday. Usually appearing in public with a hippie-style flowered shirt and a guitar, Oglesby fit perfectly with the public image of the sixties political radical—an individual with one foot in the counterculture and the other in left-wing politics. Above all, Oglesby was known for naming the enemy of the radical youth in a public speech given at an antiwar SDS-sponsored rally in the nation's capital. Following the example of his predecessor in SDS, Paul Potter, who six months earlier had demanded that the movement "name the system," and who then continued to attack it without naming it, Oglesby gave the speech of his career. There was a name for the system, he opined in a speech presented to cheering throngs—it was "corporate liberalism." Speaking at a March on Washington held on October 15, 1965, as 100,000 people in fifty other cities across America met at similar rallies organized by an umbrella coalition named the Vietnam Day Committee, Oglesby threw out the challenge. The president and his advisors were not monsters, he told the crowd. Indeed, they were "all honorable men. They are all liberals." Their morality was that of servant of the corporate liberal system, and unless the system was changed, atrocities such as the war in Vietnam would not end.[1]

For Oglesby and his followers, the system in America was essentially akin to fascism, a fascism with a human face, protected by the thin veneer of so-called corporate liberalism. To justify their perspective, the SDS youth turned to the words of an old and respected philosopher, Herbert Marcuse.[2] A refugee from Nazi Germany, where in Weimar days he was part of the radical Frankfurt School of social theory, Marcuse had penned what became perhaps the single most influential essay of the New Left, on "repressive tolerance." Protest was allowed in repressive America, Marcuse argued, as a mechanism to siphon off emerging revolutionary currents. Apparent freedom was in reality un-freedom—an argument that took much from the analytical skills of Karl Marx, who argued in a similar dialectical vein that apparently free wage labor was actually the equivalent of slave labor. Protest was but a safety valve, and real substantive change could never be achieved within the system. The student Left was thereby justified in turning its attention to both street battles, such as the kind that would erupt at the Chicago Democratic convention, and violent upheavals on the nation's campuses.

Given his radical inclinations, it was not surprising to find that Oglesby and SDS thought little of the brigades of college youth who flocked to help Gene McCarthy in his New Hampshire primary campaign, and who shaving their beards and getting rid of their old torn Levis, came to be dubbed the "clean for Gene" brigade. SDS, after all, had originally coined the phrase "part of the way with LBJ," to indicate their lukewarm support for the president in his 1964 campaign against Barry Goldwater. When Johnson won, in the eyes of SDS, he quickly implemented Goldwater's campaign promises to escalate the war. Now, Gene McCarthy appeared as a Johnny-come-lately who held out the whimsical hope that working within the hated system could produce meaningful change. Oglesby's broadside, "A Message for McCarthy Voters," had more effect on the radical SDS members than on the senator's young supporters.[3]

A vote for McCarthy, Olgesby claimed, was a vote for the system that had produced the war. Rather than a force to change America, the SDS leader charged, McCarthy and his legions represented "an attempt to emasculate that protest" which SDS had already inaugurated. Aside from opposing the war, Oglesby charged, the senator saw no need to change any aspect of American foreign policy. McCarthy's case against the war was that of a "traditional case for anti-Communist containment." Radicals, unlike liberals, understood the hidden benefits of the war they despised. The U.S. policy of aggression was cracking apart the Atlantic Alliance, the very NATO forces people like Eugene McCarthy wanted to preserve. At best, Oglesby wrote, McCarthy's campaign was the "Leftmost ideological position at which political realism still endures." It was understood that realism was a bad thing—it was no substitute for idealism.

Oglesby continued to point out that while it was true that some on the Left had endorsed McCarthy, it was not because they thought the senator "would join the Vietcong," as SDS cadre would have liked. Rather, they worked for him because they hoped he would "bring off the capitulation [of the United States] without totally freaking everybody out." As for the real Left, it had to be utopian in the terms demanded by Marcuse—preaching socialism rather than reformed capitalism, withdrawal from the war rather than endless negotiations. Above all, it had to oppose "defense of the same American Empire" that Gene McCarthy clearly revered and which the New Left knew was "flatly insupportable." McCarthy and his kind wanted to end the war in order to revamp American imperialism. The goal of the New Left had to be clear—working for a revolution at home through support of a Vietcong victory in Indochina.

Oglesby's position shifted the New Left considerably further leftward, and pinpointed the critical differences between the liberal opposition of an Allard Lowenstein and the antiwar view of the New Left. Lowenstein was clear that he wanted the American political system to work. To Oglesby, those with that goal were the real reactionaries. To support McCarthy was to adulterate the "necessary critique of the war," and meant obscuring "its sources in the system of American expansionism." Indeed, Oglesby even opposed the path Robert Kennedy espoused—that of support for a coalition government in Vietnam including the National Liberation Front or Vietcong. Such a move, Oglesby protested, would force the NLF "into a coalition whose other elements are precisely the forces which the NLF has been struggling to expel." In other words, nothing less than an NLF victory in Vietnam was acceptable! The Left knew this, he surmised, and those of their ranks backing McCarthy were cynically seeking a way to make their own "dissent look respectable and 'legitimate.'" It was McCarthy who needed the ranks of the New Left, not they who needed him.

McCarthy, he stressed, was an anti-Communist. Not only was Communism not a threat, but rather it was "the primary form taken on by the struggles of the forcibly dispossessed to repossess themselves of their identity and destiny." It was for this reason that within the United States, the New Left welcomed the "militant nationalism of American blacks." Not the integrated democracy of Martin Luther King, but the separatist black nation demanded by the followers of Malcolm X would be the forces to which the white New Left gave its support. Their goal was simple: complete socialization of the world's wealth, a goal that anyone could see was unobtainable through the very system which had produced Vietnam.

Oglesby's path, however, was obviously self-defeating, at least for those who sought political influence and an actual end to American involvement in Vietnam. Hence many others of the radical Left, especially those a bit older than the SDS generation, offered Eugene McCarthy, and later Robert Kennedy, their support. Martin Peretz and the Cambridge New Left were strong McCarthy backers. There was, as historian Herbert Parmet has written, a national climate favoring another Democratic presidential candidate, one not so closely tied to waging war in Southeast Asia. The emergence of such a figure within the Democratic Party mainstream was not long in coming. General William Westmoreland had called for a vast increase in the U.S. military presence. In response, a group of some of the nation's leading "wise men," as they were called, including Clark Clifford, Robert McNamara, and McGeorge Bundy, advised the president to cut bait and prepare to move away from the commitment to war. The bombing of North Vietnam in particular, the president was told, had proved ineffective, and to send in a few hundred thousand more American troops clearly would produce an even more volatile response from dissenters at home.[4]

Once Eugene McCarthy entered the race, the concern over U.S. policy in Vietnam could no longer be said to be exclusively that of the far-out counterculture, or the politically irrelevant and extreme New Left. The media paid close attention to the well-scrubbed and groomed young people who traveled to New Hampshire for the primary, and who looked so respectable and different from the Haight-Ashbury hippies or the campus radicals with their torn clothes and unkempt appearance.

Now Allard Lowenstein worked to create yet another new group, this time one formed precisely to pressure the administration to back down on Vietnam. Called the Conference of Concerned Democrats (CCD), the new body would become the base for those who sought a concrete electoral challenge to the president. Speaking to the organization, national ADA student chairman Elliott Abrams let it be known that college students would not abide by ADA's decision not to take part in a dump-Johnson movement. Showing the intellectual toughness for which he was later known during the Reagan administration, Abrams announced that "we will not be eunuchs." Lowenstein provided the inspiration for his cadre to stand firm. Traveling from campus to campus, where he stayed up in all-night sessions eating junk food and chatting with dedicated young activists, Lowenstein kept promising that a candidate "of great prominence" would come forth shortly. He had been in touch with both Robert Kennedy and George McGovern, he announced, but as yet he found that neither man was willing to commit themselves to such an effort. But his group was building a viable base for such a candidacy, and hence Lowenstein was confident that "leaders will come along later."[5]

At first, Lowenstein and his friends were actually skeptical that they could pull their promises off. But the growing intense opposition to the war encouraged them greatly, and their early doubts were eased. Gerald N. Hill, president of the ultraliberal California Democratic Council (CDC), met with Lowenstein during the summer of 1967 to discuss what strategy Democratic leaders opposed to the war should take. Citing "antipathy to the war on many grounds," Hill wrote General James Gavin and pointed out to him that 95 percent of antiwar activists were registered Democrats, and the "belief that Johnson will control the Democratic convention is posited on his being a candidate." Hill explained to the general, whom he hoped might consider a run, that the president's "well founded fear of defeat might well drive [him] . . . out of the race."

Since Republicans would try to prove that Johnson was so unpopular that he could not be reelected, broad opposition within the Democratic Party was the only way to demonstrate the depth of the opposition to LBJ among Democratic voters. Only that strategy could effectively undercut Republican hopes, Hill implied. New Hampshire, Hill correctly observed, "looms large as a bellwether." Charming as they might be, the New Politics crowd's hopes of a King-Spock ticket would not do the job. To end the war they needed a "major candidate with responsible credentials."

Divided They Fell

At that moment, being desperate for such a candidate, Hill and Lowenstein hoped that the general might be that man. If their chosen candidate, Hill argued, succeeded in getting Johnson to lose New Hampshire, he would then have credibility. Two more similar losses and the president would be finished. Even if he received a majority of the delegates pledged to him at the convention, 50 percent of voting Democrats would have by that time announced their rejection of Johnson's candidacy. Thus, any candidate opposed to the war *had* to run in a Democratic primary, rather than on the Republican ticket. Only a primary victory, Hill argued, would "blow the situation wide open."[6]

Hill, of course, turned out to be right about that prediction. At the time, however, he was wrong about the candidate. Having been turned down by General Gavin, as well as by George McGovern, Hill and Lowenstein would settle on the only candidate who agreed to take the bait, the then relatively unknown senator from Minnesota, Eugene F. McCarthy. And his candidacy coincided with the desire of mainstream center liberals such as Galbraith and Schlesinger to have the liberal ranks move as swiftly as possible toward an antiwar position. It was Galbraith who advised Lowenstein that he should seek out McCarthy.

Others have claimed that they had sent the dump-Johnson people and Lowenstein to the senator. But McGovern, speaking years later to journalist Charles Kaiser, recalled that he had sent some of those people over to McCarthy to raise the issue of his candidacy, and that the senator's answer virtually stunned him. McGovern, although he was fully committed to opposing U.S. policy in Vietnam, faced reelection in 1968, and was therefore reluctant to take up the cudgels. McCarthy, however, would be in office until 1970, and an imminent electoral battle for maintenance of his Senate seat was not a consideration. Approaching McCarthy on the Senate floor, he told him that he had told some of Lowenstein's people to talk to him about running in the primaries against Johnson. "Yeah, I talked to them," McCarthy answered. "I think I may do it." McGovern could not believe it. As he recalled, he had only sent them to McCarthy "as a way of getting these people off my back."[7]

The result, of course, was McCarthy's announcement of his candidacy on November 30, 1967. The Senator did so in a press conference held in the caucus room of the Senate Office Building, where he announced his intention of entering at least four different primaries—Wisconsin, Oregon, California, Nebraska—and possibly Massachusetts and New Hampshire. McCarthy stressed that he was doing this not to challenge LBJ personally, but rather to oppose the president's position on the Vietnam War. Emphasizing the folly of that effort, McCarthy talked about the "physical destruction of much of a small and weak nation by military operations of the most powerful nation in the world," and the futility of a monthly American expense that ran somewhere between 2 and 3 billion dollars. By running, he hoped, he would be able to alleviate the "deepening moral crisis in America," by working for "an honorable, rational, and political solution to this war." Writing decades later, journalist Kaiser viewed McCarthy as a heroic figure, one of the few politicians around who would even consider undertaking what Kaiser saw as a "reputedly hopeless quest." Viewing McCarthy as an "enigmatic iconoclast," Kaiser argues that his unique qualities made him "the ideal candidate for the challenge."[8]

Yet not all the Democrats opposed to the war thought that McCarthy was the right man to pull this off. At the time, other leading left-leaning journalists were not so sure. "Let the unhappy brutal truth come out," wrote one of the movement's leading journalistic lights, Jack Newfield, during the late winter of 1967. "Eugene McCarthy's campaign is a disaster ... Mc-

Carthy's speeches are dull, vague, and without either balls or poetry. He is lazy and vain."9 Even Lowenstein's own supporters
were disappointed by the senator's performance. A visit to Michigan by McCarthy, Peter Mandler wrote to Lowenstein, turned
out to be only a "mixed blessing." Some activists had set up a
McCarthy-for-President Committee, but the senator himself
"did little to lend credibility to the seriousness of his candidacy."
Instead of giving a rousing speech, he stated "dispassionately his
conclusion that [the war] was not morally justified." Even worse,
McCarthy had not made any real effort "to persuade with argument or arouse with passion." What he had to do was relate the
war to central domestic concerns; to speak with Democrats like
Pat Moynihan, and to meet with "some angry Negro leaders,"
since, Mandler advised, McCarthy was "innocent about these
matters."10

In New York, Lowenstein found that he faced another familiar
trouble: opposition from the legions of Communists, fellow-
travelers, and self-proclaimed "progressives" who were active in
New York Democratic circles. A prominent Reform Democratic
grouping, the [Greenwich] Village Reform Democrats, reversed
a pro-Israel resolution because of what one of Joe Rauh's correspondents termed a "mass turnout of Stalinists . . . pro-Russian,
pro-Hanoi, pro-Castro." These Stalinist elements were hiding
behind the McCarthy movement, Rauh's source noted, "because
a large segment of liberal and progressive politicals . . . have such
an aversion to Johnson." What this writer feared was a repetition
of "the Communist seizure of the [Henry] Wallace movement,"
which meant that Lowenstein and McCarthy might be "sitting
on a political dungheap without being aware of it." Since the reform movement could be destroyed by Communist infiltration,
activist Al Glotzer wrote, it was necessary to continually reiterate

that opposition to the war did not mean "support for Hanoi and the Vietcong."[11]

Rauh agreed, and told Glotzer that if Gene McCarthy really decided "to go for broke" and run an "affirmative campaign for president" rather than a symbolic dump-Johnson effort, he and others would agree to offer him their support, thereby offsetting the far Leftists who were then signing up. Of course, Rauh added, he hoped and trusted that McCarthy "has the will and ability to keep out the [Wallace] people."[12] Rauh saw himself as actually being strongly opposed to Lowenstein's dump-Johnson movement, as well as to the Concerned Democrats organization that was being created. But since McCarthy was running with their support, and had not announced early enough, the job was to get "responsible people into the various state McCarthy organizations." It seemed, he wrote, that "Gene not only has to have ADA [and] not Wallace or New Left types in his various organizations, but he also has to put more fire into the campaign." Overall, Rauh felt that McCarthy had given them a "political way to work against the war," and hence he supported him as much as "an act of faith" as a reasoned "act of political judgment." And once again, he bemoaned the fact that the war in Vietnam "divides and disaffects" the old liberal movement.[13]

It was clear that the animosity to LBJ was so great that even Lowenstein—perhaps especially Lowenstein, who was close to the sentiment of most young activists—contemplated voting Republican if the president regained the nomination. Lowenstein was so adamant that he even told one friend "he would vote for Reagan or any other alternative to Johnson if the Democratic Party didn't dump LBJ." He had come far from the early spring, when anti-Communism was still Lowenstein's line in the sand. Lowenstein even told the chairman of Minnesota's Democratic-

Farmer Labor Party that if Minnesota's Democrats did not support his dump-Johnson movement, he would fight them tooth and nail. Specifically, Lowenstein suggested putting up alternative slates of candidates in each precinct caucus, a suggestion that led Marilyn Gottlieb of the DFL to comment that she could not "imagine a 28-year-old who is not stupid being so out of touch with political reality." On her part, she felt that liberals had to overlook the president's personality, because it was necessary for them so support LBJ's domestic agenda. Lowenstein's anti-Johnson stance, she wrote, upset her so much that it almost made people like her want "to defend LBJ all the way."[14] But from his perspective, Lowenstein saw his attempts blocked by a coalition of both the far Left and the "establishment liberals." The radicals, he commented, saw his attempt to "dump LBJ" as a trick to destroy the peace movement, while the liberals were against opposing the president without a committed major candidate running against him. They were backing a formation of peace advocates whose sponsors would endorse Johnson.[15]

Most of McCarthy's backers were more supportive. Martin Peretz, then a graduate student in political science at Harvard University, praised McCarthy's courage in deciding to run against the president in the primaries. Peretz stressed that continuation of war in Vietnam was beyond "the endurance of moral men." Although Peretz agreed that McCarthy had little charisma, he saw the senator as "reflective, self-conscious, and honest," and he rejected the argument of those who said the United States could afford to fund domestic reform programs and civil rights legislation while at the same time it waged war abroad. What America needed, Peretz suggested, was an active minority that could set limits to the exercise of American power, and it was his own hope that electoral work could galvanize people "into such a community of shared values and effort."

Although others saw Peretz as part of the Left, he went out of his way to aim salvos at the sectarians of SDS and the New Left, whom he thought were demanding "an ideological posture from McCarthy which they know he does not hold." What Peretz called for were "new coalitions with an active Left that is conscious of the need for vision in politics." As for the centrists, Peretz and the moderate Left had to be frank about not giving their support to those he dubbed timid ADA types, who were nothing but "cautious trimmers" who held dogmas "of the Cold War in its most dubious manifestations." They certainly did not need the company of Arthur Schlesinger, whom Peretz called the "ideologist of our squalid little war against the Cubans."[16]

Writing to the senator, Peretz made his actual feelings more clear. His concern, he informed McCarthy, to whom he and his wife were giving substantial sums of money for the campaign, was with the positions taken by liberal Democratic professionals such as Schlesinger and Rauh. Efforts to reconcile them to the Johnson ticket, he thought, would "end up in your being in a very closed box." But McCarthy, he advised, should not worry about the course they took. These men were Cold War liberals, the "intellectual pastorate for some of the worst incidents of the Cold War" and hence were "ill suited to lead Americans away from the fatal assumptions which they first so successfully peddled." Peretz, in fact, hoped that they would not join the McCarthy bandwagon, because if they did, it would serve to blunt the "critical rub of your candidacy" and McCarthy's own constituency would have no compelling reason to vote for him.[17]

Peretz, then, was privately pushing McCarthy to move toward the Left, a position he blunted in his public pronouncements, such as his article for the Social-Democratic journal, *Dissent.* There his concern was to modify the harshness of the extreme elements of the New Left, and hope that they would abandon their sectarianism and work constructively within the McCarthy campaign. But to the senator, Peretz sought to have McCarthy differentiate his proposals from those of people like the despised Robert Kennedy, whom Peretz and others were angry at for jumping in and thereby harming the possibilities of a successful McCarthy candidacy. Proposals to selectively bomb North Vietnamese supply routes, rather than free fire zones, appealed to RFK-type trimmers, a group Peretz denounced as "the bane of our national moral life." Yet he informed McCarthy that he understood his "reluctance to be identified as a captive of the New Left," and therefore he thought that McCarthy's going on the offensive in New Hampshire was both "brilliant and marvelous." As for those who were trying to claim that McCarthy was a secret New Leftist, Peretz told the senator he knew that was pure sham. Peretz did not feel that the Left could provide McCarthy with the "masses that will carry the cause to victory." The senator would have to do that by himself, and take "assistance where it is available and anxious to work."[18]

Privately, Peretz was much harsher in his judgment, and revealed that he actually did want McCarthy to become more forceful in his criticism of U.S. policy. The destruction of the Vietnamese towns of Bentre and Hue, he wrote to McCarthy, revealed the "strategic bankruptcy and moral depravity of America's venture in Vietnam." Positing that Americans were being purposefully bombed in order to terrorize them not to support the NLF, Peretz compared U.S. policy to "Nazi retaliation against hapless civilians, harboring or living in close contact with people of the Resistance." Calling for full-scale attack on the Johnson administration, Peretz complained that "no one on your staff appears even interested in that."[19]

McCarthy stunned the country, of course, with his astounding triumph in New Hampshire. The effort of the "clean with Gene" brigade had paid off. Suddenly, the McCarthy candidacy fueled the hopes that LBJ could be defeated, and that a turnabout in U.S. policy in Vietnam could be accomplished.[20] "McCarthy's cause," Charles Kaiser wrote, "attracted some of the youngest, smartest, most independent, best-educated, and worst-paid staff members in the history of American politics."[21] Of course, some were radical. But as Allard Lowenstein recalled, "for every person that worked the campaign who was a radical giving the system a dubious last chance, there were a hundred who were fraternity or Smith girls."[22] Some, of course, could not refrain from being critical. The radical journalist I.F. Stone quipped that McCarthy was a dilettante at both poetry and politics. More seriously, the historian Herbert Parmet has emphasized the truly quixotic nature of the senator's campaign. Subordinating partisanship, and concentrating on issues alone, McCarthy ignored the Democratic Party and its traditions, and sought instead to identify himself with the civil rights, health, and educational programs of the past decade. He was, in fact, the direct descendant of the late Adlai Stevenson, the patrician reformer whose own presidential campaigns had floundered badly, but who had become the darling of college educated Americans, liberals, and professionals.

One has but to contrast Lowenstein's stridency with McCarthy's own measured and somewhat academic stance when both spoke before the critical meeting of the Conference of Concerned Democrats. "It was not a time for storming the walls," McCarthy wrote in his own memoirs of the campaign, "but for beginning a long march."[23] Calling for a "reasonable" settlement of the war, McCarthy was a serene follow-up to Lowenstein, who had revved up the youthful crowd with a tough anti-LBJ talk. In contrast, McCarthy quoted Arnold Toynbee and referred back to the ancient Greeks. He did criticize the "mistakes" of the administration, but refused to personalize his criticism by attacking the president. The United States, he said, had to seek "an honorable, rational, and political solution," but not seek "peace at any price." In his own memoir, the senator acknowledged his weak beginning. His entry into the race, a friend of Rauh had told him, "is the greatest thing that could happen to Johnson; he's so weak he makes even Johnson look good."[24]

But McCarthy continued to stun the pros. In Minnesota, the Johnson-Humphrey forces were humiliated, as McCarthy's people gained control of precinct caucuses in three out of the state's five congressional districts. The fighting was so fierce that it amounted to the worst Democratic Farmer-Labor infighting since the late 1940s, when Gene McCarthy had worked with Humphrey and Walter Mondale to weaken and expel pro-Communists and fellow-travelers from their organization. Tet had begun to turn the nation against the war. The McCarthy forces in New Hampshire, led by Herbert Gans, pulled out all the stops. Gans told Charles Kaiser that they ran radio commercials every half an hour in the state during the campaign's last two days. "Think how it would feel to wake up Wednesday morning to find out that Gene McCarthy had won the New Hampshire primary [and] find out that New Hampshire had changed the course of American politics." They bought every single billboard space, enough literature for each voter three times over, and even what later would become commonplace—an inundation of movie stars, such as Paul Newman, who arrived to campaign for the senator.[25]

McCarthy had reason to be elated. He had received 23,280 votes in the New Hampshire primary, 42.4 percent of the entire vote, a tremendous showing compared to the president's attainment of 27,243, which amounted to 49.5 percent of the total votes cast. To come so close to the incumbent president was widely interpreted as a presidential defeat and a strong showing for the antiwar elements in the party. And McCarthy had done just as well in getting delegates to the convention. There, the insurgents actually won, gaining twenty of the twenty-four allotted delegates from the state. McCarthy and his supporters actually began to smell the scent of impending victory. Gerry Studds, the future congressman, had been campaigning with McCarthy. Studds explained that McCarthy had campaigned in areas where Democratic candidates did not usually go, such as the southernmost towns of New Hampshire. In one of those, Salem, McCarthy won with 53 percent, and the president received only 40 percent. Realizing that the southern tier was expanding, the campaign gave it full attention, and their effort paid off. Thus, as Studds put it, they beat the president in towns which always had been "reliable organization towns." No wonder the president's backers were "absolutely stunned."[26] Some did point out, to no avail, that McCarthy's showing was not necessarily a mandate for peace. Polls indicated that some New Hampshire residents voted for him out of anger over the president's not being tough enough with the Vietnamese; indeed, three out of five had deserted LBJ for not being hawkish enough.

Whatever McCarthy's early hopes, they were to be dashed when four short days after his dramatic New Hampshire showing, Robert F. Kennedy announced that he was entering the race for president. McCarthy and his young followers were furious. McCarthy, and not Kennedy, had taken the plunge. Indeed, Kennedy had consistently refused to run, even when so counseled by supporters such as Jack Newfield, and by McCarthy himself, who months earlier had told Kennedy that if he opted to enter the race, he would step aside. "Kennedy simply didn't take seriously McCarthy as a candidate," Lowenstein recalled. Hence Kennedy's backers never grasped the "depth of gratitude to McCarthy that he made the fight when Kennedy wouldn't." Not only did the New York senator show little interest in a challenge, he admonished Lowenstein not to work with the California Democratic Council, the state's liberal body which Kennedy commented was composed of "radicals and kooks." When Kennedy finally did enter, Lowenstein commented, McCarthy appeared as a "pure knight who had been put upon by this opportunist."[27]

Privately, as Lowenstein's biographer has noted, he had always seen Robert Kennedy as the ideal candidate to beat LBJ. Indeed, at a famous meeting held in the senator's home in Virginia in September 1967, Jack Newfield and Lowenstein argued in favor of his entering the race, while James Loeb and Arthur Schlesinger urged against. When the latter two argued in favor of Rauh's peak plank tactic, Kennedy retorted: "When was the last time millions of people rallied behind a plank?"[28] Thus McCarthy had always been Lowenstein's second choice. McCarthy's decision to run, and later Kennedy's, was indeed a personal triumph for Lowenstein. "His success in putting together a mainstream Democratic effort to defeat a sitting president," historian and Lowenstein biographer William Chafe writes, "was one of the most remarkable political achievements of contemporary American history. With unerring singleness of purpose, Lowenstein identified his objective, created a brilliant strategy, and mobilized an elite battalion of supporters to achieve his goal."[29]

The case for Kennedy that Lowenstein surreptitiously supported was spelled out most clearly by one of his key associates, Professor Arnold S. Kaufman of the University of Michigan, who had written a book proclaiming himself a practitioner of the "radical middle." Concerned with the possibility that the egos of the proclaimed candidates would "squander this opportunity to reverse catastrophic Johnson policies," Kaufman stressed that the primary task was to replace the president with a leader who would have the will to end the war. Hence they needed enough delegate votes to deny Johnson the presidency on the first ballot. From that perspective, Kaufman argued, the entry into the race by McCarthy was a first step, and Kennedy's candidacy was "the likely consequences of initial success." Thus it was welcome since those who thought they were only "tilting at windmills" would now take them seriously.[30]

First, Kaufman continued, fence-sitters and LBJ supporters would switch to Kennedy. Second, others who were cautious earlier now were deciding to back McCarthy, even though previously they had hedged. Third, individuals still backing the president were acting differently, and legitimizing the protest candidacies of both contenders. Thus defections to both McCarthy and Kennedy would mount, and might in some states even win a majority of the delegates to the convention. McCarthy appealed to rural voters and Republicans; radicals on the fringe would eventually support him, and Kennedy appealed to college students. The result, he posited, was that New Hampshire, combined with RFK's entry, created "an overall energizing and widening of the anti-Johnson, antiwar political effort." Those who wanted a Democratic dove were on the same side. If they came to see either antiwar candidate as each other's main enemy, they only played "into the hands of the prowar forces." The McCarthy supporters had "flushed the junior senator from New York," and Kaufman thought they should be proud of that accomplishment. Indeed, he thought it possible that RFK's entry could lead to a California primary victory. With that effect, they might "dislodge the president before August rolls around." And that could be done by turning the "trickle of defectors into a flood," by beating the president in the primaries, by winning in California, and hence by "smashing the pro-Johnson forces."

And the way to do that was by having both Kennedy and McCarthy cooperate to roll up a high vote in California, assuring that the president came in third.

Lowenstein had more than one foot in the Kennedy campaign. As Chafe writes, "at the heart of Eugene McCarthy's intense dislike of Lowenstein was the latter's deep and transparent devotion to Robert Kennedy."[31] While publicly committed to McCarthy, Lowenstein worked closely behind the scenes with Robert Kennedy. While Lowenstein's public position was that "he was committed to Eugene McCarthy's nomination . . . until the end of the Democratic convention," Chafe explains, "such claims were disingenuous," since he was for McCarthy verbally but favored Kennedy emotionally.[32]

As Kennedy saw things, McCarthy never had a chance to become president, and although he gave him grudging praise for proving that anti-Johnson sentiment was so strong, he believed that it made sense for a real candidate who had a potential to unseat Johnson at the convention to take the president on. But McCarthy's supporters were livid with rage. "Kennedy thinks that American youth belongs to him at the bequest of his brother," columnist and McCarthy backer Mary McGrory wrote. "Seeing the romance flower between them and McCarthy, he moved with the ruthlessness of a Victorian father whose daughter has fallen in love with a dustman."[33] Murray Kempton, the dean of New York's liberal pundits, went further: "He has, in the naked display of his rage at Eugene McCarthy for having survived on the lonely road he dared not walk himself, done with a single great gesture something very few public men have ever been able to do: In one day, he managed to confirm the worst things his enemies have ever said about him."[34]

As historians Irwin and Debi Unger have written, "the Democratic Party seemed to be decomposing into its constituent elements."[35] Or, to put it more bluntly, the leaders were bleeding in an ongoing and ever nastier fratricidal war. The Tet offensive had given McCarthy's campaign a boost, and now Robert Kennedy threatened to be a spoiler. And there was still the problem of what the official liberal organization, ADA, was going to do. Traditionalists favored no endorsement of a candidate until the Democratic convention; antiwar activists were demanding that ADA endorse McCarthy. Finally, in February, the ADA board voted to endorse Eugene McCarthy—the first time since its formation it had not backed an incumbent Democratic candidate. Now the split within was irreversible. Immediately, Johnson loyalist John P. Roche resigned, as did three major trade union leaders—I.W. Abel of the United Steelworkers, Louis Stulberg of the International Ladies Garment Workers Union, and Joseph Bierne of the Communications Workers of America. By the ADA convention in mid-May, the dissenters were gone, and the younger antiwar activists reaffirmed the board's endorsement of McCarthy. The logic of Joe Rauh was persuasive. Unless a peace candidate was on the ticket in 1968, he told a New York gathering, "the rioting at the Pentagon would look like a pantywaist tea party." If ADA failed to back McCarthy, he warned that he and other moderates, those condemned by the New Left as Cold War liberals, "would have been in truth what the fellow-travelers and New Left have always wanted to paint us—total and complete captives of any Democratic administration." Galbraith added that ADA members simply could not compromise on matters of principle. The war, columnist James Wechsler added, had created new coalitions, and the price might have to be the abandonment of the new liberalism by the leadership of organized labor.[36]

McCarthy, unfortunately, had a set of glaring weaknesses. From the perspective of the nineties, it was clear that the senator ignored the growing cultural and social issues that would eventually help produce the new conservatism of the seventies and eighties. If McCarthy wanted to be taken seriously, one of his backers commented, he would have to add a "not-so-liberal" plank on law and order, and link support to crime prevention—a tough stance on criminals, with support to civil rights. Nixon, as Wechsler shrewdly put it, intended to make crime in the streets a major issue, and that alone would prove effective in gaining the support of the middle class. Since many conservatives respected McCarthy for his courageous entry into the race—the senator, he noted, had obviously received many Republican crossover votes in the New Hampshire primary—he could broaden his appeal by taking a tough stand on law enforcement. McCarthy would still keep his necessary liberal backing, but would immediately pick up support from conservatives and middle-of-the-roaders. "It may be that Senator McCarthy is already committed to a hard 100 percent ACLU . . . position," Michael Armstrong wrote. "If so," the writer quipped, "you can make several large paper gliders out of this letter."[37] It might not have been clear at the time, but in an interview conducted years later, McCarthy himself claimed to oppose a contest with Nixon over the issue of which party "provided the most welfare." In a democratic society, McCarthy told journalist Ben Wattenberg, "affirmative action [was] contrary to kind of an open free competitive society." McCarthy, however, was still furious at what he claimed was a particularly false and vicious attack levied on him by Robert Kennedy. During the California campaign, Kennedy had charged that McCarthy planned to take 10,000 people out of Watts and move them to Orange County. That, McCarthy said, was plain and simple racial demagoguery. He refused to accept the criticism that while Bobby Kennedy had the support of both the white working class and minorities, he (McCarthy) only had a base of the white upper class and the college students.[38]

At the time Kennedy made the charge, the two candidates were appearing together on a televised debate. At issue, Mc-Carthy may have forgotten over the years, was the desire of both to gain support in ultraconservative Orange County. McCarthy had made the argument that the ghettos had to be broken up, otherwise America would have its own form of apartheid. He then explained that it was necessary to take housing out of the ghetto "so there is a distribution of races throughout the whole structure of our cities and on into our rural areas." To that construct, Kennedy replied that McCarthy was going to try and "take 10,000 black people and move them into Orange County," a statement that made it appear that McCarthy's solution to the racial crisis would prove horrendous for the upper middle-class residents of the California suburb. He was for integration, naturally, but Kennedy was hinting to the constituency in Orange County that he understood that if urban blacks were taken out of the ghetto, where "they can't afford the housing, where their children can't keep up with the schools, and where they don't have the skills for the jobs, it is just going to be catastrophic." Of course, McCarthy had not really said quite what Kennedy charged he had said. Kennedy had merely taken hold of an opportunity to score a point. But it proved to be a spot that neither McCarthy nor his young supporters ever forgot.[39]

It seemed, as one looks back, that McCarthy's most committed supporters were more open to compromise with the Kennedy forces than the senator was himself. Seymour Martin Lipset, the highly regarded political scientist, recommended that McCarthy "do nothing which might reduce the possibility of his coming out as a compromise candidate." Lipset thought McCarthy should not pull out of the race if he had fewer delegates than Bobby Kennedy. If it turned out that both Kennedy and Johnson had 1,000 committed delegates, and McCarthy had only three hundred or four hundred, the convention might turn to him as the only compromise alternative. But for McCarthy to get the nomination, Lipset warned, he had to "avoid as much as possible any action or statement which might identify him with the extreme left." This was especially so since Kennedy would have the support of both moderates and political bosses, and McCarthy's support, unfortunately, "disproportionately will come from the left." The public would accept that, Lipset thought, as long as McCarthy did nothing to make people fear "that he is a captive of the Left."[40]

While the debate was raging, Lyndon B. Johnson made a stunning announcement, for which the nation, as well as the Democratic Party, was completely unprepared. In mid-April the president was scheduled to give a speech in which it was widely assumed he would announce another pause in the bombing, a tactical maneuver that the peace camp saw as a blatant and meaningless attempt to trim their sails in an attempt to offset the primary challenges. Some thirty-five minutes into his address, at which point many Americans had already turned off their television sets, Lyndon B. Johnson paused and said: "I shall not seek, and will not accept, the nomination of my party for another term as your president." With that one sentence, the president had changed the game. The race for a candidate was now apparently wide open.[41]

All of this put the liberals in a state of total confusion. Some were torn between voting for their beloved favorite, Gene McCarthy, or shifting to Robert Kennedy, whom many of them despised but whom they thought had a chance to gain the nomination. But to vote for either of the two antiwar candidates meant they would be standing against the old warhorse for their own liberal cause, Hubert H. Humphrey, the sitting vice president and hence the apparent front-runner. But the liberals were so angry at the president that abandoning the vice president was easy, especially since Humphrey had inherited the backing of those who had stood by LBJ, including labor leaders and many businessmen. Then, on June 5, the critical California primary was held. When Robert Kennedy appeared to address his supporters in the ballroom of the Ambassador Hotel, he knew he had won, and he and his supporters also realized they were on the verge of gaining the party's nomination. The bullet fired by Sirhan Sirhan that took Kennedy's life showed the nation once again how a single act of violence could change the political landscape overnight. That tragic event left Gene McCarthy as the only remaining serious challenge to Hubert Humphrey, and many of Kennedy's loyal followers were not prepared to turn to him.

As for Humphrey, Arthur Schlesinger wrote, he was making "a disastrous error if he continues to pursue the nomination along his present road . . . backroom manipulation of delegates and without serious discussion of issues." Accusing the vice president of avoiding confrontation in both the primaries and in debates, Schlesinger predicted that if Humphrey won the Democratic nomination, he would "face a bitter party," with the greatest bitterness existing among "issue-oriented activists, whose support is essential for a Democratic victory."[42]

As the noted liberal historian saw things, Humphrey was going on the belief that he could ignore the liberals, who would all unite around him once the campaign began and Nixon had received the Republican nomination. At that moment, Schlesinger could not conceive that in fact, he would do precisely what Humphrey had hoped—support his presidential bid once all other options had evaporated. But in July, Schlesinger actually argued that "if we are to have a stupid and reactionary foreign policy, it should be carried out by a Republican administration." He even argued that Democrats should have elected Barry Goldwater in 1964, since a revolt against his Vietnam policy would have taken place years earlier, "and saved the country a lot of trouble and lives."

The United States, Schlesinger continued, was pursuing "idiot" policies in Southeast Asia, and better such policies be carried out by a Nixon than a Humphrey administration. Citing a bit of Humphrey campaign rhetoric, when the vice president asserted in May that he and Nixon were actually not that far apart, Schlesinger proclaimed: "then give me Nixon." Politics is politics, he understood, but it is incomprehensible that "Humphrey *really* believes in this ghastly war." If so, this was a "catastrophic misapplication of honorable ideas—the idea of containment of aggression and the idea of a global New Deal." Hearing the vice president talk about the need for a Marshall Plan for the nation's cities—once a shibboleth of liberal politics—Schlesinger wept over Humphrey's "failure of imagination and sympathy," and bemoaned the fact that Humphrey and his staff had "produced a condition of arrested intellectual growth for so many bright people." Humphrey's generation, he posited, had imposed the truth of containment on a changed world. As a Kennedy Democrat, Schlesinger acknowledged that he regarded Eugene McCarthy "with contempt." But at present, he simply could not "support Hubert."

Much to his chagrin, Schlesinger learned that his friend David Ginsburg promptly gave the vice president a copy of the letter containing these remarks. The result was that Humphrey himself took up the challenge. John F. Kennedy, he wrote to Schlesinger, got nominated "exactly the way I am trying to get nominated, namely by the delegates. He surely didn't get the nomination because he was in the primaries." Both McCarthy and Robert Kennedy, Humphrey noted, worked with and supported the political bosses, who gave candidates the nomination. Moreover,

Humphrey noted that he had run neck and neck with Bobby in California, where he had not even entered the race, and hence the results of that primary could not be construed as a political defeat.

Vowing to "stack up my record of liberalism against anyone's," Humphrey responded that his ideas about Southeast Asia were hardly idiotic. Moreover, he took credit for being an expert on urban affairs, and he assumed that when he used the Marshall Plan as a goal, intelligent voters knew what he meant. "You write history," the vice president snidely commented, while "I help make it." Rather than being caught up in the past, Humphrey felt his problem was that he was "too far ahead of the times." On the basis of Schlesinger's "earlier and more mature liberal convictions," Humphrey scolded, he should be supporting, and not opposing, his run against Nixon. If he did not, it only meant that the liberal historian was helping to destroy "a healthy sense of liberalism."[43]

The vice president's response only strengthened Schlesinger's admonition that he would not—simply could not—endorse him. Despite Robert Kennedy's death, Schlesinger promised that he would not endorse Humphrey or anyone else. Agreeing that Humphrey would be far better on "racial justice, urban problems, and poverty than McCarthy," he told the vice president that there was still solid reason for "principled . . . opposition to your candidacy," and that there were "sound *public* reasons for a certain anger and bitterness today." With his position on the Vietnam War, Schlesinger wrote the vice president, he had lost his "own sense of reality." Accusing Humphrey of holding a "hectoring and evasive" position, Schlesinger let Humphrey know that he saw it as a "fantastic" view that disregarded the fact that the United States was neither "omnipotent nor omniscient."[44]

Divided They Fell

There were still other issues that disturbed some of the old liberals, even if Schlesinger himself no longer saw them as critical. Marvin Rosenberg, a noted New York lawyer and ADA stalwart, was most upset to find that just as others had feared months earlier, there were clearly Communist Party members heavily involved in the McCarthy campaign. Rosenberg had attended a meeting for delegates from New York's 17th Congressional District, which included the ultraliberal Upper West Side, the habitat of many holdovers from the Old "progressive" Left. Eleanor Clark French chaired the session, and Rosenberg described how leaflets were handed out by those trying to discredit the Humphrey candidacy, by falsely claiming that at the 1964 Democratic convention, Humphrey and Joe Rauh had conspired "to sell out the Mississippi Freedom Democratic Party in order to assure the vice presidential nomination of Hubert Humphrey." When he attempted to take the leaflet home, French grabbed it from him. "More and more," Rosenberg complained, "they [referring to McCarthy's supporters] are adopting the style and practices of the Stalinists—breaking up meetings and rewriting history."[45] Rauh was chagrined. But all he could reply was to let his old friend know that he was "at least as uncomfortable with the Old and New Left supporting McCarthy as you must be with some of the people on your side."[46]

The assassination of Robert Kennedy, of course, strengthened Hubert Humphrey's position immeasurably. Kennedy's California primary victory had given strong evidence that McCarthy could not get the kind of widespread support he needed for a victory. Hence a dilemma for McCarthy's supporters. Should they mount a major effort, and try hard to obtain the backing of Robert Kennedy's formerly hostile and committed supporters? Or should they call it in, support a peace plank, and rally around

Hubert Humphrey, now likely to be the Democratic Party's standard-bearer?

The answers were forthcoming immediately. When a story appeared that members of McCarthy's finance committee were talking to Humphrey and were considering giving him their support, Marty Peretz hit the ceiling. He simply could not conceive of voting for Humphrey, he noted in a memo to himself. As for what Peretz called "Humphrey's desperate search for a verbal formula to conciliate opponents of the war and McCarthy supporters," that simply demonstrated to Peretz that Humphrey "cannot be trusted." A record of "zealous enthusiasm for American policy in Vietnam," Peretz thought, "cannot be neutralized by a few happy dovish phrases."[47]

Peretz's hostility was repeated in a statement issued by former leading McCarthy supporters, including Peretz, Vietnam moratorium organizer Sam Brown, Harold Ickes, Jr.,—later to be a campaign manager for Governor Bill Clinton's presidential effort in New York—political scientist Curtis Gans, and the activist New York alternative radio personality Paul Gorman. This influential group saw Humphrey as sharing responsibility with Lyndon Johnson for the war, as well as for the violence [which had taken place at the 1968 Democratic Party convention]. Both domestic and foreign events, the prestigious group claimed, revealed the "reliance of the Democratic Party leadership on violence and repression as responses to popular demands for change." Hence the group announced that they could not and would not vote to "entrust to Hubert H. Humphrey's coalition—Cold War liberals, military-industrial lobbyists, big labor, big city machines, Southern governors—the solution of the problem . . . brought about in large measure by that very coalition." It was significant that in rejecting any support to

Humphrey, thereby implicitly endorsing Nixon under the guise of the "worse the better," the group sounded the very themes of the far Left they had previously urged rejecting. Instead of voting Democratic, they trumpeted the need for creation of a new majority movement for change in America.[48]

Some of Kennedy's former supporters did their own part to push away any backing of McCarthy. One of Gene McCarthy's backers was furious to find that twenty-four brief hours after Robert Kennedy's burial, Arthur Schlesinger appeared on television and attacked McCarthy for having "no interest in the poor or the colored." Such an attack on the only remaining peace candidate, the McCarthy backer argued, was "ill-timed, ill-tempered, intemperate, and stupid." He saw Schlesinger's criticism as a "vicious" attack made on a day of mourning.[49]

Be that as it may, the end result of the effort to challenge Johnson was to push the Democratic Party to the Left. Even the Lowenstein dump-Johnson movement inevitably had that effect, notwithstanding Lowenstein's own objectives. As his astute biographer points out, "to isolate and defeat the Left," Lowenstein "had to show that the politics of the center could work in addressing grievances identified by the Left and shared by liberals. Thus, he had to reach out to the mainstream and simultaneously move it leftward, cultivating a heightened consciousness among 'moderates' about the dimension of the problems that existed."[50] In that manner, while defeating the overt left wing of the Party, Allard Lowenstein's work had the inevitable effect of keeping the struggle within the system, but also of defeating the Johnson center and Right of the party—the so-called hawks—at the same time. When it became clear that LBJ was out, and that nevertheless the party standard-bearer was still a man of the political center, the moderates and center-left voted with their ballots against Hubert Humphrey's candidacy, and thereby saw to it that the election of Richard M. Nixon was guaranteed. They had taught the Democrats a lesson, many of their members said in glee, and they were heartened that their efforts alone had caused defeat for their own party. Surely in the annals of American party history there has rarely been such a naïve view of defeat. Not just to punish Humphrey centrists, this defeat was thought by the Left to be strategic, for Nixon would take the full blame for "the system," which surely had to fall. Instead, however, it was another step on the slide to the Left that would continue to burden the Democrats for the next two decades. The Lowenstein challenge may very well, as William Chafe writes, have instituted a "program of political protest that promised to redeem the faith of Americans in peaceful change through democratic processes."[51] But it also assured that the goals they sought would not be achieved, and that the center would be pushed into the hands of the Republican right wing. The center, after all that work, did not hold.

5

THE CHICAGO CONVENTION

The New Left Strikes Back

As the Democrats faced their 1968 Convention, it appeared that their organization was in shambles. The assassination of Robert Kennedy had left the Senator's supporters alone and bitter, and refusing to give their backing to Eugene McCarthy. It was a given that the nomination would go to Vice-President Hubert Humphrey, a man whose support of Lyndon Johnson's Vietnam policy had made him anathema to left and liberal Democrats. Antiwar activists and their supporters in the New Left saw that the situation was ripe for them to enter. The result would be a convention that few who were there would ever forget.

Gene McCarthy had run out of steam. The Kennedy camp was more than hostile to his candidacy, and the left wing of the party, without Kennedy and with McCarthy doomed to defeat, was planning a politics of revenge to teach the standard bearers a lesson for not turning against the hated war. Still, McCarthy had a few stalwart and established supporters. In particular, McCarthy had gained the backing of Stephen A. Mitchell, the leader of the Democratic Party machinery and former leader of Adlai Stevenson's campaign during the Illinois governor's presidential bid in 1952. McCarthy had first come to Mitchell's attention, indeed, during the year of the Stevenson campaign, when he saw McCarthy hit a home run during a baseball game. "I can still see his long frame stretched out running the bases," Mitchell recalled. "Here indeed was a competitor!" Later, Mitchell came to see him as a very practical and pragmatic politician, a man who was willing to withdraw from his vice presidential quest in 1964 when it was clear liberals were firmly behind Hubert Humphrey. McCarthy, Mitchell thought, withdrew with dignity "before President Johnson carried out all of the final charades which led to his announcement for Humphrey as if it were a double-thriller." McCarthy, he remembered fondly, was "not willing to be Johnson's mouse."[1]

McCarthy, as Mitchell told him, deserved his New Hampshire victory, and he predicted similar results in the forthcoming Wisconsin and Oregon primaries. Nevertheless, Mitchell confessed that he was "deeply troubled about your prospects over the whole course," and was especially "disgusted with Senator Kennedy."[2] Mitchell, moreover, knew that to gain a victory for McCarthy, the politics of confrontation had to be avoided. New tactics, he argued, were necessary to get the senator the nomination. He had to achieve a 10- to 15-percent gain in the polls, and wage a successful campaign on behalf of an open convention. Those party stalwarts who valued regularity over principle had to be convinced to accept the candidate of an irregular campaign. The focus of McCarthy's effort had to be "to link Humphrey inextricably with the Johnson-Humphrey administration and to continuously remind the American public of the verdict of the primaries—that the mass of people want a change." That meant a professional rather than an amateurish operation. A petition of Democrats threatening to bolt the party if their candidate did not get the nomination would be more likely to antagonize than to persuade. And speakers who stressed McCarthy's positive virtues, Mitchell emphasized, were likely to be better received than someone who railed against an "'insane and genocidal war.' A rally that is conducted nonviolently is more conducive to building support than a massive effort at civil disobedience." Hence the senator's grassroots and campus Left backers had to be integrated into a regular delegate operation.[3]

McCarthy was getting his share of regular delegates whose visceral hatred of the Vietnam War led them to look for an alternative. One such supporter was Don Peterson, chairman of the Wisconsin delegation at the 1968 convention. The Wisconsin delegates, Peterson said, felt that McCarthy was providing the kind of fresh leadership they needed, and had "shown the inspirational quality" so necessary to a leader. "We need to squarely and honestly face our disastrous plight in Vietnam," Peterson explained, as well as to "forthrightly face and fully deal with the plight of minorities, particularly the blacks." To the liberal Peterson, the goal was to "uplift economically deprived people of America, black and white," and to not "stand by and watch the erosion of our cities." It was for that purpose they had to unite to undo the Unit Rule, a mechanism that enabled the political establishment to dominate the convention machinery, by bringing state delegations under the voting domination of a group that without the rule would have only been able to obtain a slim majority, creating what historian Herbert Parmet has called "an efficacious means of keeping control in the hands of certain powerful state leaders."[4] Peterson's goal, to the contrary, was to elect as delegates "only people who are truly representative of the liberal principles of the Democratic Party."[5]

For such an old fighter, working for the first time against the party leadership and the Johnson administration, the effort was worth fighting for—even at the convention. Mitchell's chosen strategy, given his candidate's frank admission that he was not going to be able to win the nomination, was to challenge the Democratic Party at its gut—to attack the apparatus by waging a fight first against the Johnson camp's control of the nomination process at the convention, and second by attacking head-on their political and ideological principles.

Mitchell, as he explained in a long memo to the McCarthy committee, had taken aggressive action at the New Mexico Democratic state convention, where, as he put it, "the McCarthy forces set back the Anderson-Montoya old line [political machine] organization," where a resolution favoring proportional representation in the choosing of delegates carried by seven votes, thereby giving them twenty-two delegates for McCarthy and twenty-six for Humphrey. Conferring at the Blackstone Hotel in Chicago with McCarthy, Richard Goodwin, columnist Mary McGrory, and Tom Finney, an old political veteran who had joined the McCarthy forces, Mitchell argued that his aggressive stance would be seen "by my urging of the fight on the Unit Rule and the domination of the committee by Texas and Oklahoma allies." In this effort, Mitchell reflected, he was facing the opposition of the McCarthy volunteers, which included among the wheat the chaff—"camp followers of what I call 'McCarthy's Coxey's Army' because it is so very disorganized." The only thing they seemed to have in common, besides supporting McCarthy, was "an enormous appetite" which led them to clean out the home of a McCarthy supporter on Lake Shore Drive of all food and drink.[6]

In addition, McCarthy's campaign had serious financial problems. Mitchell found from Finney and Tom McCoy, the financial manager of the campaign, that they were $800,000 in debt, and had budgeted expenses over $1,700,000. Mitchell also began to distrust Finney, with whom he had worked both during the '52 Stevenson campaign and the effort to win Los Angeles for the governor. Mitchell thought that Finney "does not have a full grasp of political campaigns," that he was actually simply a "Washington lawyer-lobbyist" who would work with whomever won the nomination in the capital, and who was actually against "an aggressive action at the convention itself" and who favored quiet negotiation combined with influence and persuasion aimed at gaining support during the final roll call. Thus Mitchell came to "suspect that Finney's ties and sympathies with Johnson and with Humphrey and with the Oklahoma leaders . . . are too strong to permit him to run any risk even if . . . his loyalties to Gene might make him wish to do so." Since his own backstabbing only aided Humphrey and his side, Mitchell thought that it was possible Finney was "an operative in the McCarthy camp for the president and Humphrey."[7]

What Mitchell proposed to do was to hit at the one-hundred-four-vote Texas delegation, then controlled by Governor John Connally. Mitchell had explained the real purpose of his strategy to McCarthy in San Francisco in early June, and the Minnesotan "grasped it and all of its implications immediately." Indeed, the senator was willing to release his own delegates in order to achieve a vote for himself on the first convention ballot.[8] What Mitchell sought, simply, was to box Hubert Humphrey into the position of opposing reform, a tactic, as Herbert Parmet has commented, which would "merely confirm his conservative course and further alienate his opposition."[9] If Humphrey surprised everyone by supporting abolition of the Unit Rule, Mc-

Carthy's camp would also still come out ahead. Were Humphrey to do that, he would offend the Southern delegations that regularly used the device, as well as offend Lyndon Johnson. Whatever path was taken, then, Humphrey was bound to come out a loser.

The strategy was to be put into effect by having Texas McCarthy supporters send two hundred people to the Chicago convention, to dramatize their contention that only 5 percent of Texas residents controlled the selection of Connally-backed delegates. What Mitchell hoped to produce was some kind of a deal with the governor, even getting him to agree to run with McCarthy as his vice presidential candidate. Mitchell and McCarthy quickly found that although he had promised LBJ that he would support the Unit Rule, Hubert Humphrey let it be known that he would support the reformers in their quest. Connally, in the meantime, toyed with the idea of accepting the McCarthy camp's desire to gain his backing by acceptance of the VP spot. But when asked whether he would approve, McCarthy backed down.

As the work progressed, George McGovern suddenly came forth hoping that some would back him as a more left alternative to the centrist McCarthy. Few did. Jesse Unruh, the head of the California delegation, moved to gain the support of Chicago's powerful boss Mayor Daley to rally behind Edward Kennedy, the one remaining member of the plagued Kennedy dynasty. But Kennedy, still young and wary of an effort, told the pros that if nominated, he would move to withdraw his name.

As Humphrey began to worry that his nomination was in danger, he informed the Texas delegation that he was in favor of changing the Unit Rule for future conventions, but not the present one. He also backed down from accepting a compromise over Vietnam, a move that he feared would fully endanger his support from hawkish elements among the delegates. The antiwar forces had introduced a proposal for a negotiated settlement, including eventual withdrawal of American troops, an end to the bombing of North Vietnam, movement toward a coalition government in the South composed of National Liberation Front and South Vietnamese participants, and a reduction of military offensives in the countryside. Instead of supporting this McCarthy-McGovern resolution, Humphrey and the convention called for a "stop [to] all bombing of North Vietnam when this action would not endanger the lives of our troops in the field; this action should take into account the response from Hanoi."[10] This resolution, weak from the point of view of the antiwar forces, passed by 1,567 to 1,041, and Humphrey was soon to achieve his coveted first-ballot nomination. The vice president easily defeated McCarthy, who lost by 1,760 1/4 to 601, with George McGovern getting 146 1/2 delegate votes, putting him in line for a future run as a major antiwar voice.

While McCarthy lost, the fight waged against the Unit Rule was successful. Mitchell, for one, was more than satisfied. The McCarthy campaign, he wrote a friend, had brought together "such a large group of extraordinary people." Moreover, Mitchell believed that they had accomplished "some fundamental changes in the party system through abolishing the Unit Rule and insisting that delegates in the future be chosen by processes in which the public has a right to full participation." Texas, he mused, "will never be the same again!"[11] The reformers, then, had won a fight that later would begin the Democratic Party's slow decline, as activists within the party had more power than most long-time Democrats to determine the party's agenda. At the 1968 convention, for the first time, delegates were able to override the all-white Mississippi delegation and seat a biracial group instead. Similarly, in Georgia, seats were shared by the former SNCC leader Julian Bond and the segregationist governor Lester Maddox, whose delegates refused to accept the arrangement and left the convention. Both voting and party representation were opened up as a result of the McCarthy-Mitchell effort.

Before the convention actually began, the McCarthy supporters were hopeful that their efforts, if not leading to victory for their candidate, would lead to further opposition to the war. Convention speeches, Jean Calhoun wrote to Mitchell, should be "as brilliant as possible" and presented by delegates who were eloquent and were decidedly "un-Conventional," and the demonstrations at the convention for McCarthy should be "free of hoopla and silliness." America, this correspondent put it, was in a "bloody, terrible, unconvincing war," and it was simply awful that the Republicans saw that as an opportunity to capture the seat of government. Escalation of police power as a mechanism for dealing with antiwar protest, she predicted, would be met by force on the part of the antiwar groups and turn America's cities into "internal Vietnams." Thus they had to stage a convention demonstration more meaningful and sober than those of past years. "Let's try to provide a model," Calhoun urged, "for the spirit of the 'new politics.'"[12]

Calhoun's plea, given what was to transpire, has elements of high irony. Unbeknownst to moderate McCarthy backers, the convention was to erupt into an orgy of violence, orchestrated in a confrontation of New Left and "Yippie" militants on the one hand, and the Chicago police of Mayor Richard Daley on the other. In hindsight, the Democratic convention of 1968 would evoke memories not of the efforts of the McCarthy campaign, nor of the complicated fight to undo the Unit Rule, but rather of the demonstrations in the street and the fierce police crackdown which came to dominate the proceedings on the convention floor itself. As it turned out, more than 10,000 young antiwar militants, a composite of the most Far Left elements of the antiwar movement, would descend *en masse* in Chicago—ready to provoke a confrontation that would show the entire world their disenchantment with the Democratic Party and its chosen course.

After the events the Walker Commission, called together to investigate the causes of the violence, found that most protesters had wanted to express "by peaceful means their dissent either from society generally or from the administration's policies on Vietnam." As for the major fighting that culminated in night-long pitched battles between police and activists at nearby Lincoln Park that extended to the streets and hotel lobbies themselves, the Walker Commission termed these occurrences a "police riot."[13]

This conclusion, however well meaning, was made too close to the events, and in the atmosphere of backlash over the obvious mean-spiritedness of the Chicago police when faced with the accumulated wrath of unarmed young demonstrators. As they moved on the streets with TV cameras glaring, shouting that "the whole world is watching," they reminded many observers of Eastern Europe, where Czech youth bravely faced invading Soviet troops and tanks as a slow movement toward "socialism with a human face" was crushed in Prague. The New Left had a ready name for the Convention city—"Czechago." Yet the Walker Commission's scolding of Mayor Daley's police was not the last word on the causes and meaning of the Chicago demonstrations. In fact, the tactics of the demonstrators meshed well with those employed by the vicious Daley machine's police forces. New Left forces had planned for confrontation and violence in advance.

The previous March, more than one-hundred antiwar groups met at a mobilization meeting in Illinois, under the leadership of what quickly came to be dubbed "the Mobe," short for the National Mobilization to End the War in Vietnam. Led by a veteran pacifist and Socialist, Dave Dellinger, the meeting also included SDS leader Tom Hayden, and radical activist Rennie Davis. They would soon be joined in organizing for a counterdemonstration by the so-called "Yippie" leaders, the late Jerry Rubin and the late Abbie Hoffman.

The term Yippie, as the writings of Hoffman and Rubin explained, was born one morning after they and some friends were coming down from an LSD trip, and the duo came up with the idea of forming the Youth International Party, a vehicle for dramatizing their personal version of countercultural rebellion. The purpose of Yippies, Hoffman explained, was to create a "blending of pot and politics into a political grass leaves movement—a cross-fertilization of the hippie and New Left philosophies."[14] With their influence preeminent in the planning and creation of the Chicago demonstrations, it was bound to become not a moderate protest of the war, but an assault of the counterculture against the existing system, an event meant to polarize, confront, and discredit the political establishment, including the Democratic Party.

Some of the older pacifists and traditional Left activists, of course, were more than wary of interaction with denizens of the drug culture. As one activist put it in Dellinger's pacifist magazine, *Liberation*, drugs were "basically a diversion, a distraction, an irrelevance, an impertinence, a conceit, a siphoning off of energies desperately needed elsewhere, a way of opting out that is heartlessly unfair to those who are left."[15] Nevertheless, the Old Left stalwarts found they had nowhere else to go. Having decided to get into bed with the counterculture, they could not opt out when their more radical counterparts scheduled a mass action. SDS, whose leaders already were soured on the McCarthy campaign and were most concerned with getting more bodies into their own organization, saw the event as a natural recruiting ground. The SDS national office at first opposed the action, but as one of the historians of the organization explained, it wanted to "get the McCarthy kids out of their bag and into SDS chapters in the fall."[16]

In his autobiography, Tom Hayden remembered these days and rendered his verdict on the events. Recounting the fiery and incendiary speech given by Black Panther Party leader Bobby Seale—who spoke to the assembled young crowd about the necessity of "picking up the gun"—Hayden recalled that it was "a measure of the alienation of the times that what seem now to be caricatures of rebellion could have been taken seriously, but they were."[17] As for the violence, which Hayden accurately recounts in graphic detail, he emphasizes that "it is too simple to place the primary blame for [Hubert] Humphrey's defeat on the New Left or the demonstrators in Chicago." Richard Nixon's subsequent electoral victory, Hayden argues, could not be blamed on the radicalism of Chicago. Nor could the violence at the convention be blamed on the protesters. The Johnson White House and the Democratic Party, Hayden asserts, were responsible for their own destruction. He presents the final rationale: "Our cause was both just and rational, even if all our methods were not. Our values were decent ones, even if we could not always live up to them . . . *We arrived at a confrontational stance not out of political preference but only as a last resort.*"[18] (author's emphasis)

Certainly, given widespread discontent with the war in Vietnam and with the Johnson administration policy, dissent and protest were welcome and within the rights of American citizens. But was Hayden correct that the stance of confrontation, and the subsequent violence, could not be put at the hands of the New Left, who only moved in that direction when all other mechanisms of protest were closed to them? That conclusion, so accepted by many, is not borne out by a careful examination of the events preceding the nights of rioting.

Fortunately, a thorough and meticulously documented history of the events in Chicago exists. Written by David Farber, a young historian sympathetic to the goals of the New Left at Chicago, this definitive account makes it quite clear that for most of the leaders of the event, including Tom Hayden, confrontation and polarization was their first choice, and not a grudging response to police repression and administration reluctance to negotiate an end to the war.[19] Indeed, Chicago was in many ways the culmination of the previous few years of New Left activity. As another historian has written, the New Left actions at Chicago "represented a self-conscious synthesis of slogans and tactics and icons drawn from the year's previous events and confrontations. The images and influence of Paris were reflected in the Situationist aspects of cultural confrontation and Yippies. The impact of Tet was reflected in the Vietcong flags and the almost universal call for NLF victory. There were also token appearances by Black Panthers. A number of protesters referred to the repression in Prague; and varying attitudes toward Eugene McCarthy's candidacy were expressed. As a result, overall the demonstrations presented one of the oddest spectacles in the whole history of the New Left."[20]

The day-by-day account in Farber's book makes it clear that while all hopes of an antiwar liberal candidacy were doomed, the New Left was able to provoke a police riot, and hence achieve the very polarization its leadership desperately sought. The New Left sought to undermine the entire "corporate system." What it attained, instead, was a shocked response to the police repression unleashed against them by the mainstream liberal community, garnered by watching the bloodshed on TV. Once police let go and unleashed their fury on the youth gathered at Grant and

Lincoln Parks, and began to beat them into oblivion, the New Left's victory was won. But as for who started it, Nigel Young appropriately writes, "the offensive guerrilla tactics of the militant minority at Chicago were consciously chosen . . . the eventual SDS decision to 'bring the war home' was made largely independently of Daley's police." Chicago was not meant to be another mass peaceful mobilization. "Certainly and predictably," as Young argues, "the clashes were provoked, and many demonstrators carried weapons."[21]

Many of those who had come to demonstrate at the Chicago convention were already firmly committed to what they termed revolutionary action. The previous year's march on the Pentagon—which produced Norman Mailer's classic *Armies of the Night*—led these radicals to argue that the American people might be lulled by such protest into thinking that "the 'democratic' process in America functions in a meaningful way."[22] At first organizers Tom Hayden and Rennie Davis sought a coalition of groups to come to Chicago, and they warned against violent tactics. "The campaign should not plan violence and disruption against the Democratic national convention," they said at the start, since some 300,000 demonstrators could not "charge into 30,000 paratroopers." Moreover, these shrewd politicos knew that "any plan of deliberate disruption will drive people away." Instead, they favored the kind of action that would pressure the Democrats to change Vietnam policy, as well as work to radicalize a divided peace movement.[23]

By the time their followers had arrived in Chicago, however, Hayden and his associates were caught up in the gale of revolutionary ardor that seemed to grip the very best of the SDS founders. Lyndon Johnson's surprise announcement that he would not seek renomination was met almost with fear by the antiwar leaders. Rather than rejoice at the chance a peace might be arranged, they expressed fear that LBJ's move deprived them of an easy enemy to target. Sid Lens, a leading Chicago activist and MOBE leader, thought that demonstrations would be so un-eventful he planned a vacation during the period the convention would be in town. To deal with this attitude, Dellinger, Hayden, and others argued consistently that any peace talks and Humphrey candidacy would not lead to a real antiwar settle-ment; that goal had to be won in the streets. No one had done more to spread the doctrine than Hayden, despite his contempo-rary proclamations to the contrary. After the Columbia Univer-sity SDS and black militant strike, in which Hayden played a cel-ebrated role, he had publicly argued that a major turning point had been reached. When the student rebellion at Columbia Uni-versity took place, Hayden had quickly arrived at the scene, and was captured in a famous photo crawling into one of the occu-pied buildings through an open window. Reflecting on that event, Hayden wrote at the time that Columbia presaged "a new tactical stage in the resistance movement," one that would grow from building occupations to "permanent occupation," from civil disobedience "to revolutionary committees."[24]

Reading Hayden in the 1960s, and comparing him to his own later account of what he believed in that earlier decade, reveals that the author has rewritten his own history to square with later entrance into Democratic Party politics as a responsible moder-ate—a man slightly to the political right of the Democratic Left. At the time, it was quite clear what Hayden, Rubin, and the SDS leaders meant when they spoke of revolutionary actions. SDS, one has to remember, was at the time the single largest member-ship organization within the broad and somewhat amorphous New Left. Estimates of its membership vary, but it hovered around 50,000 members who belonged to some 350 college chapters. In 1968, the group was led by a *troika* of self-pro-claimed revolutionaries—Mike Klonsky, Fred Gordon, and Bernardine Dohrn. Others, as David Farber carefully notes, saw Chicago as a truly golden opportunity. Jeff Jones, later a Weather Underground leader, favored rough action in the streets, the kind that would prove to naïve McCarthy supporters where real leadership lay. But Hayden had no equal in the strength of his rhetoric.

On the very eve of the convention, Tom Hayden rallied his troops. "We are coming to Chicago to vomit on the 'politics of joy,'" Hayden wrote, alluding to Hubert Humphrey's campaign slogan. "We are coming . . . to expose the secret decisions, upset the night club orgies, and face the Democratic Party with its illegitimacy and criminality." The purpose was not to transform the party, but rather to destroy it. Hayden proclaimed, in the radical rhetoric of those times, "the government of the United States is an outlaw institution under the control of war criminals."[25]

The convention, as we have seen, did not move in the direction favored by McCarthy and the antiwar forces. Although some 80 percent of Democratic primary voters had cast their ballots for either Gene McCarthy or Robert Kennedy, the convention delegates saw things differently. Hubert Humphrey resisted all admonitions that he endorse the peace plank as a bridge to the antiwar constituencies, and the result was the overwhelming defeat of the plank by a vote of 1,567 3/4 to 104 1/2. After that, the peace forces were even more inclined to action in the streets. On Wednesday afternoon of the convention some 10,000 met at Grant Park for a giant antiwar rally. It was here that a demonstrator, rumored to be a Chicago undercover police agent, scaled the flagpole to bring down the American flag. The immediate response was total pandemonium, as demonstrators threw objects at the police and they in turn used Mace, tear gas, and a full panoply of billy clubs on the demonstrators. The crowd began what became its mantra—"the whole world is watching."

The park stood directly opposite the Conrad Hilton Hotel, the site of both the Humphrey and McCarthy campaign headquarters. Thousands gathered in front. At the convention nomination speeches proceeded as scheduled. Outside, hundreds of people were repeatedly beaten and clubbed. Looking at the events from his hotel window, McCarthy reflected that the police were "reminiscent of the formations of Hannibal's last battle," the event looked to him like "a surrealistic dance—the ballet of purgatory."[26] Others, like George McGovern, compared the occurrences to Nazi Germany. On the convention floor, Senator Abraham Ribicoff told the delegates that thousands of young people were being beaten on the streets of Chicago, and that if George McGovern were president, "we would not have to have such Gestapo tactics."[27]

Hayden made the same comparison, saying that America was at the same stage as pre-Nazi Weimar. Therefore, he argued, "our victory lies in progressively demystifying a false democracy."[28] The message and intent were clear. Confrontation and polarization were necessary to lay bare the fascist reality behind the apparently liberal political mechanism.

This was evident from the scene and impromptu rallies held at Lincoln Park, where most of the demonstrators made their unofficial headquarters and outdoors home. Before the Grant Park riot, for example, the assembled young people heard the incendiary comments of Black Panther Party leader Bobby Seale, who played to the emotions of the crowd. Seale, now more well known for his Southern barbecue cookbooks and his benign image on the "Ben and Jerry" ice cream poster pitching their vanilla flavor, had a far different message in 1968. Since the power structure ruled America by force, he told the crowd, the "people" had to use force. "If a pig comes up to us and starts swinging a billy club," Seale yelled, "and you check around and you got your piece—you gotta down that pig in defense of yourself." Urging them to "pick up a gun," Seale urged them to "shoot it well" and then "keep shooting."[29] This message made some Yippie participants uneasy. The poet/author/singer Ed Sanders, whose group "The Fugs" was a New York area counter-culture standard-bearer, was frankly upset. "I'm sick and tired of hearing people talk like this," he told Abbie Hoffman, who was advocating looting and pillaging. "You're urging people to go out and get killed for nothing."[30]

There was ample reason for the police to feel quite wary. When various intelligence units reported to them that demonstrators were coming with oven cleaners and ammonia to use as weapons, the atmosphere of tension increased. On the demonstrators' side, the expectations of violence kept away middle-class peaceful demonstrators from groups like Women for Peace, a Communist front that recruited from antiwar mothers and housewives. SDS, especially, was upping the ante. If the police chose to prevent the demonstrators from sleeping in Lincoln Park, Hoffman and Rubin advised, they should "leave the parks in small groups and do what is necessary, make them pay. . . ."[31] It is not surprising that local columnists justified whatever measures the police had in mind. As one of them wrote, the New Left was constantly threatening various "sophisticated forms of sabotage," from spreading nails on the expressways to poisoning of delegates' food.[32]

As the official report of the events concluded, a "police riot" did ensue, and demonstrators and bystanders alike were brutally beaten by Chicago's finest, often in blatant disregard of both the law and the instructions issued by their own commissioner. But given the first night's attack, the demonstrators' decision to march the next night toward the Amphitheater and Grant Park was provocative. There they were met by SDS leaders, who urged the crowd to take their protest to the streets of Chicago. The police decision to lob powerful tear gas grenades into the crowd only intensified the protesters' anger and reinforced the position of the radicals who were continually urging confrontation. As usual with these kinds of events, the two extremes met each other in the middle, resulting in a giant conflagration that the world watched on their daily television news reports.

The effect of the police attack was to push many of the moderates into the waiting arms of the far Left. Arthur Waskow was then a left-wing historian and a McCarthy delegate from the District of Columbia. Looking at the large group gathered at Grant Park, Waskow told a reporter that the Chicago demonstrations were becoming a "complete victory . . . *the difference between the movement and the liberals in the party is declining, disappearing.*"[33] (author's emphasis) Waskow was typical of those slightly older left/liberals who sought an opening toward the younger and more militant SDS activists. He saw interaction between the two groups, even in violence, as positive. Waskow and others could not see it at the time, but it was that very coming together of the two elements that would produce the eventual decline and growing isolation of the once-proud Democratic Party.

At that moment, however, future left-wing Democratic leader Hayden had a slightly different goal. Speaking to the assembled body at Grant Park, Hayden claimed that their "primary struggle has not been to expose the bankruptcy of the Democratic Party; they have done that for themselves." Rather, it was to "struggle for our survival as a movement." The next step was to march the following day on the convention, and to take control "by any means necessary."[34] When the ten to fifteen thousand people finally met on the day of Humphrey's nomination at Grant Park, it seemed that Waskow's hopes had been met. As historian Farber notes, the rally included scores of older and conservatively dressed people, including a large number "of increasingly bitter McCarthy supporters."[35] What they heard was a ringing call for confrontation. Recorded for future use by a Naval Intelligence Officer assigned to monitor the rally, Jerry Rubin promised that they would "take the same risks the blacks take." Emphasizing their rejection of wealth and the property system, Rubin—who would die a millionaire businessman in 1994—shouted: "The hell with property . . . it has been shown that white people are going to take to the streets to become fighters to try to take the country away from the people who run it and that's how we are going to join the blacks, by joining them on the streets. See you in the streets tonight."[36] Other speakers, according to Jason Epstein's account, followed with more of the same. After stalwart pacifist Dellinger informed the assembled multitude of the nonviolent option, he was followed by Tom Neuman, who urged the crowd to move out and "defend ourselves in any way we can." Although Dellinger evidently found this call for violence to be anathema, he did not condemn it, since he was loyal to the all-inclusive politics of the antiwar Mobe.

The final speaker, once again, was Tom Hayden. The future politician did little to promote calm. Instead, Hayden told the crowd: "If blood is going to flow, let it flow all over the city . . . if we are going to be disrupted . . . let this whole stinking city be disrupted and violated . . . I'll see you in the streets."[37] The Walker Commission, commenting on the violence that followed, reached the conclusion that although it was not "a one-way street . . . the preponderance of violence came from the police." This conclusion has stuck, and has become something of a shibboleth, especially since few looking back want to be in the position of supporting the subsequent prosecution of the Chicago Seven, which was based on the claim that the violence was a deliberate plan of the so-called conspirators, Rubin, Dellinger, Hoffman, and their codefendants.

While there certainly was no conspiracy—violence had not been planned intentionally in advance—it was clear that the politics of key movement leaders, including those of the Students for a Democratic Society, were intent on provoking violence and creating confrontation as their key strategy for exposing the fascist reality that they believed lay behind the facade of the liberal political structure. The police violence was quite real, extreme, and unwarranted. As Farber reports, while scores of police acted responsibly and asked demonstrators to leave, in the face of verbal taunts and assaults with garbage, rocks, and bottles, others lost control and began to club uncontrollably, and "dozens of enraged officers [were] screaming curses, us[ing] their clubs, fists, knees, and Mace to hurt people." At the same time, many of the demonstrators used sticks, rocks, and concrete chunks, and "punched, kicked and struck."[38]

Upstairs in his hotel suite, George McGovern watched the violence. Turning to those with him, he asked: "Do you see what those sons of bitches are doing to those kids down there?"[39] At that moment, perhaps, the future division of the Party came into full flower, as the man who would lead the Democrats into defeat assumed the mantle of leadership of the party's antiwar forces. From that moment on, the extent of the police violence seemed to have the effect precisely desired by the radicals—that of polarization and weakening of the Democratic Party's traditional base. With the nomination firmly in the hands of the liberal Hubert Humphrey, former antiwar moderates vowed in droves not to support his candidacy—even if that act guaranteed the subsequent victory of the much-hated Richard M. Nixon.

New Left leaders drew their own lessons. Rennie Davis urged the crowds in Grant Park to "build a National Liberation Front for America." Tom Hayden reiterated a message he had received from an SDS member visiting Cuba—"While we heard of the Revolution in Cuba," the member had wired Hayden, "you held it sacred in Chicago. Create two, three Chicagos." Hayden modified it: the movement should create "two hundred or three hundred Chicagos everywhere." As Farber writes, each speaker was more radical than the previous ones. Jeff Jones, a future leader of the "Weatherman" extremist SDS faction, minced no words: "Fight it out," he told the crowd. "Build a strong base and knock those motherfuckers on their ass."[40] Moderates like Arthur Waskow now espoused what he called "guerrilla politics," a phrase meant to show his hope that New Left tactics could be used in the political process. Like the radicals, Waskow agreed that events at Chicago "had challenged the most important liberal dogma . . . that America is a free and democratic society with only a few major faults that need to be reformed."[41]

With the demonstrators moving toward the extreme, liberal moderates had to choose between Humphrey and the Revolution. Humphrey formally backed Daley's handling of the events. "The city of Chicago," the vice president stated, "didn't do a thing that was wrong. . . . There are certain people in the United States who feel that all you have to do is riot and you can get your way. I have no time for that."[42] That kind of statement infuriated antiwar moderates, who saw it as further confirmation that Humphrey would prove unable to break with Lyndon Johnson's disastrous Vietnam policy. Warily, their disdain for Humphrey pushed them into the hands of the waiting New Left.

Even old radicals like Socialist Party leader Norman Thomas—the moderate grand old man of American radicalism—held no brief for Humphrey. Writing to his party's members on the eve of the Democratic convention, Thomas informed them "it is my thought that all our strength should be devoted to helping" Eugene McCarthy win the nomination. If he lost, Thomas believed that the Socialist Party should advise a vote for the Democratic candidate, but leave a final decision up to each member's personal conscience. As for himself, Thomas was strongly for McCarthy, because he thought the senator "represents a sincere and determined effort to get us out of the war, far more nearly than Nixon or Humphrey."[43] When it became clear that McCarthy was not in the running, it became virtually unthinkable for many of his former backers to swallow their pride and vote for—not to speak of endorse—Hubert Humphrey.

Thus Martin Peretz, reading a story in the *Boston Globe* that indicated McCarthy was considering trying to "help" Humphrey in his campaign against Nixon, advised the senator that "the young would indeed think support for Humphrey constituted a sell-out." As Peretz and other moderates on the Left saw things, Humphrey was still defending the same "nonsense about imposing governments on the South Vietnamese," and his position on bombing halts was rigid. Moreover, the fact that Averell Harriman, whom Peretz termed an "elegant facade for the thugs," had given Humphrey his support, proved that the vice president was not worthy of the presidency. Peretz was incensed that just days earlier, Humphrey had attacked young activists as "storm-troopers and anarchists," an opprobrius assessment that decades later, Peretz himself would acknowledge was not far from the mark.[44]

Peretz's disdain for Humphrey reflected a more serious disillusionment with American democracy from the new intellectual class. Typical was the writing of the influential young historian, Christopher Lasch, whose writing regularly graced the pages of *New York Review of Books*. Reflecting on the meaning of Chicago, Lasch explained that the center in American politics had increasingly adopted "the policies and outlook of the right." In his eyes—as with so many others of the Democratic Left—Hubert Humphrey was indistinguishable from Richard Nixon. Indeed, Lasch claimed that the centrist liberals were seeking to outmaneuver the Right by preempting their policies, and only worked to contribute to the growth of the Right.

Thus, in Lasch's analysis, "the focus of American politics has shifted to the right. Domestic discontent was bought off, as Lasch saw things, by building roads and cars by which inhabitants of prosperous white ethnic communities would escape from the cities to the "summer paradise of the suburbs," a strategy he thought had worked until Vietnam, ghetto riots, and the events in Chicago had taken place. But with Chicago, Lasch wrote, "its utter bankruptcy [stood] fully revealed." The system would defend its interests only with savage repression and by counting on "the most reactionary forces in American life." Indeed, Lasch saw a "fascist mentality" triumphant in America—one that could, under the right conditions, move toward total fascism once "politicians like Nixon and Humphrey" who retained "some lingering commitment, however tenuous, to democratic procedures," faded as the rulers embrace fascist means to restore law and order.

For the then-radical Lasch, the McCarthy and Kennedy campaigns represented "the last chance to maintain the American empire under liberal auspices." The Humphrey campaign, by contrast, was the cutting edge of entrance to the future fascist order—Lasch cited in particular "the cruel battle waging in the streets while Humphrey sat undistracted before the televised unreality of the roll call," combined with his refusal "to disavow the actions of Daley's thugs," demonstrating "the price that must now be paid by those willing to carry on the politics of American world power." The answer for Lasch was clear: "Radicalism [was] the only long-term hope for America." Liberals like Humphrey could not even undertake palliative reforms. The only kind of liberalism that had a slight chance to stave off revolution was what Lasch called a "radicalized liberalism," one in which traditional Democratic Party liberals made alliances with the new radicals.[45] Lasch may have favored that path, but his analysis fed the illusions of the New Left, which desired not a change in the system, but its overthrow. As part of that revolutionary thrust, the destruction of the Democratic Party, and the illusion that it offered the working class and the poor, was of paramount importance.

The influence of Lasch's analysis was extensive. A former moderate who did not grow up in a left-wing household, and a man with bona fide academic credentials, he symbolized the growing estrangement and radicalization of the new young intellectual class. Little did Lasch and his followers realize, however, that his prescription of a new left-wing liberalism that "would force concessions to the Negroes, forestall disastrous military adventures abroad, turn back the right-wing assault against . . . civil liberties, and thereby postpone the collapse of liberal capitalism," would overtake and come to control the very Democratic Party Lasch saw as bankrupt a scant four years later.

It was no wonder that the leaders of the old Democratic Party were suffering a great despair. Speaking to the Democratic National Committee shortly after the New Year, and the election of Richard M. Nixon to the presidency, Hubert Humphrey showed the good humor for which he was always highly regarded. "All I can say," Humphrey told the DNC, "is that when midnight, December 31 came and the hour was 12:01, January 1, 1969, I said to my wife . . . 'Well, thank goodness 1968 is gone. That was year that I could have gotten along without very, very well.'" That, perhaps, was the understatement of the year. When it came to the politics of 1968, however, Humphrey was not the slightest bit recalcitrant. Indeed, he reaffirmed to the DNC the politics of the old New Deal–Fair Deal labor-liberal coalition. His support, he noted, had come not just from the wealthy, but from the "black leadership of the trade union movement" as well as "our friends in the labor movement." Their backing, he thought, was essential "in any election victory for progressive government."

As for Chicago, Humphrey believed "that some day there will be the proper perspective on Chicago. There were two Chicagos," he thought; "one outside the Convention Hall, and one inside. The one I liked was the one inside . . . it was historic." Most important was implementation of the criteria for delegate selection adopted at the Atlantic City 1964 Convention, as well as the vote to eliminate the Unit Rule. The result, Humphrey thought, would be the revitalization of the party he had served for decades.[46]

The Democratic Party would be revitalized, but not in the direction preferred by Hubert Humphrey. The direction to be taken by the Democrats would be decided in the contest for the 1972 nomination—a contest that pitted Humphrey's logical successor, the state of Washington's beloved senator, Henry "Scoop" Jackson, against the senator from the state of South Dakota, George McGovern, who had made his name as a strong and early opponent of the war in Vietnam. McGovern's victory, and the changes instituted in party rules prior to the 1972 convention, would be two of the most important elements in the transformation of the Democratic Party into a radicalized organization far removed from the needs of mainstream America.

6

McGOVERNISM AND THE CAPTURED PARTY

The Democrats and Party Reform

Hubert Humphrey had made a valiant attempt to win the Presidency. He had managed to win back the support of some of his erstwhile antiwar opponents late in the campaign. Despite the advice of key supporters, even Eugene McCarthy and the Americans for Democratic Action came through for the vice president. But it was not enough. The liberals' arch-nemesis, Richard M. Nixon, managed to squeak through. He received a vast majority west of the Mississippi, and came out with 302 electoral college votes. Humphrey garnered only 191, and most of them came from the state of Michigan—the stronghold of the United Auto Workers—and from the Northeast in general. Nixon's victory came despite the votes he lost in the South to George Wallace, whose independent candidacy got 45 electoral votes from the old Confederate states.

Indeed, the outcome of the vote might have shown the Democrats that it was a bad time for traditional New Deal–Fair Deal liberalism. Some 57 percent of the electorate had voted for Nixon or Wallace. Only Texas remained Democratic, and a study of the vote would have revealed a new shift—traditional Democratic blue-collar voters, who considered themselves mainstream middle-class Americans, had begun to shift toward the Republican slot. Later they would be named "Reagan Democrats" in reference to former white ethnics who left the Democratic ranks to cast their votes for Ronald Reagan in 1984. Hubert Humphrey had only gathered 38 percent of the white vote.[1]

Given these results, the Democrats might have reevaluated their direction. But the fierceness of the debate over Vietnam, combined with the leftward drift of key Democratic Party activists, proved too much of an obstacle. Rather than look at the meaning of results, pressure was developing to push even farther toward the political Left. The key pressure group was the newly formed New Democratic Coalition, or NDC. As historian Herbert Parmet has written, "the Democratic Party had a choice. It could seek to unify around a centrist coalition that would hold out the bait of national success every four years or it could sacrifice components of the coalition for ideological purity."[2] By 1972 the fateful choice had been made.

The entire purpose of the NDC, as two of its original proponents described the organization, was to create a "new national liberal movement" after the "fiasco" and "debacle" of both the 1968 convention and the presidential race. Instead of a party run by a coalition of big labor, farmers, city bosses, and the Old South, the NDC would group itself around "the McCarthy, Kennedy, and McGovern Democrats, minority groups, the youth, the intellectuals, enlightened labor and business, and peace and civil liberty groups," all united for the sole purpose of forging a new coalition "of liberal Democratic interest groups strong enough to put the Democratic Party back into national office."[3]

Central to the New Politics argument was the belief that organized labor—once the mainstay of the Democratic Party during the heyday of the New Deal—was no longer a group that worked to shift the party to the left. Indeed, the New Politics group argued that organized labor had "basically achieved its end," that of a good standard of living for American workers, and therefore, "it has become conservative." The social revolution was now from the ranks of "the impoverished of the nation," and their desire for change was described by these NDC stalwarts as "a direct threat to the job of the blue collar worker," who resented paying higher taxes to finance welfare for the poor. Hence their solution: "to weld the McCarthy, Kennedy, and McGovern Democrats" into a force that could overcome labor to reform the party from within.

While the authors of the draft described themselves as liberals, the thrust of their argument for the New Politics was essentially that of the far Left in Students for a Democratic Society. The SDSers and others in the ranks of the New Left similarly viewed labor as a moribund reactionary force, and not as a movement that sought rights for working people. And like the New Left, the NDC looked for the engine of change in America as coming from the most oppressed—the blacks and the poor. It was a definition for identity-group politics that would become more common in a decade, and it was a recipe for political disaster.

The authors, however, had their finger on something. Parties, they realized, were becoming increasingly irrelevant, since candidates and the campaigns they waged were frequently independent of the party mechanism. As they saw it, the problem was that the party organizations were not responsive to the "will of the people," a will which the NDC group assumed it alone represented. Hence they sought "broad citizen participation" that would guarantee responsiveness to the people's needs. No longer could they rely on the "stale liberalism" of the past, that of the New Deal which they saw as "irrelevant to the issues of contemporary America." Hence the liberal community failed to rally around the issue of poverty, as it had to the cause of civil rights. Their group could forge the new philosophy that would ostensibly remedy the problem.

The hopes for the NDC would be stillborn. Twenty states had NDC clubs in 1968, but by 1970, possibly because their sectarianism did not appeal to most mainstream Democrats, the national office had closed and the enthusiasm for the organization, outside of major liberal centers such as New York City, had ebbed. Yet the direction the NDC group had sought was quickly becoming the orientation of the Democratic Party itself. Nowhere was this more evident than in the mechanism for party reform called for by the 1968 convention. The Credentials Committee of the convention had mandated a study of how delegates for national conventions in each state were chosen. The result was creation of the Commission on Party Structure and Delegate Selection, which came under the chairmanship of Senator George McGovern, and a Rules Commission chaired by Rep. James O'Hara, a liberal Michigan congressman. It was a choice, party chairman Larry O'Brien commented later, that was "clearly weighted toward the liberal wing of the party, rather than being representative of the party as a whole."[4]

The McGovern Commission was highly controversial. During the spring and summer of 1969, the Commission held hearings in seventeen cities and heard more than five hundred witnesses.

The purpose of the Commission, according to guidelines created by the Democratic National Committee and prepared by political scientist Alexander M. Bickel and historian Richard Wade, was the belief that the "chief danger to the continued stability of the American political system is the erosion among some groups . . . of a sense of the legitimacy of the system's decisions and choices." According to the two Democratic academics, the way to "counteract that danger [was] by ensuring the participation of political minorities," precisely the groups whose sense of the legitimacy of the process was impaired.[5] A similar case was made by the stalwart liberal Joe Rauh, who saw the reform as a continuation of the efforts on behalf of civil rights he had fought for at the 1964 convention. The Democratic Party structure, Rauh argued, needed "genuine participation by the underprivileged, the minorities, the alienated . . . the intellectual community," or, he thought, these forces would turn to a new party that would then threaten the Democrat's majority status or perhaps even lead to the complete destruction of the Democratic Party itself. Rauh favored a structure that would bring these "vital elements of change in our social order" into control of the party structure. To that end, he favored annual conventions of the party, more rank-and-file participation, and the selection of delegates to national conventions not through state committees, but through a voting process in primaries.[6]

The rules being promoted were clearly the left's revenge for the 1968 riots. Even Gene McCarthy saw the new rules as necessary to get those who left and had refused to vote for Humphrey back into the party's ranks. At Grant Park, he told the Commission hearings, he swore to the activists that he wouldn't ask them to work in the party unless it changed along with the policies it stood for. But "rational choice was almost impossible," and many activists felt compelled to stay outside the orbit of both political parties. The Democratic Party had to change its procedures so that popular judgments could be translated into party positions, and so that state delegations at national conventions would reflect the strength of support for issues, such as opposition to the war, that activist delegates supported.[7]

As for the hearings, George McGovern was euphoric over the results. "We have heard from every conceivable ideological point of view," he told the DNC, "from the young, the old, the black, and the white in every region of our country." McGovern did not seem to realize that he was identifying ethnic and racial groups, and terming them "ideological," as if their racial or age group signified their ideas. Indeed, McGovern noted that they even heard from one witness who doubled as a member of "the state Central Democratic Committee and a local SDS." What they found was more than upsetting. Women, the Senator reported, comprised only 13 percent of delegates to the last convention, and blacks, who made up 11 percent of the population, had given Humphrey 20 percent of the vote he received for president, and yet they comprised a mere 5 percent of delegates to the party's convention. Moreover, people under the age of thirty were almost omitted entirely. For the party to win, McGovern thought, it had to capture the youth vote.[8]

In that one argument, George McGovern ironically underscored precisely the reasons for the decline of the Democratic Party. Gearing the party to liberal constituency groups and activists rather than to the traditional Democratic electorate, and the organizations that regularly represented their needs and interests, McGovern was opening up the party to a course that would over the decades result in a steady loss of electoral support. At the hearings, many delegates complained about the very existence of a convention, and they favored national nominating primaries in its place for each political party. Eventually, most favored keeping the national conventions, but developing other methods for the choice of delegates. In twenty states, they pointed out, one-half to 10 percent of delegates were chosen the year before the convention. When Gene McCarthy declared his candidacy, the report of the Commission noted, "nearly one-third of the delegates had in effect already been selected."[9]

By September of 1969, the Commission had announced its guidelines. Most of the attention and controversy was focused on two sections of their report. The first directed state parties to "overcome the effects of past discrimination by affirmative steps to encourage minority group participation, including representation of minority groups on the national convention delegation in reasonable relationship to the group's presence in the population of the state." The other section called for ending the "effects of past discrimination by affirmative steps to encourage representation on the national convention delegation of young people . . . and women in responsible relationship to their presence in the population of the state."[10]

The problem was one of implementation. The Commission noted in a footnote that they rejected "mandatory imposition of quotas." But their denial amounted to a rather meaningless *pro forma* statement—precisely the kind of statement one would become quite used to in the 1970s and eighties, when liberal Democrats would regularly argue that their requirements for minority representation were still not quotas. In reality, everyone who composed the statements understood well that their goals would not be attainable without what in effect *were* quotas. McGovern himself boasted, in an interview with the *National Journal*, that "the way we got the quota thing through was by not using the word 'quotas.'"[11] Moreover, as Herbert Parmet has noted, the guidelines had been adopted by a scant ten to nine vote out of a twenty-eight member body, and tellingly, a major old-line labor leader, I.W. Abel, president of the United Steelworkers of America, had been so angry he boycotted the meeting in protest.

The results were a foregone conclusion. The Democratic National Committee adopted the Commission's guidelines on February 19, 1971, and made them part of the Call for the 1972 Convention. Similarly, the parallel O'Hara Commission on party rules also included a directive that committee members chosen by states had to be balanced by the sexes and take into account "due regard to the race and age of the men and women elected." The results meant that traditional Democratic mainstays, such as organized labor, were now regarded as "special interests," a term that denoted groups to which the party should not kowtow. No longer could labor, which since the New Deal era had pulled out the votes for Democratic candidates, be counted on to have their desires taken into consideration by the Democratic Party. Since 75 percent of delegates had to be selected at congressional district levels, it also meant that older, established Democratic Party leaders now might even face the humiliation of not receiving seats and credentials for attendance at the national convention itself.

The results of the reforms, future Republican, then Democrat, Jeane Kirkpatrick concluded in a massive study of the changes, was creation of what she called "a part of the process of the continuing transformation of American parties and political life." Writing in 1975, a short time before she would become one of the first of a generation that created a new political force—neoconservatism—Kirkpatrick noted that the "policy-oriented liberal who makes his own party and country the object of his reformist zeal is as familiar as the policy-oriented conservative whose goals are first to capture his party and then to restore his nation to traditional virtues."[12]

The conflict, Kirkpatrick understood, was as much cultural as political. The astute political scientist put it this way:

> Popular descriptions of 1972 Democratic politics painted the conflict within the Democratic Party in large part as a contest between oldtimers and newcomers. The former were presumably found among the supporters of traditional 'establishment' candidates . . . said to be the people who had dominated American politics for decades, had made a mess of things at home and abroad. . . . Juxtaposed to them were the newcomers, who, legend had it, had been stimulated by passionate concern with the issues of the late 1960s—civil rights, war, ecology—to enter the political arena. . . . The McGovern movement was frequently described as a product of this surge into politics of thousands of Americans who had a rising sense of social justice and social outrage.[13]

It was, in other words, the beginning of a new ideological politics, unlike that of the old style in which Democrats like FDR and Truman had responded to the economic needs of their constituency. It was that of the group Kirkpatrick dubbed the "new presidential elite," a group of Democratic Party elites which were dominated by men and women who were urban and suburban college-educated, with high incomes, largely Jewish, and generally on the political left of the spectrum.

It was precisely this development that traditional Democrats were worried about. Writing in *Commentary*, a Jewish journal of opinion which soon was to become the leading voice of the neoconservatism edited by young Norman Podhoretz, Penn Kemble, then a Democratic Socialist active in the Norman Thomas wing of American socialism, wrote of the threat to the Democrats caused by emergence of the New Politics movement:

To the extent that any force in American politics embodies the interests of the new intelligentsia, this does—or at least is attempting to. . . . The strategy of the New Politics movement has been to concentrate on its own favorites, regardless of their importance to the larger political picture, and in a manner completely independent of—and occasionally in conflict with—the other major liberal blocs.[14]

The result, according to Kemble and his colleague Joshua Muravchik (later to become an influential neoconservative foreign policy analyst but at that time national chairman of the Young People's Socialist League), was the hijacking of the nomination. "The reforms," the two young Social-Democrats wrote, "have left one of the major institutions of American democracy in a shambles." The staff of the commission, they argued, was composed of a majority of New Politics supporters, backers of either Eugene McCarthy or George McGovern, including a leader of the Vietnam Moratorium Committee. In November 1969, the die was cast. At that meeting, staff "introduced the proposal for a quota system for representation at national conventions," not only for blacks, who had been consistently denied participation in Democratic Party affairs in the South, but "for two newly classified victims of political discrimination, women, and youth." But the commission went even further, claiming for itself complete decision-making power in forging the process of delegate selection.[15]

Years later, McGovern recalled that the reason he had taken the chairmanship of the Commission was that other leaders, including Hubert Humphrey, Fred Harris, and Walter Reuther, knew he "had impeccable credentials with the antiwar so-called New Politics people," and he himself believed that the new rules would protect the party "against the kind of explosive divisions that erupted in 1968."[16] McGovern, however, implicitly denied the kind of argument made at the time by Kemble and Muravchik. His convention victory was fair, he said, since he won according to the "way the rules were then." For his part, McGovern argued that he won the nomination because "I did a better job of getting people to vote for me in ten crucial primary states including New York and California, the two big ones, than anybody else." He did admit, however, that the rules helped him to do "better in the caucuses and the state conventions than might otherwise have been the case."[17]

The DNC assured McGovern's success at its February 19, 1971, meeting. Convened to authorize the call for the 1972 convention—a meeting that set apportionment of delegates and rules for delegate certification—the body saw to it that the reform guidelines would become part and parcel of the convention call, thereby having binding force on the state Democratic Party organizations. At the meeting, Joe Califano argued that the guidelines were not within the power of the DNC to change, and had to be adopted. Similarly the Credentials Committee of the Democratic Party convention could have modified the guidelines, but it too went along with the steamroller put into effect by the McGovern forces. Speaking to that body, Califano told them that these were the "rules that have been set up and adopted by your national party. They are no longer the McGovern Commission Rules . . . they are the Democratic Party Rules." Thus, wrote Kemble and Muravchik, "the party had been radically transformed by an agency which through bluff and maneuver had successfully avoided all mechanisms of democratic review."[18]

Their view was documented in a letter and report to Democratic activist and fund-raiser Stanley Sheinbaum, by the young Left-liberal activist and future political journalist, Ken Bode. Writing in October of 1971, Bode was worried that Larry

Divided They Fell

O'Brien and the DNC had "dealt a number of blows to the party's reform wing." Believing that O'Brien only honored reform rhetorically, Bode worried that O'Brien would overturn the new "apportionment formula," and that the DNC would join with their paid staff and the AFL-CIO to defeat meaningful reform. Predicting O'Brien's "last hurrah," Bode argued that they had to "fight O'Brien's influence and that of the National Committee." That meant a policy of picking reform-minded staff, preparing challenge procedures against conservative delegates, and working for major rules changes, such as "mandatory proportional representation for future national conventions," and making these "tied to support for the national ticket."[19]

What the Commission had done was nothing less than a radical reinterpretation of the traditional view that supported equality of opportunity for all Americans, once the mainstay of the Democrats' approach toward politics. The new doctrine of demographic representation, Jeane Kirkpatrick commented in her seminal study, assumed that sex or race have "special, unique, or definitive relevance to political perspectives, roles, or outcomes," and it left the decision as to representation to these very groups, so that blacks, for example, could choose only blacks to represent them if they desired. "The demographic approach to representation," explained Kirkpatrick, "requires that someone other than voters determine which of the many statuses of a person are in fact most important: the McGovern Commission decided in favor of sex, race, and age."[20]

There was some argument against the Commission. At a closed caucus held by House Democrats on June 28, shortly before the Miami convention, the assembled congressmen approved a resolution denouncing the reforms as "not in the best interests of the Democratic Party," and demanding "further investigation and study." Congressman Wayne Hays of Ohio, one of the group, stated the hidden truth boldly. "The Democratic Party is in shambles," Hays asserted, "and this isn't going to make a better shambles."[21]

Months before the Miami convention, it was not apparent that the candidate of the Democratic Party would be George McGovern. Indeed, the front-runner was the dutiful centrist and well-regarded Edmund Muskie, and lots of old-time regular Democrats still thought there was a chance that the former vice president, Hubert Humphrey, was in the running. The Democrats also faced a major challenge from George Wallace, whose stunning 42 percent plurality win in the eleven-candidate Florida primary had been the single greatest victory of his political career.

Wallace, long regarded simply as a racist and demagogue by Northern liberals and minority groups, had since 1968 been developing a campaign based on a new kind of populism—as the representative of the forgotten blue-collar workers and middle class, whose needs and concerns had seemingly been replaced within the Democratic Party by those of urban, college-educated, and elitist Northern radicals. But as one of his most recent biographers has well pointed out, there was much more to Wallace than the issue of race. The themes he emphasized in 1968 and in his stillborn 1972 campaign, destroyed by the bungled assassination attempt which left him paralyzed and in constant pain thereafter, were those echoed through the decades by Richard Nixon, Jimmy Carter, Ronald Reagan, George Bush, and eventually Bill Clinton. Wallace called for being tough on crime, for limiting the power of the federal government, for restoring traditional values that had eroded, for returning the Supreme Court to a path of judicial conservatism, and most important of all, he urged that the administration start paying "attention to a beleaguered middle class, balance the budget, reduce waste, and reform welfare."[22] As his most recent biographer, historian Dan T. Carter argues, "two decades after his disappearance from national politics, the Alabama governor seems vindicated by history. If he did not create the conservative groundswell that transformed American politics in the 1980s, he anticipated most of its themes. . . . If George Wallace did not create this mood of national skepticism, he anticipated and exploited the political transformation it precipitated. His attacks on the federal government have become the gospel of modern conservatism; his angry rhetoric, the foundation for the new ground rules of political warfare."[23]

Wallace, in other words, emphasized the centrality to American politics of the factor Richard M. Scammon and Ben J. Wattenberg had dubbed "the social issue" in their seminal 1970 bestseller, *The Real Majority*. In their evaluation of Wallace, written some three years before the 1972 campaign, Scammon and Wattenberg argued that regardless of Wallace's own political fortunes, Wallaceism as a political force was growing more potent on a daily basis, and would not fade away. Indeed, they claimed that when he was perceived as a racist, the social issues he put stress on lost all force—the electorate did not want its answers from one perceived as an extremist and a racist. It was a message Wallace well understood. If he moved to the center—enunciating more clearly the concerns of the average people he always said he represented—his votes could easily reappear, and he or someone following in his footsteps would be a threat to any candidate who eschewed the critical social issues.[24]

Wallace did not have to read Scammon and Wattenberg. His campaign was based on a gut understanding of the arguments they made, and his success at the polls indicated the validity of their analysis. Wallace, as the left-wing historian Michael Kazin perceptively argues in his book *The Populist Persuasion*, appealed to those left out of the eroding postwar prosperity, "newly 'middle-class' consumers dependent upon but wary of the liberal state." No longer did such people attack the monopolists as they did at the turn of the century; now they attacked big government, whose representatives spent taxpayers' hard-earned dollars on the unworthy poor. Thus they blamed "liberals, those 'big people' in Washington, who got the blame for leading the nation into a shooting war it couldn't win and a war on poverty whose promise grossly overshot its achievements."[25]

By the time he had won election as governor of Alabama, Wallace had consciously begun to devalue the issue of segregation, much as Scammon and Wattenberg had predicted. He sent out careful signals, his biographer notes, that "he would want a rapprochement with those who controlled the black votes in Alabama."[26] Wallace's ultimate target, of course, was the presidency itself. The first step was in March 1972, when he decided to compete in his first primary campaign, in the state of Florida. Turning for help to the liberal activist millionaire Morris Dees, Wallace was steered in the direction of a new young conservative who worked in the direct-mail business, Richard Viguerie. Running one of the most well-financed Democratic campaigns, and touching base with all of the varied Democratic constituencies, Wallace managed, again and again, to articulate the hopes and frustrations of average citizens. On the eve of his announcement that he would enter the Florida primary, Wallace noted: "I have no illusions about the ultimate outcome. But we gonna shake up the Democratic party. We gonna shake it to its eye-teeth."[27]

That is precisely what George Wallace did. As he told a crowd at a Bradenton, Florida rally:

We're here tonight because the average citizen in this country—the man who pays his taxes and works for a living and holds this country together—the average citizen is fed up with much of this liberal-ism and this kowtowing to the exotic few. The big-time media is here too, and they're not here because of me but because of you . . . they didn't listen to us in the past—but they have to listen now.[28]

Wallace hit all the themes of what would become a familiar refrain in the Reagan-Bush eighties, a refrain that would lead scores of working-class Democrats to leave the party that once represented their economic hopes and dreams, and to vote *en masse* for self-proclaimed conservative Republicans. For Wallace, it looked like it was going to pay off. He spoke to sellout crowds who displayed wild enthusiasm. His major message, spoken over and over again, Stephan Lesher notes, was his 'passionate apotheosis of the frustrated, overlooked middle class."[29] Unlike other candidates, who tended to group these people into an amorphous bunch—"the masses," as both Old and New Left liked to talk of them—Wallace named them in his speeches: the "taxi driver, a little businessman, or a beautician or a barber or a farmer." The result was a striking 42 percent of the Florida vote—more than half a million people. Wallace carried each Florida county, including urban Miami, suburban Fort Lauderdale, and wealthy Palm Beach. Hubert Humphrey came in second with 18 percent, Scoop Jackson third with 13 percent, and Edmund Muskie, already out of the race because of his "crying" on camera after his wife was attacked in a conservative New Hampshire paper, came in last with 9 percent. Wallace was ecstatic. "We beat the face cards of the Democratic deck," he boasted. "We have turned the Democratic Party around." *Time*, the weekly newsmagazine, went even further. Wallace, it noted, had "turned the party inside out." Muskie, who had been perceived as front-runner, was furious, and let out a vicious blast. Wallace, the now-defeated candidate said, is "a demagogue of the worst kind." The Florida primary, Muskie said in his election night speech, revealed "some of the worst instincts of which human beings are capable."[30]

Yet Wallace, *pace* Muskie, was no longer seen as an extremist, and his appeal to Northern blue-collar working-class voters was more and more evident. By branding him as a blatant racist, Muskie missed the point. As *Time* explained to its readers, millions of Floridians "share none of Wallace's residual racism but do keenly feel the sense of alienation from the system that his little-man populism plays to." McGovern, taking the high ground, emphasized that he understood that "40 percent of the vote that went to George Wallace was [not] a racist vote," but a "protest against the way things are."[31] Even in Wisconsin, where initial polls showed him receiving a scant 8 percent, and with only eight days in which to campaign, Wallace received a stunning 22 percent of the votes, putting him in second place, ahead of Hubert Humphrey, one of labor's favorites, and only eight points behind the front-runner, George McGovern.

Clearly, Wallace's entry into the race was a factor that all the announced candidates—Ed Muskie of Maine, Hubert Humphrey of Minnesota, George McGovern of South Dakota, Henry "Scoop" Jackson of Washington, and John Lindsay of New York—would have to take into consideration. Wallace, as *Time* noted, could simply not be dismissed "as a redneck rabble-rouser."[32] Those who did, such as New York's Mayor John Lindsay, who attacked him as "no man of the people" and as an advocate of "perpetual racial segregation," received few votes—a scant 7 percent for Lindsay in the Florida primary. In Texas, it was a bad omen for liberals when they learned that Wallace ran well in urban liberal areas, and that he had across-the-board electoral support from all income classes. And in Maryland, where Wallace had entered the primary, he and Hubert Humphrey were tied in the polls as the two favorites. In Pennsylvania, a key industrial state where the AFL-CIO pulled out all the stops for Humphrey, the former vice president received a 35% victory, his first primary win in three presidential campaigns. But Wallace showed his strength by tying for second place with George McGovern. And as expected, Wallace won all races in the Southern states, including Tennessee and North Carolina.[33]

Because of the nature of the primary systems, which awarded convention seats to delegates on the basis of pluralities in congressional districts, rather than apportioning delegates on the basis of popular vote, Wallace did not have the number of delegates he felt the vote should justly have awarded him. Nevertheless, he hoped he would have between 300 and 400 delegates by the time of the Miami convention, enough to block a first- or second-ballot nomination of either Humphrey or McGovern. According to that scenario, Wallace could then either become a major broker, or even receive the Party's nomination. All the speculation about Wallace's apparent strength, however, came to a halt at a shopping center in Laurel, Maryland, where the governor was appearing at a campaign rally. Wallace had high hopes for an expected victory in that state, and his polls gave him new confidence. But lurking in the crowd in suburban Laurel was one Arthur Bremer, who had followed the governor from a previous rally and after his campaign speech pumped him full of five shots from a 38-caliber revolver. The effect was to give Wallace new sympathy, from the electorate as well as his opponents. He would win the Maryland primary by a narrow margin and the Michigan primary, where big labor sought ineffectively to oppose him, by an even wider margin. Wallace took the prolabor sanctuary by a margin of 51 percent to 27 percent for McGovern and only 16 percent for Humphrey, labor's favorite. Wallace polled more than

3,300,000 votes cast, a million more than McGovern and 700,000 more than Humphrey.

Nevertheless, Wallace's new physical disabilities meant in reality that his campaign was stillborn. Much of his appeal and growing political strength depended upon his fiery personal appearances, and these would come to an end. He had his ideas and his program—the message that the Democratic Party had to move toward the Right—but as Stephan Lesher so well put it, "the power of ideas alone, divorced from a convincing sachem crusading for them, has rarely been enough in American politics to forge a wide and stable constituency."[34]

The last great opportunity for the Democrats before Bill Clinton came in the form of Scoop Jackson's 1972 candidacy. His differences with the eventual winner, George McGovern, could not have been more stark. His similarities to the 1992 Clinton are also stark. His failure, sadly, showed how the Vietnam issue had been transformed into a culture war.

George McGovern had always been on the left wing of his party, and part of its antiwar wing. He had fought valiantly in World War II, where, as he liked to point out, he served his country as a bomber pilot, flying thirty-five combat missions over Nazi Germany as part of the 15th Air Force.[35] After the war, however, McGovern already was revolving in the orbit of the American Left. In 1948, he supported the third-party candidacy of Henry A. Wallace, who ran for president on the Progressive Party ticket, a party that was organized and controlled by the Communist Party of the United States, and that had as its main focus opposition to what it termed the anti-Soviet and Cold War foreign policy of the Truman Administration. Later, McGovern did not like to advertise the fact of his support of that party. As his biographer pointed out, his own summary for his 1959 Congressional race made no reference to the 1948 campaign. McGovern's "campaign propaganda," Robert Sam Anson wrote, "conveys the impression that his beliefs have never been anything except the most regular Democratic kind." Anson excused this reluctance as McGovern's need to avoid fierce "red-baiting," to which he had been regularly subjected in every one of his South Dakota races. But, as Anson correctly notes, McGovern's support of Henry A. Wallace "was more than ordinary political support. Intellectually, emotionally, politically, McGovern was committed to Wallace and to what he perceived as the cause he stood for."[36] In a letter to the editor of his local paper, written in 1948, McGovern wrote: "I take off my hat to this much smeared man who has had the fortitude to take his stand against the powerful forces of fear, militarism, nationalism, and greed," and he noted that he was tired of hearing the "thoughtless jeers" of 'Communist' being thrown his way."[37] When McGovern attended the Progressive Party convention, however, he claimed to have supported the efforts of the Vermont delegation, whose members had introduced a resolution for a foreign policy independent of all powers, a stance that suggested criticism of the Soviet Union. That plank was voted down by the pro-Communist delegates, and McGovern claims that as a result, he voted for Truman at election time.[38]

By 1953, McGovern had become the executive of the South Dakota Democratic Party, a full-time organizational job. In a Republican state, McGovern ran for Congress, and in 1956, he became South Dakota's first Democratic representative in twenty years. In his race for that seat, in a stance prescient of that he would take in 1972, he positioned himself as a peace candidate. "I resent the false charge," he told South Dakotans, "that the Democratic Party is less interested in peace than the Republican

Party. It has been my observation that a bullet hurts a Democrat just as much as a Republican." Those right-wing Republicans who had accused the Democratic administration of sacrificing American lives in Korea, McGovern said, "forget that they did their best to persuade President Truman that the war should be carried to the Chinese mainland." McGovern told his audience that when his navigator was killed during a bombing mission, he decided that if he survived, "I would dedicate the rest of my life to the cause of peace."[39]

His peace position had made McGovern a natural enemy of Joseph McCarthy's supporters in the Senate. Karl Mundt, a right-wing Republican who was first a representative from South Dakota and later senator, had been coauthor with Rep. Richard Nixon of the Mundt-Nixon Bill, a precursor of the McCarran Internal Security Act, which asked all American Communists and fellow-travelers to register with the government as "subversives." Mundt, Stephen Mitchell wrote to Sam Rayburn, tried to use "every low and false device of the McCarthy type that they thought could beat McGovern. They tried to brand him a traitor, or at least a Communist sympathizer," because McGovern had five years earlier remarked to a church group that he favored negotiating with the Chinese Communists at the table rather than fighting them on the battlefield. Mundt, Mitchell revealed, had dug McGovern's name out of a HUAC listing as someone who was "possibly" a member of a Communist front group—undoubtedly a reference to McGovern's membership in the left-leaning American Veterans Committee at the end of the war. Nevertheless, Mitchell assured Rayburn that McGovern had an "absolutely clean record," and he staked his entire record on a voucher for McGovern's "loyalty and honesty." He would definitely have, Mitchell predicted, a great future in the Democratic Party.[40]

But what Mitchell did not see was that McGovern's politics, and the support that party activists gave him, would eventually prove the turning point that led the party to eventual decline. Of all the candidates vying for the nomination, a retrospective look back suggests that Henry "Scoop" Jackson, the beloved senator from the state of Washington and a favorite of AFL-CIO leader George Meany, might have had the kind of approach and support that, had he been able to make a strong race, might have propelled the Democratic Party to political victory. Jackson was an old New Dealer, an advocate of New and Fair Deal welfare state policies, a hawk on defense issues, and a man who understood that attention to social issues would be the factor that would make or break the Democratic Party. Jackson, however, would come to face the fierce opposition of the party's new left wing, which unfairly and consistently branded him as prowar, right-wing, and even racist. The same activists who were coalescing around the war in Vietnam and supporting candidates who made opposition to that war their main issue, viewed Jackson with nothing but complete hatred and disdain.

Jackson was fully aware of the hurdles he faced. As some of his supporters noted, the road ahead for their preferred candidate was unknown, particularly because in New York City's ultraliberal circles, Jackson was regarded as a superhawk. Yet, even in New York City, Robert A. Low emphasized, Jackson's views "essentially coincide with what a very broad cross-section of people are looking for." Hence, it was essential to their game plan that "Scoop appear to be a middle-of-the-road candidate," not, in other words, a right-winger who happened to be a Democrat. As part of this scenario, Low thought it prudent that they not be propelled by Southern Democrats who favored others, and more important, that they "have Muskie pictured generally as a candidate of the left, that is, the militants who supported Senator Mc-Carthy or Senator Kennedy in 1968."[41]

Once Jackson decided to run, he turned to none other than Ben Wattenberg as a campaign manager. Wattenberg's argument about the social issues as preeminent, brought forth in the best-seller he wrote with Richard Scammon, became in effect the guidebook for the Scoop Jackson candidacy. In a long and critical memo for Jackson's aide, Sterling Munro, Wattenberg traced out what he thought had to be the essentials for a Jackson candidacy. *"To gain the support he needs (in the polls, in the primaries),"* Wattenberg wrote, *"he must emerge all over the nation as a candidate starkly different from the others; but to avoid the political New Left veto that might well operate at the Convention, he shouldn't further alienate the left-liberals."* (Wattenberg's emphasis) Wattenberg saw this as potentially the only damaging contradiction for a Jackson campaign. After all, in distancing himself from the New Left while appeasing Democratic left-liberals, he risked alienating those who might gravitate to his candidacy but who wanted precisely such a rupture with the Left.[42]

Wattenberg suggested one way for Jackson to escape such a trap. It was a simple answer: "Attack the New Left. Now. Bluntly." Jackson needed mass support, Wattenberg understood, and he could not get it without antagonizing the New Left. At that moment, the convention was still more than one year away, and perhaps he could neutralize the Left and befriend them if his mass support emerged. Then, perhaps, the New Left might decide to back its own third-party candidate—which would only help a moderate Democrat. Wattenberg's argument may have made sense, but he neglected one outcome—that the New Left presence in the Party would become so prominent that its approach would be the one to gather enough internal strength so that its preferred candidate would come out victorious.

It was precisely because Jackson had his own independent stance that was authentically different from others that Wattenberg thought he could gain national support more rapidly than someone like Indiana's Senator Birch Bayh. Wattenberg, in fact, compared Jackson's chances of becoming a known factor to those of two previous Democratic unknowns—George Wallace and Eugene McCarthy. Wattenberg then traced out the three main areas in which he hoped Jackson would come to the fore. The first was the economic issue. Since most Democrats agreed on the fundamentals—they supported reduced inflation and more jobs—there was little to be gained from making it a major theme. The second was foreign policy, especially Vietnam and national defense. To Wattenberg, that was a "central issue" in the 1970s, but it lacked "political sex appeal." He was sure that a "responsible" position on Vietnam—for negotiations and a continued commitment to the South Vietnamese—had more support than the polls indicated, but "it is still probably a minus issue." Certainly Jackson differed on these issues, but emphasizing them was not enough to stand out. Thus, he concluded, it was the "social issue" that he thought Jackson had to emphasize. "In its various manifestations," Wattenberg wrote, "it is still the issue that is honestly most troubling to most Americans." For Wattenberg, the social issue meant such items as forced busing to achieve integration, school choice, and the erosion of moral values—all of which the public deeply cared about, but which most Democrats did not understand as the "coequal" of economic and foreign policy concerns. The other candidates, Wattenberg wrote, had "ignored it, downgraded it, or forgotten it." Therefore, it made sense for Jackson to sharply stand out in front on these concerns.[43]

Having laid out the path to follow, Wattenberg proceeded to cite the key factors that composed "the meat of the Social Issue":

First, still, *crime*—'law and order.' Second, still, *race*—not antiblack necessarily, but probably antibusing, and anti-bending-over-backward. Beyond these, there are other facets. *Patriotism*: the spectacle of marchers with V.C. flags, of U.S. senators chatting pleasantly with shaggy demonstrators in the park, of Senator Edward Kennedy saying that it's 'America on the skids' in Laos . . . *Elitism* . . . particularly vis-a-vis the ecological purists. *Values*: People are not prepared to vote for a candidate who is saying *America Has Failed*, and that would seem to be the perception many people have of the Democrats-of-Despair.[44]

Jackson had to identify "with those who are fed up in a way that is clear and direct," Wattenberg argued. He had to become more passionate—and show that he too was fed up with elitist liberals who could not understand crime was a real issue. "If this means attacking other Democrats," Wattenberg emphasized, "so be it." Wattenberg understood that any Democrat had to support civil rights, but, he noted "he must condemn apologists for black violence." In other words, Wattenberg favored a new kind of liberalism, one that emphasized the need for "social stability" and that would cast him [Jackson] as the "voice of the workingmen in America, black and white," who had just resentment against the elitists who continually put them down. He hoped that would be something Jackson could accomplish, given that Wattenberg thought "that the Democrats of the left have gone berserk." If Jackson could articulate that, he would become a major public figure and his standing would go up in the polls. Stretching an analogy perhaps a bit too far, Wattenberg argued that Jackson might be the equivalent of "Winston Churchill in the 1930s," and his election could produce a different history than might otherwise take place. To gain funds and support for major primary races, Jackson had to do one main thing: be "seen as a man (and the only one) crying out against the Left/Berserk flank of the party." With that as his goal, he would create a new constituency.

Despite Jackson's efforts to take Wattenberg's advice, or perhaps because they feared he might just be effective, his opponents smeared him. Thus an ADA report prepared by Steven Brill quoted Jackson as saying in April of 1972 that "I want to end government welfare payments. . . . Work is the answer to the nation's poor problem; able-bodied welfare recipients want a handout, and I want to end that handout." It also painted Jackson as an opponent of civil rights and as a supporter of George Wallace. Brill neglected to point out that Jackson was a key supporter of AFL-CIO programs for working-class Americans, and a devoted supporter of liberal (i.e., big government) programs to promote jobs and full employment. The conclusion the Brill report reached—that "in Senator Jackson's long public career there is no such event, no issue large or small, where time has proved him right and all the others wrong"—is perhaps the most incorrect conclusion one could have reached.[45]

Those who supported George McGovern had good reason to paint such a dark picture of Henry Jackson. But was it correct? The report, for example, singled out scores of quotes from various years—most taken from the early period of U.S. action in Vietnam, the early 1960s, to indicate that Jackson favored U.S. defense of South Vietnam, and saw American policy as part of a worldwide effort to oppose Communist expansionism. It accused him of showing "Cold War combativeness," at a time when, in fact, the Cold War was on in full force, and a case could be made for opposing Soviet interests—a factor the ADA by omission seemed to regard as purely benign.

As for McGovern's views on foreign policy, he boldly put it this way:

I saw the Soviet desire to control the political alignment of its Western neighbors . . . not as the beginning of a Soviet march across Europe, Hitler-style; rather, it was a Soviet reaction, however regrettable, to two world wars. . . . Without excusing the aggressive behavior of the Soviets in Eastern Europe after 1945, I have always believed that we not only overreacted to it, but indeed helped to trigger it by our own post–World War II fears.[46]

McGovern's candid statement of his approach toward the Soviets, brought forth in his 1978 autobiography, possibly reveals more than he intended. McGovern, himself a professional historian, clearly lay in the camp of the left-wing Cold War revisionists, who were creating an entire field of scholarship dedicated to proving that the responsibility for the Cold War lay entirely with the United States, and that American provocation unleashed the unnecessary furor of the Soviets, who acted only in self-defense. McGovern may have thought he was not "excusing" Soviet actions in Eastern Europe, but that, of course, was precisely what he *was* doing. The clear implication of his words was that Soviet actions would not have taken place if not for aggressive American actions. In McGovern's eyes, clearly, the United States was the culprit, the power responsible for whatever problems were creating turmoil in the world.

As he told Milton Viorst in a *Playboy* magazine interview, McGovern believed that Americans had to "abandon our paranoia about Russia's ambition to dominate the world." The Soviets, he believed, no longer held "messianic" views, and were interested only "in a security zone to protect them from another invasion from the West, from revived German militarism," and saw U.S. power as pro-German and created for the purpose of "building a nuclear cordon." That, and not a desire of the Soviets to control and dominate Eastern Europe for their own sphere, was "the real reason they wanted a cushion of Communist states on their Western border, from Poland to the Mediterranean." As for the arms race, it took place because the Soviets needed to "offset" the "enormous American buildup after World War II." Had we been soft on the Soviets, McGovern claimed, "they might have been less fearful and therefore, less belligerent."[47] To McGovern, obviously, the Soviets were blameless for the Cold War, and whatever tensions existed between the two superpowers, the blame for them lay with the United States.

Jackson, on the other hand, stood squarely in the Truman/FDR tradition of the old Democratic Party. His own view of the Soviet Union, and how to deal with it, was miles away from the McGovern position. In a major speech made after the 1972 Nixon victory, Jackson took on what he called the "blindness" of American liberals on Soviet power and policy. First, Jackson made it clear he stood with those in the liberal era who opposed Henry Wallace, liberals who "were among the first after World War II to recognize the dangers the aggressive Soviet totalitarian state posed." And yet, even after the Soviet invasion of Czechoslovakia in 1968, a new breed of liberals had emerged, liberals who now seemed to regard the Soviet Union as just another nation-state, trying to defend its own legitimate interests. In Jackson's eyes, the invasion of Czechoslovakia "and the tightened grip on Eastern Europe reflect clear Soviet determination to maintain effective control of these states and peoples." Jackson saw this as part and parcel of Soviet policy on Berlin, the entrance of Soviet arms into Egypt, and what he called "the steady flow of Soviet supplies for the invasion of South Vietnam from the North." All of these, Jackson argued, testified "to the growing power and outward thrust of the Soviet Union."[48]

What upset, indeed infuriated, the senator, was that so many of his colleagues "look at the Soviet Union with an air of benign neglect." As he put it:

> I suspect that the first cause of the changed American vision of the Soviet Union is the long, costly war in distant Vietnam. . . . The longest war in our history, fought over television, the prize of our mass media, the subject of deep and bitter political conflict, has so embroiled Americans that our political leaders and our public all fail to see North Vietnamese troops operating in neighboring countries. . . . The faults and flaws of the Saigon government have become so much a part of our culture that the policies of the Soviet Union, Communist China, and North Vietnam have become beneficent, if not benign. Before his death, Ho Chi Minh, as murderous and aggressive in his territory as was Stalin, was as popular among some Americans as . . . Winston Churchill in 1940. In short, the unthinking emotionalism caused by this prolonged, nasty, devilish war has destroyed the good sense and the perspective of many of our countrymen, especially of our liberal intellectuals.[49]

These new liberals had become so "demoralized by these overwhelming social issues"—poverty, the decay of the cities, violence in everyday life—that they seemed to prefer the peace of totalitarian states. "If only the sympathy and support lavished on the Black Panthers by some of our wealthy," he quipped, "could be devoted to the relatives of those massacred in Hue or to refugees from Czechoslovakia!" And, in an age before anyone spoke of "political correctness" as a disease afflicting the nation's campuses, Jackson saw the new liberalism as a result of the influence of the revolution in higher education, in which a new educated liberal elite became the main base to which candidates had to appeal. It was from this elite that Cold War revisionism had arisen. Looking ahead, Jackson made a prophetic argument: "Another school," he predicted, "will almost inevitably rewrite the volumes which today find Stalin blameless and Truman responsible for the Berlin blockade, the Korean War, and even the Communist seizure of Prague in 1948."[50]

Summing up, Jackson condemned these new liberals as "both arrogant and romantic." He saw them as "remote from the real world," a group that scorned workers and farmers, whom Jackson still believed were the "backbone" of American liberalism. He saw "liberalism . . . under siege around the world," and he was upset that liberals were responding to the crusades of the revolutionary young, instead of trying to resurrect their movement on the basis of well-proven strengths. Liberals, he bemoaned, seemed to be exhausted.

His entire campaign was an effort to define and create a center for the Democratic Party in the sixties—a forlorn job, perhaps, at a period when the raging war eroded the possibility of a vital centrist position, and those espousing it were regularly and unfairly condemned as Cold War reactionaries. In a May 1971 speech to Democrats in San Diego, principally written by Ben Wattenberg, he charged that the Democrats were "in danger of snatching defeat from the jaws of victory." The average workingman, he said, was threatened by both Republican follies on the Right and the "absolute radical left fringe that is attempting to steal the Democratic Party from the people." The radicals, he noted, lacked any tolerance for those who differed with them, and practiced the politics of the "Emotional Binge."[51]

Some on the Left even wanted an atmosphere of political repression in which they thought they could thrive, and if they succeeded, he thought "they will have brought us closer to the totalitarianism which is so abhorrent." In the name of preserving the environment, Jackson argued, they sought to "identify a conspiracy," and to see technology and economic growth as the sole villain. Their solution was that of the Luddites—to "shut down factories, turn workers out, and turn the clock back to a simple age." Jackson was for clear air and water and sensible environmental controls, but programs of "spartan vigor" would only hurt the average American, who would "take it on the chin." Jackson also singled out for criticism the Left's attack on the universities as "imperialist, militarist, racist, fascist, capitalist, Byzantine institutions." Liberals should support funds for higher education, and not the closing down of these essential institutions. Finally, Jackson criticized the Left's argument that calling for law and order was a "codeword for racism," and he noted that the elderly, the poor, blacks, and Hispanics could not walk the streets safely in their own neighborhoods.

But it was in the realm of foreign policy, Jackson argued, that the Left's position held the most danger. There they revealed what he called a "streak of irrationality" as well as "reactionary emotion" about America's world role. It was one thing to say they did not like defense spending, another to argue that the Soviets were no longer a threat to American national interests. To argue against the draft, they made the assertion that "America is imperialist and genocidal." And if they wanted more money for domestic programs, they had a simple answer: "cut the defense budget by $40 billion." If such a step meant that Israel would be threatened, that was something to "think about later." What it boiled down to, Jackson asserted, was that the Left has *"lost faith in America."* The Left had tried to paint America as a "guilty" nation, and to maintain that a concept of "patriotism is . . . only for squares." There were but two choices, to listen "to the siren song of the radical fringe, cater to it, condone it, apologize for it—and gain the scorn of the majority of Americans for leading the country and the party into a sick and dangerous era."[52] Or, the Democrats could "look to our roots," to those who wanted to build "a fairer and more prosperous nation," who did not seek to listen to those who held America virtually in contempt.

McGovern, of course, was smart enough to eschew and reject the label of radical. As he put it then, "it's nothing radical to call this nation to the principles on which it was founded."[53] As late as the 1980s, McGovern would complain that he was unfairly perceived as a radical, as part of a "counterculture, splinter group that really wasn't part of the mainstream of American life."[54] And he claimed to be representative of the best, rather than the darkest, side of the sixties: the movement for civil rights, open government, and concern for the small man against big corporations. Yet, on specific issues, McGovern epitomized just such a radical position. One could, for example, contrast the positions enunciated by Jackson and McGovern on the controversial and misunderstood issue of opposition to busing of white schoolchildren to formerly all-black schools.

Jackson, who, as even his opponents admitted, voted for all major civil rights legislation in the Johnson era, argued forcefully that whites who backed equality of opportunity and civil rights for black Americans could also resent and oppose forced busing, which they saw as government encroachment which would take their own children out of decent neighborhood schools. With that kind of solution for past discrimination, the burden of adjustment would be put on working-class whites, who already saw their standard of living and their neighborhoods in danger of erosion. With George Wallace emphasizing antibusing in his campaign throughout the North, and with Muskie, Humphrey, McGovern, and Lindsay all supporting busing, this left Jackson as the only other candidate besides Wallace questioning the accepted liberal pieties. Humphrey, for example, said he opposed "massive compulsory busing that has as its sole objective racial balance based on a mathematical formula;" but went on to say it was "fit, right and proper that you bus a child from an inferior school to a good school."[55] Jackson sought to gain the middle ground by firmly rejecting racism while opposing the tactic of forced busing as a solution for past grievances. *Time*, however, called Jackson's stance "an antibusing position just a shade short of Wallace's." That meant that Jackson sought a constitutional amendment for choice in schools and the right of individuals to send their small children to neighborhood institutions, along with increased federal aid to inferior schools. His purpose was clear. As one of his aides put it, Jackson sought to reach the middle-aged, middle-class suburbanite who didn't like the bus ride his kid was taking but who couldn't vote for Wallace on other principles."[56] The magazine called Jackson a "Wallace in spats," which one might take as a euphemism that Jackson was a gentleman racist.

Of course, another major issue on which the two candidates differed was Vietnam. Most people do not recall that McGovern, unlike Allard Lowenstein, was only critical of the United States role, and by implication, favored the North Vietnamese, whom he thought represented authentic Vietnamese nationalism. Journalist Robert Novak queried McGovern on NBC's popular "Meet the Press" as to whether the North Vietnamese troops invading Cambodia and hiding in southern Laos represented the "right" side of Asian nationalism. McGovern responded that these Vietnamese soldiers were "a lot closer to the nationalistic aspirations of their people than the American troops who are there."[57] And in his *Playboy* interview with Milton Viorst, McGovern responded favorably to Viorst's suggestion that Ho Chi Minh was the George Washington of North Vietnam.[58] He also told Viorst that he sympathized with the nationalist aspirations of the Vietcong, although he eschewed the terror they and the North Vietnamese had adopted as a tactic. Yet, when it came to viewing any side in the war as "war criminals," McGovern felt, as he told a New Hampshire audience during the campaign, that "the real war criminals are the people that deceived the Congress . . . about this war," the members of the Kennedy and Johnson administrations.[59] And in his first mass mailing fund-raising letter, sent to prospective friendly Democrats in 1971, McGovern argued that it was "not enough merely to favor withdrawal from Vietnam." One had to elect a president "whose thinking is completely free from the last vestiges of the Cold War paranoia which led to our Vietnam involvement in the first place." McGovern went on to suggest that keeping NATO forces in Europe was perhaps unnecessary, and he backed Senator Mark Hatfield's resolution to cut the NATO force in half.[60]

Jackson has widely been regarded as the polar opposite—a candidate who stood for a fight to the finish, who regarded the American commitment as wise, and who was a fierce opponent of peace. Such a view has elements of truth, but is quite skewed. Jackson clearly did believe in the original commitment to Vietnam, but the outcome of the war disturbed him deeply. Indeed, in the early sixties, Jackson shared the assumptions of the Kennedy and Johnson administrations that led them to up the level of the original commitment. There was no alternative to U.S. involvement, Jackson thought at first. "Our sacrifices in this dirty war in little Vietnam," he said in a speech, "will make a dirtier and bigger war less likely. It is on this basis that we ask young Americans to fight in the jungles and mountains of Vietnam." Moreover, Jackson thought the bombing raids carried out by the Johnson administration were successful, and had limited North Vietnam's ability to sustain large-scale offensives in the South. He then favored more air raids on power installations and port facilities.[61] There was no substantial body of opinion, Jackson said in April of 1968, that favored abandoning Vietnam to the Communists. The only debate was how to move toward negotiations, and how to compromise with an enemy that wanted only victory. Americans, Jackson thought then, should not settle "for a one-sided de-escalation of the fighting that risks more American lives and that would sell out South Vietnam to the aggressor." The only solution was what he called an "honorable political settlement."[62]

Jackson did support the so-called Domino Theory, and in 1967, he had said "if all Vietnam were Communist, it would only be a matter of time before Thailand, Cambodia, and Laos would be Communist. Next it would be Malaya . . . and so it would go . . . if they took over Asia, they would then have the land mass, people, industry, and raw materials to destroy the balance of forces in Europe. Europe would very probably fall to the Communists."[63] Jackson's invoking of what is now widely understood to have been a faulty and simplistic syllogism was perhaps the weakest part of his analysis. But, as the *Congressional Quarterly* noted, Jackson was "relatively moderate in his recommendations on how to prosecute [the war] particularly in 1970 and 1971. He opposed President Nixon's May 1970 decision to send U.S. troops into Cambodia." Jackson favored orderly withdrawal from Vietnam, and saw the Cambodian incursion as a reversal of that decision. He also favored an extension of the 1970 Christmas truce to promote efforts for a standstill ceasefire.[64] Americans, he thought, should not fire unless fired upon. If North Vietnam violated such a ceasefire, it would have showed the world it rejects "the desire for peace to which it lays claim." In his eyes, Hanoi had to be put in the position of explaining to the people of South Vietnam how such a proposal was a "perfidious scheme," which is what the North Vietnamese government had called Jackson's proposal.[65]

Privately, Jackson was quite thoughtful and sanguine. The

powerful Democratic figure Edward N. Costikyan had written Jackson about his thoughts on the war. Costikyan did not desire "mea culpas" or "ex-post-facto justifications" for decisions made. But he did want to know what Jackson and other candidates would do, "knowing what we know now" if faced with the question of whether or not to get involved in Vietnam back in 1965. Costikyan himself thought that the whole war was a "disaster," and favored immediate withdrawal. But he wanted to support Jackson, and demanded an answer as to "where we would be going under your leadership as President if you were faced with the decision about involving American troops in . . . the Vietnamese War."[66]

Like Costikyan, Jackson emphasized that the key issues facing America would be domestic. And on these issues, he favored a traditional liberal agenda: "a massive housing program, tripling the federal investment in public education, and providing decent health care for every citizen." But he viewed Costikyan's comments on Vietnam as "hard, tough questions," and Jackson agreed that with hindsight, "almost everyone today would have made different decisions in 1965 if we had known then what we know now." Arguing that the Vietnam War had taught Americans "many lessons," Jackson thought above all it made clear that "the United States must consider with extreme care the times and places it chooses to get actively and militarily involved." Moreover, Jackson agreed that another "basic lesson is that we should never get involved again in a war of attrition—a long, drawn-out, protracted conflict."[67] Jackson, in other words, was not that far apart from many moderate opponents of the war. Jackson, in fact, voted for the Cooper-Church Amendment, because he opposed widening of the Vietnam conflict. Jackson argued that the United States should get out of the war as quickly as possible, that the ground troops should be withdrawn, and the war wound down. He was fond of saying that he was "neither a hawk nor a dove," and preferred Americans to be the "wise owl."

Jackson, as one might expect, vigorously opposed the McGovern-Hatfield Amendment, which would have sought an end to U.S. involvement in Vietnam in an eighteen-month period, by December of 1971. If adopted, Jackson argued, such a measure would diminish the influence of the South Vietnamese government, and any hope of a negotiated settlement would end. Announcing a withdrawal more than a year in advance would only give comfort to the North Vietnamese. "The result," Jackson argued, "is to place oneself in the hands of the North Vietnamese, politically, in the sense that action taken by them, and beyond our control, could be politically catastrophic." American losses would then be traced to a military deterioration "resulting from the amendment." Yet Jackson said he would support the resolution if it could be proved that American opinion was "deeply against the war," and if it would heal divisions within the nation. But the polls suggested the opposite. Instead, it would not pass the House, and would only "further polarize and divide the country." The war would continue, and the "loss of life would be greater rather than less." McGovern would then be responsible for a protracted war, and "a highly likely bloodbath if the South Vietnamese were to be militarily defeated."[68]

Jackson tended, therefore, to support the Nixon administration's policy on Vietnam, particularly the January 1972 efforts for a standstill ceasefire, release of American POWs, and the demand for free elections, including candidates of the National Liberation Front, that would be supervised by an electoral commission that included NLF representatives. Jackson was also concerned about Muskie's criticism of the Nixon policy, although he acknowledged that Muskie favored a "prudent defense posture" while McGovern favored a drastic cut in the defense budget amounting to an almost 50-percent cut. On Vietnam, Jackson stressed a "bipartisan effort . . . to try to find an area of agreement," and he praised President Nixon for laying out the basis for continued negotiations. Muskie, he argued, was moving "more and more to the left," and thereby joining McGovern.[69]

The valiant attempt of Scoop Jackson to gain the nomination as an alternative to McGovern on the Left, Muskie at the Center-Left and Wallace on the Right, was doomed to failure. The McGovern steamroller was in full swing, and the new party rules, the result of the McGovern Commission hearings, assured a victory for the candidate who gained the greatest support in the primaries among partisan activists. Essentially, as the race began, the leading Democratic candidates were agreed on economic issues, and, as Wattenberg argued, the key differences were cultural. All the candidates, the shrewd political observer Michael Barone noted, "agreed that the Vietnam war now needed to be wound down and ended . . . but they disagreed on their attitude toward it. For McGovern it was a purely immoral assertion of power; for Wallace, a patriotic cause subverted by Washington and media intellectuals; for Jackson, a war which had been strategically unwise but not supported strongly enough once it was undertaken; for Muskie, a sadly mistaken policy."[70]

The problem was that the Democratic Party was not a unified body, and old economically based coalitions were collapsing because of new cultural attitudes. Once Ed Muskie fell apart after conservative publisher William Loeb attacked him in the *Manchester Union Leader*, causing him to appear as if he were crying in front of the paper's offices, McGovern, the second-place New Hampshire finisher, began to emerge as a serious contender for the presidency. And, as Michael Barone has noted, after the attempted assassination of George Wallace, McGovern began to improve greatly in the polls, which showed him closing the gap with Nixon by 48 percent to 41 percent. This showed, Barone writes, "that at least in his initial appearance in the spotlight Mc-Govern did not come off badly and that he might well be the strongest of the conceivable Democratic nominees; it suggested that his positions on issues and his right-from-the-start opposition to the Vietnam war might not be the electoral handicaps so many in Washington imagined."[71]

Barone, of course, turned out to be right about McGovern's capturing of the primary, although the factors that made him strong would be precisely those that led to his being swamped in the election. Thus, in speech after speech, he pledged to grant amnesty for Vietnam war-resisters, a measure that at the time was more than unpopular, and let college students know he understood their desire to experiment with drugs like marijuana and to favor abortion rights for women. All of these issues might have had great appeal to the eighteen- to twenty-year-old set, but their popularity on the campuses was equaled by their unpopularity among the general older electorate.[72]

Most important, McGovern made use of the new Democratic Party guidelines, while the other candidates, including Humphrey and Jackson, relied on the support of the old party stalwarts and professionals, from political leaders to union chieftains. A late June Gallup poll showed McGovern ahead of his rivals, with a 30 to 27 to 15 percent lead in the critical California race. He won the state by pulling a fast one. The McGovern Commission had singled out the California primary, based on the principle of "winner-take-all," as grossly unfair to political minorities. Humphrey's campaign therefore sought to gain the seating at the convention of one-hundred fifty-one Californians McGovern had not won, but to which he had claims on their backing because of the California primary rules. The Credentials

Committee of the convention met on the issue, and awarded Humphrey one-hundred six of the California delegates, with the remaining forty-five split among other minority candidates. Mc-Govern's troops opposed this ruling on the convention floor, and argued that the California rules violated "the spirit of reform."

McGovern was soon faced with a stop-McGovern coalition, centering on Hubert Humphrey, Scoop Jackson, and the AFL-CIO. Some dubbed it the A.B.M. movement, "Anybody But McGovern." Delegates asked whether McGovern's remaining one-hundred twenty delegates—the share he was entitled to after winning 44 percent of the primary vote—should be allowed to vote when the credentials question came up. They had to decide as well what would constitute a majority—the 1,509 needed to nominate, or the 1,433 representing a majority after the contested California delegates were subtracted. The issue was critical. If McGovern won California, and if he only needed 1,433 delegates, he would win the nomination. If he lost, the momentum would no longer be his, and his entire count would be called into question. The delegates debated for three days, and chairman Larry O'Brien ruled that only a majority of delegates voting—not 1,509—could decide credentials disputes.

The McGovern forces then sought to lose a feminist challenge brought by the South Carolina delegation, in order not to create a parliamentary precedent that would lead to defeat on the critical California issue. The A.B.M. group was trying to raise a point of order on the issue of what constituted a majority on challenges, in order to prevent the McGovern camp from getting the votes it needed. The majority determined by the South Carolina vote—nine women were demanding to be added to the delegation under the reform rules—would establish the rule for California. Working with campaign manager Gary Hart, McGovern picked a tested group of older political veterans to lead the fight—including Senators Frank Church, Fred Harris, Abraham Ribicoff, Gaylord Nelson, Wisconsin governor Pat Lucey, and others. Floor leaders had deputies in every state delegation, and were linked by phone to McGovern's campaign trailer, where advisor and coordinator Rick Stearns held court. McGovern's troops, of course, were ideologically committed to having more women seated. But in this case, they moved in the other direction and pulled away votes from the women's protest so that it would lose by a wide margin. Max Kampelman, Humphrey's old friend and political aide, phoned Humphrey and reported with astonishment that "they're switching their ayes to no. They don't have a majority of this convention. They're afraid."[73]

The opponents of McGovern had sought to produce a vote that fell between 1,433 and 1,509, the so-called twilight zone. At that point they wanted to introduce a point of order about a majority on challenges, bringing Larry O'Brien's ruling to a vote. Then all of the delegates except those under challenge in South Carolina could vote, and it would have been hard for McGovern's people to get the votes they needed. As the voting took place, the McGovern opponents found that the women's challenge lost by 1,555.75 to 1,429.05, and they could not raise a point of order. McGovern could now not be stopped from gaining the California vote victory he sought. Manager Hart was ecstatic. "It was one of those times when politics is really fun," he told the press. "We played South Carolina like a pipe organ." And, of course, devoted feminists were quite willing to abandon principle. Actress Shirley MacLaine, a major Hollywood supporter of McGovern, argued that there was no choice between adding a few women to a state delegation and nominating McGovern. When the California vote finally came after midnight,

1,618.28 votes were cast to give McGovern back all of his 271 delegates, and 1,238.22 opposed. Having won that fight, George McGovern's nomination was now certain.

The fight on the floor had been nasty, but it would get even nastier. The next step was for the McGovern delegates to oust the Illinois delegation, led as it was by the man they considered the evil force behind the violence in 1968, Chicago's mayor Richard J. Daley. Daley's delegation had been properly elected, but the convention rejected its credentials, on the ground that it did not have the correct proportion of women and minority group delegates to be seated. Instead, the convention seated a delegation that in fact represented no one—but was led by a man who would later be a fierce contender of the party's left wing, the then little known reverend and civil rights activist, Jesse Jackson. Daley's forces had been fairly chosen, and had won the election with more than 900,000 votes cast. And Jackson, who led the new group to gain the Illinois seats, had not even voted in the Democratic primary and at the time was not even a registered Democrat. In fact, the challenge slate was drawn up at closed meetings from which Daley's supporters had been excluded.[74] McGovern had actually sought a compromise that would have seated both Daley's people and the challengers—McGovern knew he needed Daley's support to win Illinois—but Daley would not accept that kind of deal. The McGovern delegates, purely on the principle of proportional race-and-sex delegates, voting after 3 A.M., opted to exclude the powerful mayor. The victorious delegates cheered, but commenting on the events, *Time* magazine aptly noted: "The unseating of Daley raised again the fundamental question about the democracy of the party's new guidelines. At what point does the laudable idea of opening the party to women and minorities turn into a rigid and potentially tyrannical quota system?" Daley, after all, had won in a fair election that no one had challenged on grounds of fraud. He was an old-line political boss, but he had won a majority of votes. Should that majority, *Time* asked, "be discarded in favor of a slate that more strictly adheres to prescriptions of race and sex?"[75]

McGovern may have won the primary, but during the fight, issues arose that would reveal his many weaknesses. One of his most famous campaign promises was to grant every American citizen $1,000 a year, to be financed by a progressive income tax. When taxpayers asked how this would be financed, he either answered it would cost nothing, or possibly an extra $21 per year for those who earned between $12,000 and $20,000 a year. The plan was in essence one for redistribution of existing wealth, and it did not go down well for most Americans. The socialist Michael Harrington liked to recall that in his lectures that year, audience after audience condemned the proposal although Harrington had tried to endorse its spirit. They did not like McGovern's additional proposal for a vast estate and gift tax, because they told Harrington that if they ever won the lottery, their long-sought winnings would go up in smoke.[76]

The reality, as Michael Barone pointed out, was that "most voters seemed to think they were or would be the people from whom McGovern wanted to redistribute income and wealth, rather than the beneficiaries of these redistributions."[77] Hubert Humphrey had charged that single people earning $8,000 a year would pay more under the McGovern plan than a family of four with an income of $12,000, who themselves would pay $409 per year. And, echoing Jackson, Humphrey added that McGovern's defense cuts would "halt the Minuteman procurement, half the Poseidon procurement, halt the B-1 prototype. Phase out two-hundred-thirty of our five-hundred-thirty strategic bombers. Reduce aircraft carrier force from fifteen to six. Reduce our naval air squadrons by [a large percentage]. Halt all naval surface shipbuilding. Reduce the number of cruisers from two-hundred-thirty to one-hundred-thirty. Reduce the number of submarines by eleven."[78] McGovern had no adequate answer to the kind of criticism made by both Humphrey and Scoop Jackson. He successfully gained the nomination of his party, but this kind of attack would cut deeply into his final electoral vote.

Humphrey, of course, like Scoop Jackson, had made his farewell from the race. 80 percent of the delegates at the convention were attending the event for the very first time, and the convention would go to the wee hours of the morning, finally adjourning after nominating McGovern at 6:24 A.M. Ken Bode, later a TV newsman and prominent academic and journalist, had commented that "the Democrats who convene in Miami will be the most representative group ever gathered in one spot in our party's history." It was representative—but not in the way Bode meant. Shirley MacLaine, who cavorted as part of the large California delegation, approvingly commented that the convention looked "like a couple of high schools, a grape boycott, a Black Panther rally, and four or five politicians who walked in the wrong door."[79] Joining MacLaine as prominent politicos were Marlo Thomas, Patty Duke, Warren Beatty, and Julie Christie. It was the start of what Americans would become quite used to—the entrance into politics on the side of the left-wing Democrats by members of the Hollywood elite. Also present at the Convention, roaming the hall freely where they evidently had credentials as representatives of the working press, were the radical "Yippie" leaders Jerry Rubin and Abbie Hoffman, who had gained notoriety for their leadership of the demonstrations at the Democratic convention four years earlier.

In terms of meaningful representation, the McGovern Convention was a failure. The Illinois delegation had only three Poles and one Italian—although Chicago was an ethnic city in which representatives of those groups were the very mainstay of the Democratic Party. The Iowa delegation did not have a single farmer, and no delegates over age sixty-five, although that state had more senior citizens than any other except Florida. And New York's delegation had only three representatives from the organized labor movement, although New York City was still one of the remaining strong union towns, where AFL-CIO endorsements meant a great deal to Democratic candidates. And a survey taken by the *Washington Post* revealed that 39 percent of the delegates had taken postgraduate work—compared to 4 percent of the population at large—and the annual incomes of 31 percent attending was more than $25,000 a year—far larger than the average American salary at the time.

As for McGovern, he had won the nomination with only 25 percent of the total votes cast in the primary, less than Hubert Humphrey and a bit more than George Wallace, and he had consistently shown a low standing in the polls even while he was winning caucuses and primaries. As for Scoop Jackson, who would leave the race before the convention opened, he had only 2 percent of his followers at the Convention, although a Harris poll had shown that he was the candidate whose positions were most representative of the Democratic electorate as a whole. In that sense, the fact that there were more women, blacks, and young people at the Miami convention may have warmed McGovern's heart, but it did not translate to a cross-section of electoral opinion.

The effect of the new rules was to disenfranchise working-class and lower-class Democrats, who relied on representation at conventions by union leaders and professional politicians. And since McGovern was seeking the support of affluent liberals, he responded to their needs and concerns while showing only disdain for the cultural conservatism of traditional Democrats. Furthermore, though McGovern thought he at least had the support of women and youth, the polls quickly showed that even this was not true—women opposed the ticket two to one, and Richard Nixon had the support of half of America's youth.

The bitter truth was that the McGovern nomination, and the takeover of the Party by his supporters, made the Democrats less representative of most Americans than it had ever been. No longer a coalition party pulling together diverse interests on behalf of a set of common goals, the Democrats now responded to the perceived needs of Jeane Kirkpatrick's "new presidential elites," affluent, college-educated liberals and radicals. To these people, black activists were radicals in the Black Panther Party—and not the average inner-city black resident who sought to make a good living and find a way out of the ghetto. The "people" meant to them the antiwar college students, and not working Americans who might possibly have supported the war at first, and who looked askance at the arrogance and elitism of the counterculture.

McGovern, of course, had his own problems with his new core constituency. He knew that many of them "offended" the Democratic regulars, as he put it many years later. It was a fact, McGovern said, that "some of the people inside my own campaign, who were too flamboyant, too militant, too abrasive, probably did hurt our chances of winning," and probably contributed to the landslide for Nixon. McGovern recalled walking in an Atlanta campaign parade after the convention with Martin Luther King and Leonard Woodcock of the United Automobile Workers—"a perfectly respectable group of middle-class Americans"—and as he came into the main intersection of Atlanta with TV cameras following his route, "a young man and woman appeared, wearing nothing but a torn-up American flag." The man wore the flag as a jockstrap and the woman as a bikini, and they received major television coverage, as they held up a sign "McGovern for President." In perhaps a major understatement, McGovern commented: "This was not helpful."[80]

McGovern also had a similar problem at the convention. The afternoon before it started, three hundred far Left protesters appeared at the lobby of the Doral Hotel, the main convention facility. With the TV news following them, they were there to protest McGovern's promise the prior evening, made to wives of prisoners of war, that he would retain a military capability in Southeast Asia until the POWs were released. The protesters, many from the Maoist Progressive Labor Party group and others from Students for a Democratic Society, saw this as a digression from McGovern's pledge to promote a full and immediate withdrawal from Vietnam. McGovern agreed to come and speak to the group. Although he did not give in to their demands, the meeting, covered on live television, legitimized the protesters and made it appear that McGovern was pandering to them. McGovern told them he would indeed close all U.S. bases in Thailand and remove naval forces once all the POWs were freed. The group demanded that McGovern sign a petition calling for life imprisonment for police who killed blacks in the ghettos, a demand which revealed precisely how far out they were. McGovern said flatly: "I'm not going to sign it."[81]

The debacle, of course, would soon come. By the time the Republicans met at their convention to nominate Richard Nixon for his second term run, the McGovern candidacy was already in a virtual state of collapse. In August polls McGovern was behind Nixon by 57 percent to 34 percent, and by September, after the fiasco of the withdrawal of Senator Thomas Eagleton of Missouri as McGovern's running mate, McGovern was behind by a margin of 63 percent to 29 percent for McGovern. McGovern, most tellingly of all, ran behind in small factory towns, where blue-collar Democrats rebelled against the cultural aura of the Mc-Govern campaign.

Nixon, who had continually polled at the 50 percent level, won the race with 61 percent of the popular vote to McGovern's 38 percent. Only one out of eight white Southerners voted for McGovern. But he also did poorly in the regular Democratic blue-collar areas, and he won less than 40 percent in Maine, New Jersey, Pennsylvania, West Virginia, Ohio, Indiana, and Missouri. Only in liberal Massachusetts did McGovern win the state with 54 percent of the vote. He managed to receive a total of two-hundred one electoral votes. Nixon received 57 percent of the blue-collar vote, and 52 percent of the vote of American Catholics. And despite McGovern's attempts to prove that he was pro-Israel, a significant number of liberal Jewish voters deserted the Democrats for the first time, and one-third of these voters cast their ballot for Richard Nixon. When the labor vote was counted, 54 percent of union-member households voted for the President.[82]

As for Scoop Jackson, he would always remain a Democrat close to organized labor. A 1976 press release cited the AFL-CIO report card on the 94th Congress, noting that Jackson had the best cumulative pro-labor voting record during his twenty-three years in the Senate, and that he had voted pro-labor one-hundred forty-seven times and against labor proposals only four times. In 1975 alone, labor's Committee on Political Education found, he had voted labor nineteen times and only once against.[83]

By 1976, Jackson was attacking both the "new conservatism" of Ronald Reagan and the "new radicalism" of the McGovernites who had destroyed his party. The New Left had vanished "without a trace" by that year, but Jackson saw its legacy continuing in the ranks of his own party. At the same time, he was as critical of the growing "anti-Washington syndrome" and the talk about the need to limit government power as he was of the "reckless promoters of the new" who were assailing the "liberal tradition" from all sides. Conservatives were wrong, Jackson argued, to want to dismantle "the essential agencies of the federal government which implement the social policies of the New Deal," and he worried that a new conservative mood in the country would allow those who had "narrow selfish interests to have their way again." At the same time, he strongly opposed the new "fancy packaging for the old isolationism," and he thought policies based on those assumptions would allow adversaries to take advantage of the United States.[84]

As the seventies moved on to the Reagan-Bush conservative eighties, Jackson would find that many of those who fought in his campaign, out of growing frustration with the direction taken by the Democratic Party, would leave its ranks and defect to those of the very Reagan Republicans whose policies he criticized, along with the scores of blue-collar workers who had once voted solid Democratic, but had begun to cross the line in droves to the Republican side. Ironically, the heart of the new neoconservative intellectual movement would be one of Scoop Jackson's most lasting legacies, since so many of the key workers for Jackson—Ben Wattenberg, Penn Kemble, Richard Perle, Josh Muravchik, and others—would all soon be identified as the intellectual linchpins of neoconservatism. They now supported the essence of the Reagan policies, especially on foreign policy, and on social issues tended to identify more with the policies espoused by the Republicans than by most Democrats. "We did not leave the Democratic Party, it left us," was the refrain heard more and more from many of these individuals. Some of them, of course, remained Democrats. But even among those, the ties with organized labor began to fray, as labor lost the numbers and strengths of the war years and as its leaders themselves began to espouse more and more social and economic policies identified with the left wing of the Democratic Party.

Scoop Jackson was, in retrospect, the very last of the old mainstream Democrats. He fought hard to hold together an eroding center, and he went down to defeat. The lessons he sought to instill, but for which his efforts went for naught, would haunt the Democrats for decades to come.

7

THE WILDERNESS YEARS

From Carter to Reagan-Bush

The 1972 election proved one thing above all, that the Democratic Party of old was no longer in existence. From here on, our story becomes one of continued demonstration of the irrelevance of the New Deal. All the candidates who had declared for the 1972 race had their position defined by their relation to the war in Vietnam and to the New Politics group, and the leaders of these two camps were as interested in castigating and destroying the appeal of potential opponents like Scoop Jackson as they were in possibly winning the election come November. The campaign's spirit was captured by *Rolling Stone*'s major political reporter, the founder of so-called gonzo counterculture journalism, Hunter Thompson. Using a refrain made popular by a soldier in Vietnam who was burning Vietnamese village huts, Thompson commented that "the only way to save the Democratic Party is to destroy it." Once reconstructed, it would be the only vehicle for those who were "the most committed, the most idealistic, the best minds of [the sixties] generation."[1]

Thompson, of course, was right about the boast that his idealistic supporters would successfully destroy the Democratic Party. Traditional Democrats left the party *en masse*, casting their votes for Richard M. Nixon, the candidate most hated by the liberal/left wing of the Democratic Party. Fifty-two percent of blue-collar Democrats had voted for him, and playing the new Southern strategy recommended by advisor Kevin Phillips, Nixon saw his support in the South rise from 35 percent in 1968 to 52 percent in 1972. In the House and Senate, however, Democrats still maintained their control, and Nixon's victory was more of a rejection of McGovernism and what it had done to the Democrats than it was a new electoral majority for conservative Republicanism.

With the crisis of Watergate, and the personal downfall of Richard M. Nixon, it was perhaps inevitable that the electorate's disillusionment with what the Republicans had done with the Presidency would set in. Gerald R. Ford presided over a rather undistinguished caretaker regime. Appointed by Nixon in the wake of his impending resignation, and with rumors abounding that Ford's post was the result of a deal that he would grant amnesty for the president when taking the office, thereby sparing Nixon the shame of imprisonment, Ford was off to a poor start. The full pardon he had granted Nixon one month after assuming office led to a rapid plunge in his standing in the polls, one from which he would never recover.

Ford would also make another major blunder at the start of his presidency. His decision to appoint the liberal New York Republican Nelson Rockefeller as his vice president further angered conservative Republicans. And although Ford had told the

House Judiciary Committee in October of 1974 that he had made "no deal, period," in regard to the Nixon pardon, the public did not believe him, and he continually declined in the polls. The fact, as Michael Barone has astutely noted, is that the Democrats were doing better than ever in the Congressional races. In the 1974 race, they gained forty-six seats more than they had in 1972, and the Republicans failed to gain in the South, despite the use by Nixon of the Phillips Southern strategy. In the Senate, the Democrats increased their majority by picking up four seats, including those in Vermont and New Hampshire. Six years after the 1968 debacle, as Barone writes, "the country was more Democratic than it had ever been," even more than in the landslide years of 1936 and 1964.[2]

The real race in 1976, as it turned out, would be the one waged for the nomination in the Republican Party by Ronald Reagan, and in the Democratic Party by Jimmy Carter. On the Republican side, Reagan announced his bid in October of 1975, and made it clear than he would run as an outsider—against all those in Washington who were ostensibly so out of touch with the nation's pulse. His campaign was premature, and although he gained in strength, he would not be able to oust the incumbent president at the Republican convention. Yet the case he made would be heard over and over, and would slowly gain converts. Sounding much like George Wallace, Reagan argued that Washington had become "increasingly insensitive to the needs of the American worker who supports it with his taxes."[3]

The leader at first in the race for the Democratic nomination was George Wallace. His effort to shift the party to the Right, however, led all his other opponents to close ranks and move to either win over his constituency or gain his support for their own campaign. Wallace was still burdened with his past positions on race, and when his physical condition was added to that, most

Democrats came to understand that his nomination would be a catastrophe for their party. Scoop Jackson would make yet another attempt to gain the nomination, but his campaign was once again anathema to the liberal and dovish Democrats who now made up a critical part of the party's primary voters. Humphrey was sick, and his protégé, Walter Mondale, had decided that the time was not ripe for a wearing campaign.

The stalemated situation left the position open for the entry into the campaign of the governor of Georgia, the little-known Jimmy Carter. Carter understood that the only candidate who could meet Wallace's challenge was that waged by another Southerner, and he took advantage of that situation. Many professionals had thought that Wallace would play a broker's role at the 1976 Democratic convention, and with anywhere from 30 to 40 percent of the delegates in his hand, would be able to gain the nomination for himself or choose who the standard-bearer would be. Carter put a stop to that, by letting Northern liberals understand that his candidacy was the only alternative. As he told a group of New York Democrats, Wallace votes could not be "transferred to a more liberal candidate." And to Southerners, he argued that he would carry on the legacy of the South by whittling down the size of the federal government. Wallace, he said, could only send the country a message; he gave the nation a chance to "send them a president."[4]

Carter would gain the nomination, carving out, as *Time* put it, "on his own a broad constituency of small-town and rural voters, blue-collar ethnics, white-collar suburbanites, inner-city blacks."[5] Indeed, Carter had trounced all of his opponents. He won in the Texas primary over that State's favorite Lloyd Bentsen, over Wallace in Florida, and most surprising, scored a humiliating victory over Scoop Jackson in union-strong Pennsylvania. Of course, it would be a short-lived victory. The Reagan revolution of the 1980s would reveal that the Carter victory was an anomaly, a response to the unpopularity of the Ford presidency and a reaction to the crisis of Watergate, and not a fundamental movement back toward the Democratic Party's once-strong political hegemony. For the moment, Carter's religiously based calls for a moral revival struck home, as an electorate embarrassed and saddened at what the Nixon presidency had done to the country longed for a candidate who could restore their faith in America's greatness and potential.

Democrats sensed this, and their 1976 convention reflected newfound optimism. Meeting in New York City, they thought they were witnessing the rebirth of the old labor-liberal and Southern coalition. Chicago's beleaguered mayor Richard Daley was back at his old perch, as were an array of trade union leaders. One might almost have forgiven the Democrats for thinking that 1972 had not occurred. Carter's convention speech evoked familiar left-wing Populist themes, such as attacks on the "political and economic elite" who held "special influence and privilege." Combined with the vice presidential slot going to Humphrey's protégé, the liberal Minnesotan Walter Mondale, Carter thus assured himself liberal support, while keeping the small-government rural South and conservative Democrats with promises to avoid regulation, work for a competitive system, and favor tough measures against lawbreakers. Carter himself told the press that his speech purposefully "shifted back and forth between liberal and conservative."[6] He gave something to both elements of the party faithful, and the tactic worked to guarantee support. Other liberals may have had their private and even public doubts, but they closed ranks and pulled together for a Carter victory.

The victory turned out not quite to be what the Democratic ranks had hoped for. Though the Republicans were shattered by the greatest scandal to hit the country since Teapot Dome, and though their chosen candidate, incumbent Gerald Ford, barely got the nomination from his tough challenger, Ronald Reagan, Carter's victory was a very close call. Carter's level of support had fallen deeply since the first days of the campaign, and in the final days swung somewhere between 46 percent and 54 percent. He won by a margin of 51 percent to 48 percent. Only on the surface did it look like the same kind of victory John F. Kennedy had scored in 1960—carrying the South and the large Northeastern states and losing California.

Thomas Byrne Edsall and E. J. Dionne, Jr., have pointed out that in reality a new kind of Democrat elected Carter and many Democrats in Congress. These new voters were disproportionately middle-class and suburban. The concerns and interests of their candidates were not those of the old urban, blue-collar, and minority Democrats who represented the party mainstream in the thirties and forties. Many of these voters had in fact not voted Democratic in the '76 election, and more of their ranks would quickly defect in another four years. Carter may have had liberal voters and support, but as Dionne has noted, "he was not a liberal." Free of taint of both New Deal–Fair Deal liberalism and worse, the scourge of McGovernism, Carter appealed to those constituencies who were beginning to be fed up with the Democrats, but even then he barely squeaked by with the aid of the Watergate backlash.[7] Democrats won, but their traditional blue-collar base was still disintegrating. They did not notice that they had lost the votes of low- and moderate-income whites, and had only made temporary gains by getting the electoral support of upper-income Republicans who demanded political reform.[8]

Carter's victory, won ostensibly against the party's reigning liberal factions, revealed the very weaknesses of the old liberal Democratic establishment. He was not a believer in strong federal governmental action; his moralism worked against the instincts of Northern liberals and the Left; and the conservative Southern Democrats that both he and Wallace championed were continuing to move away from the party. Later, after the fruits of Carter's victory had become apparent, Arthur M. Schlesinger, Jr., would make the now famous comment that Carter was the most conservative Democrat since Grover Cleveland. It still wasn't enough.

Scores of conservative Democrats who found Carter's religious moralism appealing began to fear that he was actually too liberal. Rather than having built a new coalition, Carter temporarily patched together different interest groups for a single vote. Carter held on to the South, but lost key industrial states that were traditionally Democratic strongholds. Clearly, a good part of the working-class Democrats who had bolted in 1972 were not yet returning to the fold, and in 1980, more of their counterparts would rejoin them in support of Ronald Reagan. The result was that rather than rebuild the old New Deal–Fair Deal coalition, "Carter provided a model for how to alienate all of its various wings simultaneously."[9]

Carter, like any president, was faced with specific problems— the Iranian hostage crisis, a rise in interest rates, and a rapid inflation along with growing unemployment. As taxes rose, the conservative tax revolt steadily took on fuel. In foreign policy, he was a bundle of contradictions. Carter stressed the primacy in American foreign policy of human rights; yet in 1977, shortly before the fall of the Iranian government, he praised the Shah of Iran and called his nation "an island of stability in one of the more troubled areas of the world." He responded to the Soviet threat with a large arms buildup, which alienated the Left, and deserted right-wing regimes like that of Somoza in Nicaragua only to find the Sandinistas in power, which angered the Right. On domestic issues, Carter also moved both Left and Right—appointing young activists to agencies concerned with the environment, consumer protection, and the like. He held traditional liberal views on civil rights, women's rights, and civil liberties, yet personally held to conservative social norms that contradicted those who favored abortion rights.

Thus Carter's policies satisfied neither Right nor Left in the Democratic Party. His April 1977 energy plan, for example, called for deregulation of oil and an increase in natural gas prices, as well as taxes on gas guzzling cars—in other words, free the oil but tax both its use and its alternative. Carter favored comprehensive welfare reform—he wanted a plan that was prowork and profamily. But when he balked at giving additional government funding to the working poor the traditional Left was outraged. Here was a dilemma that would face Bill Clinton in the nineties: When the Left is associated with activist government, any admission of mistaken policy—with a rollback—helps Republicans more than Democrats. Left Democrats went all out for passage of the Humphrey-Hawkins Full Employment bill—which would have mandated full employment as a major goal of the federal government. Carter paid little attention to it, and the Left felt betrayed. As a result, the Democratic Socialist political leader Michael Harrington, whose Democratic Socialist Organizing Committee tried to inject Socialist ideas into the maelstrom of traditional Democratic politics and constituencies, convened a large meeting in Washington of liberals, Socialists, and what he called the "broad Democratic Left" to try and push Carter further in their direction. Convened under the name "Democratic Agenda," the meeting saw Harrington try to downplay his own Socialist ideals and to create a coalition that could keep the Democratic Party on the path of liberalism. Sympathizing most with the politics espoused by Senator Edward M. Kennedy of Massachusetts, who had become the liberal's remaining standard-bearer, Harrington led a picket line in front of the Capitol to protest Carter's economic policies. For the Democratic Agenda group, Jimmy Carter had betrayed the liberal legacy, and was acting more like a Republican on the domestic front than a Democrat.[10] Carter, they pointed out, wanted the support of the organized labor movement, yet he opposed top labor musts, such as "common situs" picketing, that were priorities on the AFL-CIO's lobbying list.

Not surprisingly, as the 1980 convention loomed on the horizon, Carter faced a primary challenge from Kennedy. But Kennedy's candidacy faltered when it became evident that he did not have broad enough support within the party. Before the Iranian hostage crisis, Kennedy was way ahead of the incumbent Carter in the polls. Disaffected blue-collar workers were voting for him in the primaries, similarly to those who supported John Kennedy in 1960, but a *New York Times*/CBS postelection poll revealed that one-third of those who had supported Kennedy in the primaries eventually voted for Ronald Reagan. In short, they were protest voters, who were still registered Democrats. They were unhappy with the party, and were not pro-Teddy after all. There was a brief moment of anguish at the nominating convention, when Ted Kennedy approached the nominee on the lectern, only to turn and walk away as if he were shunning the victor.

Carter did not have much of a chance. A 1980 Gallup poll revealed that 45 percent of Americans viewed his presidency as failed, as either poor or below average. And in place of the pessimism they saw in Carter, Ronald Reagan exemplified optimism, hope, and a chance for Americans to regain a sense of national pride. The election results came as a jolt to Democrats, who were stunned and devastated. Carter took only six states. Republicans gained twelve Senate seats, defeated well-known Democratic liberals, and won thirty-three seats in the House.

Reagan had obtained 51 percent of the vote to Carter's meager 41 percent, with the third-party candidate John Anderson scoring an unimpressive 7 percent, the vote of liberal Republicans and liberal Democrats who were dissatisfied with both Reagan and Carter. The Reagan era had begun. Writing about his victory, Michael Barone commented that the results "showed that most American voters wanted limits on the growth of government at home, a more assertive foreign policy abroad, and some greater honoring of traditional moral values in their basic institutions."[11] It was what a decade later would come to be called the beginning of the conservative revolution and realignment of American politics.

The Reagan years, despite six years of a Republican Senate, would be characterized by a clear divide between presidential and legislative (and local) elections. Ronald Reagan had a clear conservative agenda. He adhered to a few basic ideas, and communicated them with deft conviction. Upon taking office, Reagan's administration cut $25 billion from welfare programs, reduced taxes over five years by $750 billion, while moving at the same time to vastly increase defense expenditures. More important, he and his followers proceeded to wage a war against the philosophy, laws, and values of the New Deal and Great Society. Instead of increased taxes to finance government programs, Reagan endorsed the concept of "supply side" economics—based on reductions in the personal income tax for the purpose of encouraging savings and investment. Dubbed "Reaganomics" by the president's liberal critics, the Republican assault on the old order was under way. But the now-divided Democrats continued to trade on incumbency advantages to cling to the House and many state legislatures.

The partisanship of the electorate responded steadily to Reagan's message. In the realm of foreign policy, it was an unmistakable truth that many Americans felt a new pride in their country. The invasion of tiny Grenada in 1983—to liberate that island from a brutal Marxist government that had just murdered its own less strident Marxist revolutionary prime minister, Maurice Bishop—was protested by the remnants of the left-liberal anti-war movement. But most Americans felt a surge of pride and triumph that the president had used armed force to restore peace and order in our own hemisphere. The president had proclaimed the end of the "Vietnam syndrome," and made it clear that his administration would use force when needed to defeat Marxist insurgencies. The policy became the focal point of a replay of the Vietnam era fight when the United States under Reagan moved to defeat revolution in nearby Central America.

In El Salvador, where a civil war between a right-wing military and left-wing guerrillas was raging, the Reagan administration promoted a moderate center government led by a Salvadoran democrat, José Napoleon Duarte. To the 100,000 protesters who marched on Washington in May of 1981, opposing the Reagan administration's economic and military aid to the Duarte government, Reagan was about to repeat the American military intervention in Vietnam—this time sending U.S. troops, they predicted, to fight nationalist guerrillas in our own hemisphere. Both sides—the Salvadoran army and the guerrillas—were guilty of serious human rights abuses. But while the Left used the army's terror tactics as an excuse to condemn the Reagan foreign policy, the administration did what it could to minimize human rights abuses by bolstering the strength of the feeble centrist government as an alternative to the military.

In nearby Nicaragua, the revolutionary Sandinistas had taken power in 1979, as they marched into the capital city of Managua to cheering throngs who welcomed the end of the corrupt and brutal Somoza dynasty's rule. The liberal-left community saw the victorious Sandinistas as moderate nationalists, who had freed their country from a right-wing dictatorship that had been backed for decades by the United States. In contrast, the Reagan administration understood—correctly, as it turned out—that the Sandinistas were a Soviet-backed Marxist movement, that sought to create yet another Soviet bastion in the Americas. As a result, the Reagan administration made the effort to weaken and oust the Sandinistas one of its primary foreign policy goals. The device adopted to gain this end was military and economic support to the so-called Nicaraguan *contras*, a policy that met with fierce resistance from Democrats, who continually passed measures to cut off funding for the resistance to the Sandinistas. Liberals argued that the Sandinistas had popular support that the *contras* lacked, and they believed that the *contras* were tainted by association with the right-wing Somoza regime that had been overthrown.

Despite Democratic interference, Reagan's policy in Central America succeeded. By 1989, continuing pressure would force the Sandinistas to permit free and monitored elections, which allowed Nicaraguans to vote them out of office by a landslide. And in El Salvador, the civil war ground to a halt, as a new elected government entered into peace negotiations with the rebels, and brought the activity of right-wing death squads to a halt. Peace had returned to the hemisphere, without a Communist victory. From Grenada to Nicaragua, Americans cheered that the age of Communist conquests had come to an end.

As 1984 approached, Reagan's economics appeared to be a raging success. Inflation was finally curbed; an expansion was underway. Democrats had little to say on the issue. It was on foreign policy that the parties squared off. But who would oppose this popular, successful, yet demonized incumbent? In contrast with Reagan and his adoption of a tough anti-Communist policy, would-be Democratic contenders courted the votes of anti-nuclear and left-wing activists in party caucuses. They vied with each other in favor of renunciation of force. Rather than seeking an increased defense budget and Star Wars missile shield, as did Ronald Reagan, the Democrats favored a nuclear freeze and numerous concessions to the Soviets. The candidate who emerged victorious over Gary Hart and others was not all that distinguishable from his opponents.

At one time in the nation's past, Walter Mondale might have been the perfect Democratic candidate. He was a minister's son from Norwegian stock. Most important, he was the heir apparent to Hubert Humphrey, and the former vice president's most able student and protégé. Having served as Carter's vice president, Mondale sought the nomination, and fully expected to win the presidency. But he had nothing new to offer the country.

Mondale's hope was to put together once again the New Deal coalition of old, and to do so by waging war against the Reagan economic program as a war against the poor. The Reagan program, he claimed during the campaign, was "class struggle on behalf of the rich." On foreign policy, Mondale thought that antiwar demonstrators had proved that Reagan's tough policy toward the Soviet Union was unpopular. After all, three-quarters of a million people had rallied in New York's Central Park on behalf of the Left's proposed nuclear freeze, and he thought this proved the dangers of a policy of confrontation with the Soviets. The giant peace rally, however, was a replay of the old World War II era Popular Front, and its sponsors readily welcomed the participation of Communists and their allies. As was the case in the 1940s, when the United States was allied with the Soviet Union, many liberals overlooked the totalitarian nature of the Soviet regime, and welcomed the cooperation of American Communists and their supporters in joint efforts on behalf of a liberal agenda.[12] And the growing conflict in Central America, according to this same Left, led them to believe that under Reagan, a new Vietnam was possible in our own hemisphere.

To gain support, Mondale opted to court those constituencies most dissatisfied with the Reagan policies. He assumed that his base lay with organized labor and the AFL-CIO, but he also reached out to new populist constituencies—the women's movement, the civil rights coalition, and especially the teachers' unions. That very tactic, however, spelled certain defeat. Mondale was not reaching out to those Democrats who were deserting their ancestor's chosen party for Reagan and the Republicans, but to the interest groups of the new middle-class elite who were rapidly becoming the Democratic Party's main base of support. The AFL-CIO endorsement meant little; many of their own membership voted against their recommendation. Mondale thought, for example, that the much touted women's vote was his, since the "gender gap," as the media called it, had indicated that women were more inclined toward peace policies and would be inclined to endorse Mondale's campaign for "fairness" as opposed to the probusiness economic policy favored by the Republicans. The tactic, as it turned out, backfired. Mondale was viewed by the electorate as pandering to self-concerned "special interest" groups—the National Organization for Women, the AFL-CIO, the black Civil Rights establishment, and the national teachers' unions. The preconvention endorsement he received from the AFL-CIO, the first time the trade union federation had ever done that for a presidential candidate, hurt Mondale more than it helped him. The similar enthusiastic endorsement of the National Education Association had the same effect. To the public, Mondale had received the backing of regulars in the political establishment and lobbyists. He did not seem to realize that the support of trade union leaders did not automatically lead to its membership's voting for him, and that unions were now viewed by the public as just another large bureaucracy removed from the public interest. Two of the most astute political journalists, Jack Germond and Jules Witcover, quoted one of Mondale's own advisors, Richard Moe, as having told the candidate in a memo the simple truth: "People simply don't want their president to be wholly owned by any group or special interest, and they inevitably react negatively to any candidate who is perceived to be so owned . . . it follows that they see candidates who pander to these groups for support—saying everything they want to hear, giving them everything they want—as very unpresidential."[13]

Mondale thought he had a chance. Governor Mario Cuomo of New York State lit up the Democratic convention in one of the best speeches of his career, telling the country how he had risen from a poor immigrant family to become governor of the greatest city in the nation, a rise that paralleled that of other immigrants to the ranks of the middle classes. The speech was great, but it was, in effect, the swan song of the old liberalism. Mondale's handing of the vice presidential spot to a woman, Geraldine Ferraro, warmed the hearts of feminists but did little to help him with the electorate.

To the nation, Reagan represented America. To Mondale's campaign charge that in Reagan's America, "no one's hurting, no one's alone. No one's hungry. No one's unemployed. No one gets old. Everybody is happy," the electorate responded as if Mondale were attacking them and their country, not their president. The results were more devastating than Mondale expected. In another landslide victory, Reagan gathered 59 percent of the vote, and forty-nine out of fifty states. Moreover, the much expected gender gap vote never materialized. Indeed, Reagan won 57 percent of the women's vote, 61 percent of the elderly, and even 60 percent of the youth vote. Reagan had asked whether Americans felt they were better off than four years earlier. The returns proved that their answer was affirmative.

To some parties, perhaps, two such resounding defeats would be cause for drastic redesign. But you can't redesign a coalition without the votes. Labor organizations were not only in decline, their members were often more Republican than Democratic. As the country's affluence continued to expand, the power of "have-not" politics continued to disappear. The best the Democrats could do was hope for external events to swing against the incumbents. Indeed, in 1988 they believed that economic and political developments could give them the chance they did not have in 1984. Most important was the Iran-Contra affair, which the Democrats had argued revealed that the Reagan administration was trading arms to Iran in exchange for the release of Western hostages held by the Iranian government. It looked, for a time, like Watergate *redux*. Dramatic Senate hearings dominated the headlines. Most sensational was the televised testimony of Lieutenant Colonel Oliver North, who had been the man who diverted money from the arms sales to Iran to illegally finance the Nicaraguan *contras*. North lied to Congress, and the Democrats thought that his exposure would embarrass and harm the administration. Instead, North appeared to the public as a brave and principled patriot, pilloried for his defense of American interests. Much to the dismay of liberals, *contra* aid now seemed popular, and was not perceived by the nation as the equivalent of another Vietnam. As for Iran-Contra, the Democrats' charge of a Reagan administration conspiracy was never proved, and the hearings, which dragged on and on, proved not to be another Watergate.

The president, despite a fall in standing over Iran-Contra,

proved that in foreign policy, his tough stance with the Soviets had paid off. Liberals had argued that during his presidency, defense spending was unnecessarily high and that the administration was courting nuclear disaster with the Soviets. Reagan had continued to uphold Jimmy Carter's decision to install Pershing II missiles in Germany, a policy that the peace movement saw as indefensible. But, during Reagan's second term, Soviet premier Mikhail Gorbachev came to the United States, and signed a treaty with Reagan for disassembling Soviet SS 20 missiles in Eastern Europe in exchange for U.S. removal of the Pershings. The Reagan defense buildup proved to have served its purpose, as the Soviets were forced to acquiesce and to make concessions to the United States. Reagan had ignored the pleas for unilateral disarmament coming from the nuclear freeze forces, and his obstinacy had paid off.

Given these realities, combined with a sound economy, Governor Michael Dukakis of Massachusetts had little chance in '88. The Democrats came into the election knowing that they had lost their old strongholds of blue-collar, Catholic, and industrial workers, as well as their old geographic base. The Republicans had won twenty-three states in the previous five elections, and now had an electoral advantage in thirty-six out of fifty states. The Democrats, rejecting old liberals like Mondale, Hubert Humphrey, or New York's Cuomo, might have had somewhat of a chance with the intelligent senator from Colorado, Gary Hart. But Hart quickly disqualified himself when caught in a series of embarrassing peccadilloes, including one with a model on a boat appropriately called "Monkey Business." In a field of competitors that included Richard Gephardt, the traditional liberal Paul Simon, and the black radical Jesse Jackson, Dukakis, who stressed his Greek immigrant roots and the supposed prosperity of his high-tech state, was able to win the Democratic nomination by appealing to "haves." But why would "haves" vote Democratic in any general election?

Dukakis tried to make it appear that he was not a liberal. Reagan, and his successor George Bush concentrated on making that term virtually anathema. To the public at large, liberalism implied not a concern for the poor and the average American, but a self-involved narcissistic attitude that was responsible for cultural decay, a rising crime wave, racial polarization, and a weakening of America abroad. Hence Dukakis told the Atlanta convention that the issue in the campaign was "competence" rather than ideology. Dukakis and his party thought the election was a sure thing, since George Bush, polls revealed, was disliked by at least 40 percent of the population. But as a candidate who stressed competence, Dukakis simply failed to offer a real alternative.

The problem was that Michael Dukakis made all issues into technocratic and legalistic ones, while Bush and the Republicans stressed the cultural implications that concerned most Americans. On Memorial Day, the Republican whiz who was running the Bush campaign, Lee Atwater, presided over a focus group in Paramus, New Jersey. Thirty voters who had declared their preference for Dukakis were informed that the governor had vetoed a law requiring that students pledge allegiance to the flag, and that he supported weekend furloughs for prisoners who committed violent crimes. Immediately, fifteen of the thirty focus group participants announced that they would shift to Bush. The message was clear. The Bush campaign realized that all they had to do to turn things around was engage in what Democrats would argue was negative campaigning, but which Republicans saw as stressing the inadequacy of the Democrats on the major social issues. Bush campaigned at a New Hampshire flag plant, and announced that unlike Dukakis, he was not a member of the American Civil Liberties Union. What got most attention was the new Republican ad campaign, the now famous Willie Horton commercial. Horton, a black prisoner guilty of rape and assault, had broken into the home of a Maryland couple on a weekend furlough, and after terrorizing them, raped the wife. "If I can make Willie Horton a household name," Atwater told the press, "we'll win the election." Democrats cried that the commercial was racist, creating a fear in whites of black felons who would invade their middle-class homes. Leading the fray was Jesse Jackson, who angrily charged that the television ads were "designed to create the most horrible psychosexual fears."[14] Republicans countered that the Horton assault took place during a furlough approved by Dukakis, and it was the policy of being soft on crime they were concentrating on, not that of race. Indeed, the ads themselves sponsored by the Bush campaign did not mention Horton's name or his race, although ads taken by independent Bush supporters did use a photo of Horton, which clearly revealed him to be black. That gave Jackson and other Democrats the excuse to charge the Bush campaign with racism. But the charge rested on the assumption that voters hated blacks more than they feared violent criminals, and on the belief that were the murderer white, they would not be enraged by the furlough policy.

Dukakis's advisors did not even understand the symbolism of his veto of the pledge law. "If Bush thinks he's going to get anywhere with this pledge stuff," the shrewd lawyer and campaign strategist Susan Estrich said, "he's crazy. We've got this Supreme Court decision." Estrich was referring to the fact that on legal grounds, Dukakis was on solid turf. But to the American public, constitutional precision has never had populist power. Dukakis had vetoed a bill that would have required schoolteachers in his state to lead students in the Pledge of Allegiance. Estrich had advised him that he had no choice, since the state's Supreme Court had said the bill was unconstitutional. Bush had said he would have signed the law, which Dukakis responded showed that Bush was "unfit" to be chief executive.[15] But the press had investigated, and found that before the Massachusetts court had ruled on the bill, Dukakis had expressed his opposition to it and asked the court for a ruling. Moreover, the court's ruling was only an advisory one, and Dukakis could have ignored it. But even if the court ruling was binding, and Dukakis had no alternative, his legalistic response made it more than clear that he did not grasp the impact of the cultural issue involved, and thought it an appropriate decision.

Liberalism was, moreover, not speaking to the social breakdown in society, and when combined with the furlough issue, Dukakis appeared as if he was in favor of the permissiveness with which the Democrats had become associated. The Pledge of Allegiance, originally written by a reformist socialist as a means for Americans to express their common sentiments toward their nation, was now defined by ACLU types as a violation of an individual's rights and liberties. Dukakis responded to Bush's swipe by saying he was proud to be a "card-carrying member of the ACLU." To the electorate, Dukakis was giving them more evidence that he just didn't get it.[16] Moreover, as Fred Siegel and others have shown, the ACLU had long ago departed from its once pristine position as a defender of civil liberties, regardless of its opinion of the views of those it was defending. Since the 1960s, in case after case, the organization had shifted ground from being a principled defender of the civil liberties of all Americans to being an organization that had become an advocacy group for select left-wing causes.

Indeed, despite consistent disclaimers, and careful avoidance of the now-hated L-word, the public saw Michael Dukakis as a secret defender of a heavily discredited liberalism. Dukakis's attempt to mold an alliance with the leader of the party's left wing, Reverend Jesse Jackson, hurt him even more. On the Monday before the Democratic convention, Dukakis convened a summit with Jackson, revealing, as *Time* reported, "fissures along racial and ideological lines that could someday threaten the foundations of the Democratic party."[17] At the meeting, it was agreed that Dukakis would employ Jackson supporters on the national campaign staff, and that Jackson himself would get a plane and funding to travel the nation. As Max Lerner, the elder statesman of American liberal columnists, explained, the problem was the structure of the Democratic Party itself. Democratic liberalism used to "be close enough to the center to make it manageable," Lerner wrote, but the policymaking bodies and the composition of its elites had "shifted so drastically that the center no longer holds." By kowtowing to Jackson and the forces he represented, Lerner argued, the nation knew that Dukakis had become "a prisoner of the party's contradictions and splits." Hence the reluctance of the candidate's managers to let Jackson speak in areas where "white marginal and centrist voters" would be put off by his radical image, and where it would harm the campaign more than help it by gaining the support of black loyalists and white leftists. To avoid an open break, Dukakis was feigning unity with Jackson, a move that Lerner correctly understood would only continue Dukakis's imprisonment.[18]

The Democrats, as Ben Wattenberg commented, were "bending over backward to be super-nice to Jackson." And since Jackson was on the "far Left of the spectrum," the message he was preaching was not the one the electorate wanted to hear. Indeed, Wattenberg argued that Democrats had lost four of the last five presidential elections because they were perceived as too liberal. Jackson had lost his bid for nomination in the primaries, yet he was demanding that the chosen candidate forge some kind of coalition with him in order to receive the Left's support. If Dukakis did not strongly repudiate Jackson, Wattenberg believed, it would become credible for the Republicans to paint him "as the leader of a party that has gone beyond what was called McGovernization and on to Jacksonization." If he does not, the columnist predicted, Dukakis would lose.[19]

The Atlanta convention only confirmed Wattenberg's predictions. The Democrats tried hard. As A.M. Rosenthal wrote, they attempted to repackage the party's image. "In Atlanta," he commented sarcastically, "it's been hard to hear that word that once was the proudly accepted label of the majority of the Democratic Party—liberal."[20] The delegates were actually more liberal than most Democratic voters, but in order to try to win, they hid their actual beliefs and tried to appear as a group not too far from the Republicans. Jackson, of course, put a brake on that. In his speech to the convention, delivered in his best rhetorical style and before a packed house of his supporters, Jackson turned Reagan's symbolism on its head and proclaimed that it was midnight in America, that the nation had abandoned its poor, its farmers, its factory workers, its elders, and its hungry. It was a classic have-not speech, delivered to a nation of comfortably middle-class citizens—a speech that, to many, indicated the true approach of so many Democrats.[21] Moreover, Jackson's speech followed a major convention debate—a fight over a platform amendment calling for the establishment of a Palestinian state on what would be formerly Israeli territory. The amendment was never brought to a vote, but it was backed by the Jackson forces and the hard left wing of the party. It was enough to lead one columnist to ask whether the "party of Franklin Delano Roosevelt and John F. Kennedy [was] becoming the party of Henry Wallace and George McGovern?"[22]

At the convention, some Democrats realized the dangers of Dukakis getting branded as an ideological liberal. As *The Washington Post* reported:

> *Even among Northern delegates, the smell of victory is tempered by fears that Dukakis could get painted into a liberal corner—that the combination of his pro-choice stance on abortion, his support of gun control, his opposition to certain weapons systems, and the controversy over Massachusetts' furlough program for criminals, could collectively be used by Bush to define the public's as yet unformed image of Dukakis as unacceptably far to the Left.*[23]

Dukakis, of course, tried his best to prove that such would not be the case. But the Left continued to argue that to win the nomination, Dukakis had to convince Democratic "progressives," the favorite self-descriptive euphemism of the Left, that he agreed with their positions. Yet conservatives and centrists within the party saw the progressive's views as extremist. One journalistic spokesman for the Left argued that Democratic aspirants to the presidency catered to activists during the campaign for nomination, only to backtrack on their promises during the campaign. "Thus," wrote journalist Eric Alterman, "the ludicrous spectacle of Michael Dukakis disavowing both the Midgetman and MX missiles in Iowa in order to pass the peace-movement litmus test, only to endorse some hypothetical . . . third land-based option once the nomination was sent up." Alterman, for one, was not taken in. Dukakis' turn was not sufficient, and he favored a new left-wing party that would oppose a new conservative Reagan Democratic and Republican party.[24] If Alterman had looked any closer, he would have seen a great deal of evidence of how Dukakis, desperate to describe himself as a nonideological moderate, was hostage to Jackson and the party's Left. One example was the foreign policy crisis in central Africa, surrounding the issue of whether the United States should continue aiding the anti-Communist forces in Angola led by Jonas Savimbi.

In that small oil-producing nation, a pro-Soviet government continued precariously in power, supported by Cuban troops who had intervened in a brutal civil war on the chosen side of the Soviets. Savimbi was despised by antiapartheid blacks, since he took military aid from the South African government. The United States was prodding the South Africans to leave nearby Namibia, in exchange for a Cuban exodus from Angola. To curry favor with Jackson, Dukakis branded U.S. policy toward Angola as bizarre, and he indicated that if elected, he would withdraw the critical U.S. aid to Savimbi's forces. President Reagan had assured Savimbi that his forces would continue to receive American aid, as long as the Soviets continued supplying arms to its Marxist client state. The policy received bipartisan support, including backing from Senator Chris Dodd of Connecticut, a major opponent of the Reagan administration's *contra* aid. But Jackson refused Savimbi's request for a meeting to state his case, and Dukakis rapidly followed suit. The effect of his action was to tell the Soviets that they did not have to make a deal; they could wait for Dukakis to get elected, when things would shift in their favor. As William Safire wrote, Dukakis was saying: "My administration would not support free elections in central Africa because Jesse Jackson does not approve of the anti-Communist candidate."[25]

The problem was, as journalist Paul A. Gigot wrote, that the Democratic Party "remains in its heart a liberal-left party, even if this year it prefers not to advertise this to the voters."[26] The best they could do was to appear ambiguous. The strategy was laid out to the party by its chairman, Paul Kirk, when he testified before the committee that wrote the party's platform in June. While the 1984 platform had more than 40,000 words, the 1988 platform had only 4,000, and they were largely devoted to attacking the record of the Reagan administration, without ever mentioning the popular president by name. "Our party should develop a winning Democratic platform," Kirk opined. "We should avoid a long list of legislative proposals and a litany of social, cultural, or ideological buzzwords . . . we have to remember those so-called 'swing voters,'" those moderate Democrats and independents who abandoned the party to vote for Ronald Reagan.[27] The delegates who heard Kirk proceeded to do just what he favored—to write a platform that was more than vague as to what the new Democratic administration would be for, a strategy that hopefully would allow Democrats of the Left, Center, and Right all to vote for Dukakis, and hope for the best after the election.

The reality, as Martin Peretz argued after the Bush victory, was that the Jackson-Dukakis coalition was what voters remembered. "The convention sticks in the people's consciousness," Peretz wrote, "not only as the apotheosis of Jesse Jackson but as the culmination of a primary campaign during which the ultimate winner said again and again he had not many fundamental differences with Jesse Jackson."[28] Others further to the Left agreed that Jackson was the key player, but argued that the Democrats should acknowledge that and make him their leader. Thus Andrew Kopkind, writing in *Nation* magazine, said that "whether the Democratic hierarchy likes it or not, Jackson became the leader of the party on November 9, and he is already its frontrunner for the nomination in 1992."[29] The primaries, in other words, were hard-fought ideological battles, and Dukakis's attempt to shift the focus of the campaign to the issue of competence did not wash. Dukakis seemed to stand for the redistributionist schemes of the Left, as well as that of the "rights liberalism" that the traditional Democratic constituency eschewed. By promising everything, Dukakis seemed to be endorsing the heart of the old liberalism. As Peretz asked: "Who among the liberals is prepared to say that mothers who cannot care for their children are not entitled to bring them into the world as burdens on society as a whole?"[30] In 1988, few Democrats were acting as if that question was even relevant. By 1996, very few would be arguing that it was not. During the '88 campaign, most Democrats were acting as if the values associated with family, defense of the nation, and patriotism were obsolete, and that those who sought to implement them would be challenged in court by the American Civil Liberties Union, with Dukakis's backing.

It was, ultimately, the social issues that led Michael Dukakis to defeat by George Bush, who many thought was highly unlikely to win at the campaign's start. Dukakis tried to shift the attention of the electorate from cultural to economic and foreign policy issues, but the ploy did not work. By July, Bush's Gallup poll ratings had risen from 37 percent to 53 percent, while Dukakis had fallen from a start of 54 percent to a new low of 46 percent. By the middle of September, Bush's ratings went up and up, as Dukakis' continued to fall. By the time of the election, Bush won with a margin of 54 percent to 46 percent, carrying forty out of fifty states.[31]

Dukakis lost because of his liberalism, which had become discredited. A *New York Times*/CBS News poll had shown that only 15 percent of voters saw themselves as liberals. Once voters saw Dukakis as a liberal, as they increasingly did as the campaign progressed, it was simply impossible for him to win an election. When an NBC/*Wall Street Journal* poll in October asked respondents whether they agreed that "Dukakis is too liberal to be a good president" or that "Bush is too conservative," 37 percent found Dukakis too liberal, while only 22% found Bush too conservative. And the election-day poll by CBS/*New York Times* revealed that four-fifths of those who called themselves liberals

voted for Dukakis, and the same number calling themselves conservatives voted for Bush. Moderates split evenly between the
two candidates. The problem for Dukakis was that by that time,
only 18 percent of the voters defined themselves as liberals, while
33 percent called themselves conservatives.

The electorate had cast Michael Dukakis in the mold of the
McGovernite liberalism they despised, and the leaders of the
party did not help in disavowing that perception. Jesse Jackson's
approach for victory was simple—to pursue the "vast number of
people who feel they've been left out—blacks, Hispanics,
women." Jackson's rhetoric appealed to guilt-ridden New Politics
white radicals, as well as to some members of these "left-out"
groups. But, as a recipe for successful politics, it was self-destruc-
tive. A coalition based on identity group politics by definition
left out the old core constituency of the Democratic Party—
white male ethnics who came from blue-collar backgrounds. By
demonizing them as part of a reactionary group whose concern
need not be addressed, Jesse Jackson had handed their votes right
over to the Republicans.

Jackson also singled out for opposition the party's embattled
moderates who, under the leadership of Democrats such as Sam
Nunn of Georgia and Chuck Robb of Virginia, had formed the
Democratic Leadership Council (DLC), a moderate group then
in the process of building a think tank—the soon-to-emerge Progressive Policy Institute—as well as a strong political arm to shift
the party back toward the center. Founded after the 1984 election, the DLC created "Super Tuesday," which moved the primaries of Southern states to one date, in order to strengthen the
chances of a moderate or conservative Democrat gaining the
nomination. In 1988, the maneuver didn't work out that way.
The one-day primary was held, but Jesse Jackson emerged as the
victor in many of the Southern states, where blacks and liberal

activists were the majority casting votes. As for Jackson's claim that the party could win by moving left and toward votes of the dispossessed, Senator Sam Nunn of Georgia commented: "If our appeal is to the dispossessed, we'll get only the dispossessed to vote for us. . . . Every time you attempt to go left, you will bring out at least equal numbers of voters against you on the right."[32]

Sam Nunn was right. It would be left to a future Democratic candidate for president, Bill Clinton, to seize that insight and develop it into the road to the White House.

8

THE CLINTON
CONTRADICTION

The Campaign and the Presidency

The Democratic Party, as George Bush and the Republicans charged, had indeed moved to the left, and Michael Dukakis did not challenge that shift. Some liberal commentators actively resisted such reasoning. Thus Hendrik Hertzberg, then politics editor of the *New Republic*, argued that "if Dukakis was too liberal than any Democrat is probably too liberal."[1] In Hertzberg's eyes, Dukakis was a centrist reformer, not a true liberal. That may technically have been true. The problem was that he continually cast himself in the language of the sixties liberalism that had become the dominant image of the party. By the election's end, it was clear that not Dukakis but Jesse Jackson had become the ascendant force in the party. Jackson used irony when he told the black journalist William Rasberry after the election, "calling me a leftist is just another way of saying 'nigger.'"[2]

Still, while Jackson was riding hard in the glow of his second-place showing, and the widely held view that he was now the party's titular leader, some Democrats were ready to seek a new direction. Joseph A. Califano, Jr., former Secretary of Health, Education, and Welfare during the Carter administration, took time out from an active law practice to ask his fellow Democrats why "so many whites perceive us as the party of blacks and special interests, soft on crime and naïve about defense." Califano raised the previously unthinkable idea—that Democrats reevaluate affirmative action, which he called "the preference of blacks over whites for slots in colleges, jobs and promotion." Califano, who hoped that the party would not abandon liberalism, was really posing the sensitive issue that Democrats redefine liberalism—away from emphasizing quotas, school busing, and the misguided belief that Democrats had to "do penance for an era of slavery and discrimination they had nothing to do with." As for Dukakis's positions during the campaign, Califano noted that "we have persisted in a dogged incantation of procedural and legalistic technicalities about protecting the rights of accused criminals without expressing comparable concern for those who have been mugged, robbed, raped, and burglarized." And on foreign policy, Califano noted that "McGovern's aggressively antidefense, antiwar campaign was considered dangerous and naïve by an overwhelming majority of Americans." Dukakis followed in that tradition, by advocating withholding of his state's National Guard from a training mission in Central America, by supporting the nuclear freeze, and by being unwilling to admit that "Reagan's defense spending . . . had helped move the Russians to sign one of the best nuclear arms agreements in history."[3]

Califano was saying, in effect, that despite all the disclaimers,

Michael Dukakis lost the election because he kept the Democratic Party moving in the direction George McGovern had taken it in 1972. The party had to move toward the Center-Right, not maintain its leftward drift. Writing in *Commentary*, Josh Muravchik saw little chance for such a course to be adopted, and predicted that "the forces now organizing to pull the Democrats down the suicidal path of the British Labor Party seem stronger and more determined to push the party back toward the Center." There were just a few isolated souls on the left of the party who acknowledged the necessity of preventing such a collapse. Jefferson Morley, writing in the *Nation*, argued that Democrats "must turn to national leaders who can perform comfortably in the culture of poor and middle-income Southern whites, like . . . Bill Clinton of Arkansas."[4]

Morley may have been the first media writer to suggest the possibility that the little-known governor of Arkansas would be a likely front-runner in 1992. Yet, if any available Democrat might be able to shift the perspective of the Democratic Party, Bill Clinton was an obvious choice. As a Southern governor of a relatively poor state, he had the support of both Southern whites and blacks. Clinton, of course, had bombed at the 1988 Democratic convention, when he gained national notoriety by his lengthy and droning nomination speech for Dukakis. But on the national scene, Clinton identified with the Democratic Leadership Council, of which he would become chairman in 1990. Sensing that participation in the DLC would be a way to reaffirm his political presence in the nation, as well as to cast himself in the framework of a party moderate, Clinton laid the base for what few would have predicted after the '88 debacle—that four years later, Bill Clinton would emerge as his party's nominee for president of the United States.

Sometime later, in July 1995 a closed meeting of the Democratic Leadership Council was held. A significant meeting, it indicated that the president's original moderate supporters were now fed up, and believed that the president's policies put the future of the Democratic Party at risk. Clinton, the DLC group understood, had run for president as a moderate Democrat, on the basis of proposals and views developed out of the DLC's think tank, the Progressive Policy Institute (PPI). As Clinton himself had said, the DLC's job was to create "a new middle ground of thinking on which someone can not only run for President but actually be elected." Though Clinton won the 1992 election with only 43 percent of the popular vote, the strategy did succeed.

The problem for the DLC in 1995 was neatly stated by Al From, the president of the group. "Since his election," From told *Time*'s political columnist, Michael Kramer, "the president's campaign agenda hasn't been his first priority." An academic advisor to Clinton and the DLC, political scientist William Galston said, "In '92 our ideas captured the country but not the party." The tension within the Clinton administration, said Galston, who himself had recently resigned from the job of White House aide, was that the president could not decide between "accommodating the liberal tendencies that still dominate the party and the centrist views the president ran on."[5]

"Clinton promised to be different," From commented, but "the fundamental change he pledged hasn't come." From was blunt. For the Democrats to continue to exist as a majority party, or to exist at all, they had to break with the party's left wing, including the civil rights establishment and the trade union movement. "A long-term majority," From understood, "will never be created around the interests represented by Jesse and the labor unions."

But the strategy faced an obvious obstacle: The forces led by

Jesse Jackson and the AFL-CIO were the two remaining solid constituency groups that could be counted on to remain in the Democratic ranks. The demise of the party was at hand. What Bill Clinton sought to do about the problem was evident in a confidential memo delivered to the White House by the president's chief pollster, Stanley Greenberg. Noting that the President's image was that of a "Tsongas Democrat," a reference to Senator Paul Tsongas, a 1992 primary challenger who was perceived as a fiscal conservative and social liberal, Greenberg informed the chief executive in 1995 that success depended upon "reestablishing that Bill Clinton identifies with the economic struggles of ordinary citizens, and that he is someone who understands their values. Bill Clinton must re-emerge as someone with an economic vision, populist instincts and as a cultural conservative." Greenberg stressed that the president's policies had cut him off from middle-class Americans, and had lost him the support of the very Reagan Democrats who had given him his margin of victory in 1992.[6]

When Bill Clinton had emerged as the front-runner in 1992, he had had all the marks of an individual capable of taking the party in a new direction. Clinton had begun his campaign with a speech to the 1991 DLC Convention, where he differentiated himself from traditional Democrats by supporting the bulk of the moderate group's programs. Clinton appeared after a speech by House Majority Leader Richard Gephardt of Missouri, who delivered what the *Washington Post* reported was "a rousing, populist address featuring a long section of Japan-bashing that appeared to put him much closer to the AFL-CIO than to the free-traders in the DLC." Clinton, then still the DLC's chairman, became "virtually the only politician who packaged the group's philosophy in what sounded to delegates like an effective stump speech." Those present, remembering Clinton's disastrous interminable nominating speech for Dukakis in 1988, were simply amazed.[7]

The differences between Clinton and past candidates, especially Michael Dukakis, was exemplified by his position on crime. Dukakis was seen as a typical ACLU member, a person who put the rights of criminal defendants over those of their victims. In contrast, Clinton was known to be a supporter of the death penalty. Indeed, some liberal Democrats were aghast when Clinton, after the election, underscored his commitment by flying home to Arkansas in January to preside over the execution of a convicted cop-killer. The party's platform, passed at the 1992 Convention, was stunning in its sharp separation from its predecessors. On the crime issue, it said that "the simplest and most direct way to restore order in our cities is to put more police on the streets." When Republicans had used that kind of argument in the Nixon campaign, Democrats had derided such calls for "law and order" as hidden racism.

Clinton ran for president as what came to be called a "New Democrat." The themes he emphasized over and over during the campaign included talking tough about crime, supporting a middle-class tax cut, emphasizing the need for "personal responsibility," proposing a new program of national service, and a firm rejection of traditional Democratic "tax and spend" programs, such as those savaged by the Republicans in their previous successful campaigns. As E. J. Dionne, Jr., wrote, "the DLC has largely won both the strategic fight over the importance of the middle class and the substantive fight over what values should be reflected in social programs. This success can be measured by the importance Clinton—and so many liberals—have accorded the issues of welfare reform, crime, national service, and the need to 'reinvent government' in a less bureaucratic form."[8]

Nowhere was the resonance that Clinton aroused as visible as among some of the intellectual Democratic community that had defected to the Republicans during the Reagan years. Clinton wooed these neoconservatives and would-be policymakers, calling them for advice and consultation, even having them draft some of his speeches, and actively seeking their endorsement. He stressed both domestic issues and a more hawkish foreign policy. It paid off. In August of 1992, a large ad appeared in the *New York Times*, paid for by the Clinton campaign endorsing Clinton for the presidency. The statement's thirty-three signers had previously met at a popular Washington restaurant with some of Clinton's key supporters, including Anthony Lake, William Galston, and Rep. Dave McCurdy, to hear why they were backing Clinton and why they thought others should.

Guests at the luncheon included a veritable who's who of moderate to conservative Democrats, including Penn Kemble, Ben Wattenberg, Joshua Muravchik, and other Democrats who were skeptical about supporting Clinton. When the ad finally appeared, it stressed Clinton's apparent support of what were considered hard-line positions in the area of foreign policy. It praised him for supporting "authentic democrats in the societies of the former Soviet Union," for his opposition to "the brutal and archaic Communist dictatorship in Beijing," and for urging firm international action, including, "if necessary, the use of U.S. air and naval forces . . . to prevent Serbia's national Communist regime from doing violence to neighboring peoples." Moreover, it praised Clinton for resisting "those at home—and in his own party—who propose reckless cuts in our national defense capabilities."[9]

Clinton next sought the talents of some of these neoconservatives (Josh Muravchik, Adrian Karynytcky, Penn Kemble, and Michael Chapman) to write what would be his single major foreign policy address, presented in Milwaukee, Wisconsin, on

October 1, 1992. The group flew to Milwaukee the day before delivery, in order to fine-tune the speech until the moment Clinton was ready to give it.[10] The speech emphasized the themes of global democracy and American leadership, and Clinton followed it up in television debates with George Bush by declaring the spread of democracy to be a major foreign policy goal of his administration, as well as the taking of a new strong stand on Bosnia.

Clinton also broke with the reigning liberal view on the matter of race. If Michael Dukakis had been perceived as a hostage of Jesse Jackson in 1988, Bill Clinton saw to it that he would seize whatever opportunity opened to avoid just such a trap. Clinton had been given this advice early in the campaign by supporters such as the powerful teachers' union leader, Al Shanker.[11] The opportunity came in June, during the convention of Jackson's group, the Rainbow Coalition. The Reverend Jackson had invited the participation of a black rap performer, Sister Souljah, who entertained the delegates as well as participating on a panel. This was a singer who had told the press after the Los Angeles riots that "If black people kill black people every day, why not have a week and kill white people? . . . so if you're a gang member and you would normally be killing somebody, why not kill a white person?"

Before Clinton was scheduled to speak, Jesse Jackson had told the audience of his pride that Sister Souljah had appeared on the previous night's program. With Jackson on the podium, Clinton proceeded to inject his strategic strike into a relatively routine speech. "You had a rap singer here last night named Sister Souljah. . . . Her comments before and after Los Angeles were filled with a kind of hatred that you do not honor." Clinton noted that "if you took the words 'white' and 'black' and reversed them, you might think David Duke was giving that speech."

Clinton's brief comments drew blood from Jackson. As the

Washington Post reporter noted, it was a "deliberate" challenge that seemed "designed to demonstrate [Clinton's] willingness to challenge core Democratic constituent groups and to begin to break his image in the public as a 'political' person who would bend to pressure from major forces within his party." Jackson was mortified and, defending the rap singer, he argued that "she represents the feelings and hopes of a whole generation of people" and hence deserved an apology.[12] Clinton's comments on Souljah, the Reverend Jackson said, were meant "purely to appeal to conservative whites by containing Jackson" and to make them at the Rainbow Coalition, moreover, "again exposed a character flaw." Clinton, for his part, vowed that he would "not back down."[13]

Clinton was positioning himself firmly in the political center. He was speaking for the neglected middle class, was taking a tough position on foreign policy questions, and with Al Gore as his running mate, he clearly rejected ticket-balancing in favor of two Southern candidates who were both regarded as political moderates, if not leaning to the conservative side. Polls showed that half of American voters regarded themselves as moderates, and that these voters were giving Clinton a seventeen-point margin. When voters looked at Clinton's other promises, "abolishing welfare as we know it," reforming health care to provide better coverage to all Americans and to reduce escalating health care costs, and finally, to create "eight million new jobs in the next four years," Clinton had come up with a winning program—one that even left-liberal Democrats could endorse while hoping for more, moderates would unite around, and conservatives could even tolerate.

On November 3, Bill Clinton became the forty-second president of the United States, gaining a sweeping electoral victory that ended a twelve-year Republican reign. Clinton had captured

30 states, winning 353 electoral college votes, to 15 states and 132 electoral votes for George Bush. The popular vote was, however, a bit closer. Clinton won only 43 percent, Bush obtained 38 percent, and Ross Perot won 19 percent, the largest vote ever obtained by a third-party candidate since Theodore Roosevelt's run in 1912. Clinton promised cheering supporters that he would bring "a new Democratic Party to Washington."[14]

The story of the next two years, however, was something different. Rather than a foreign policy hawk, welfare reformer, and tax cutter, Clinton undertook defense cuts, attempted a vast new health-care program, and raised taxes. And rather than bringing a new Democratic Party to Washington, in the midterm 1994 elections he helped usher in a new *Republican* majority in Congress.

There were signs of old Democratism early in Clinton's term. He announced that he would appoint a Cabinet that "looks like America," with the hint that many of the appointments his administration made, outside of the Cabinet level as well, would be made on the basis of race and gender. Some of the appointments were obvious. The job of Attorney General was clearly reserved for a woman, and after the first two female nominees had to be withdrawn, Clinton appointed the Florida prosecutor Janet Reno to the job. Conservative Democrats were even more upset to see Clinton placating gay rights groups. A noted gay activist was employed in the personnel office at the White House, and the lesbian activist Roberta Achtenberg—who had gained the animosity of conservatives by opposing United Way funding of the Boy Scouts because they barred gay scoutmasters—was named the Assistant Secretary of Housing and Urban Development.

When he made a change in the rules that prohibited homosexuals from serving in the armed forces as one of his first executive orders, Clinton appeared to be taking a stand on the very kind of social issue that had driven so many Democrats away from their party in the first place. The issue of gays in the military was highly symbolic and visible. Opposed by Colin Powell, then Chairman of the Joint Chiefs of Staff, as well as most of the military brass, the new policy of "don't ask, don't tell," ended up satisfying nobody, while causing anger among both the conservative majority as well as the activists of the gay community.

Clinton had made the mistake of promising unequivocally during the campaign that he would lift the ban against gays in the military. But he had also argued that he would pass a middle-class tax cut. When the latter promise was abandoned almost immediately upon his assuming the presidency, voters saw where his priorities lay.

There were two other appointments—those of Johnnetta Cole and Lani Guinier—that caused great controversy, and Clinton was forced to back off from them. Both were African-American women. Both appointees were viewed by many as radical left-wingers. When the two episodes were finished, Clinton had managed to anger everyone, from liberal Democratic blacks to conservative whites. Few people now recall the controversy over the news that Johnnetta Cole was the leading candidate for the position of secretary of education.[15] Cole's appointment was only stopped because on the very eve of her coming to Washington, the *Forward*, a national Jewish newspaper, broke her story.

Cole was well positioned to get the job. She was president of Spelman College in Atlanta, a highly regarded institution for black women, and sat on the board of directors of many corporations, including the Atlanta-based Coca-Cola as well as other Southern firms. Clinton had already made her the head of the transition team on education, labor, and the humanities, the body which had been given the responsibility of picking the candidates to head the agencies in that cluster, as well as to help re-organize and staff them for the new administration.

The only problem, either overlooked by the administration or regarded by them as unimportant, was that Johnnetta Cole was a long-standing fellow-traveler of the American Communist Party. Using material furnished to him by various sources, including myself, the *Forward*'s Washington editor David Twersky got on the case, and revealed the full story about Cole's views. Cole had been in a leadership position, it turned out, on the pro-Castro Venceremos Brigades, a group that sent American volunteers to work in and support the Castro regime in Cuba. She also held a major position on the executive board of the U.S. Peace Council, the pro-Soviet affiliate of the World Peace Council, the major "peace" organization of the still-existing Communist bloc. Cole responded when the news broke that "right-wing extremists" were after her because she had opposed the war in Vietnam, as well as the U.S. invasion of Grenada.

Yet the *Forward* was hardly right wing; it had endorsed Clinton for president. And unlike Clinton himself, Cole was not part of the mainstream opposition to the war in Vietnam, but in fact was a far-Left radical who openly supported the Communist side. When the folk-singer Joan Baez circulated a petition condemning the victorious North Vietnamese government for human rights violations and massive repression, Cole signed a letter denouncing Baez as "immoral." Printed as an ad in the *New York Times* by the U.S. Peace Council, the statement asserted that under Communist rule, Vietnam "now enjoys human rights as it has never known in history." Ample evidence existed, moreover, to show that Cole had not changed her views as the years passed. For example, she was not just an opponent of the Reagan policy toward Grenada, but was president of the U.S.–Grenada Friendship Society, a Communist-front group that offered support to the Marxist regime of Maurice Bishop. Under her signature, the group had authored a broadside that spoke of "a history of U.S. aggression and genocidal practices against people of color around the world," and that argued that the "hidden agenda" of the government was to "destroy all enemies of corporate America."

The first response of the Clinton administration to the news about Cole's views was, as press secretary Dee Dee Myers explained, that the charges against her were "silly," as well as "something we're just not concerned about." A top aide to Vice President-elect Al Gore added that she had suffered "an unfair smear." And Samuel Berger, soon to be named Deputy National Security Adviser, said the hullabaloo was about the "distant past." This support, however, produced further comments from major national columnists. Evans and Novak noted sarcastically in their syndicated column that "the Clinton administration is truly a big tent that extends to the farthest Left boundaries of the Democratic Party." And in his column in the *New York Post*, editorial page editor Eric Breindel noted that if Cole got an appointment, it would send an "inescapable" message—that the Clinton administration was not "interested in distinguishing between a Left-liberal and someone who cast her lot with the cause of Communist totalitarianism." Cole, of course, continued to receive support from the civil rights establishment, led by Jesse Jackson, who argued that "Jewish complaints" had harmed her chances for a Cabinet appointment.[16]

When it came time to make a decision, Clinton did not stand by Cole. He did not second the views of those who called her a patriot, yet neither did he chastise or drop her from the top slot in his transition team. The question remains unanswered as to why she was appointed to a top transition spot in the first place, and why she almost became Secretary of Education. The answer most probably lies in the connections Cole had with members of Hillary Clinton's inner circle, most especially with Donna Shalala, the new Secretary of Health and Human Services, and Marion Wright Edelman of the Children's Defense Fund, both of whom served on the board of trustees of Spelman College.

If Cole's near appointment was forgotten, that of Lani Guinier proved even more controversial. Guinier, a law professor, was nominated by Clinton to be head of the civil rights division of the Justice Department. Charming, brilliant, and affable, Guinier turned out to have complicated views on the issue of black representation in American politics. Republican opponents quickly branded her the "quota queen," a term that originated with a column in the *Wall Street Journal* written by Clint Bolick, head of the conservative Institute for Justice in Washington, D.C.[17] The term, itself provocative and not accurate, caught on in the press. But Guinier did hypothetically advocate what she called "proportional legislative power," going beyond proportional representation to introduce mechanisms to ensure proportional say in legislative outcomes.

Various critics read through her previously obscure law journal articles—particularly one in the November 1991 *Virginia Law Review* and another, "The Triumph of Tokenism," in the March 1991 *Michigan Law Review*—something that her good friend the president somehow had supposedly never done—and argued whether she advocated quotas for minorities in local legislatures (she did *not*); that minorities should be able to veto laws passed by majorities (she did, by calling for supermajority requirements); that the minorities in question had to be "authentic" blacks (she did *not*, but this was widely misunderstood). As she argued, "each group has a right to have its interests satisfied a fair proportion of the time." Her announced goal was "roughly equal outcomes, not merely an apparently fair process."

As the publicity about and criticism of Guinier grew, the president finally withdrew her nomination, after first responding that he would stand by her and considered her a fine and qualified candidate for the job. Again, it was lose-lose. Again he dropped a former friend; again he angered blacks and whites.

Defenders of the president would argue that once he understood Guinier's views, he did the right thing and did not appoint her, because he stood for color-blind inclusiveness. But other incidents during his first term in office indicated such was not the case. One surrounded Clinton's intervention in the New York mayoralty race between incumbent Mayor David Dinkins and his challenger, Republican Rudolph Giuliani in 1993. There were many local reasons New York City residents were rejecting Dinkins, the first African-American mayor in the city's history. Crime was up, services were deteriorating, and New Yorkers were losing confidence in Dinkins's ability to govern effectively. Facing a strong challenge from Giuliani, the president came to New York, where he intervened on Dinkins's behalf by a bold playing of the race card. In his speech to a Dinkins-for-Mayor dinner, Clinton argued that some whites who did not cast their ballot for the mayor were doing so for racist reasons. Clinton told New Yorkers that "too many of us are still too unwilling to vote for people who are different than we are." Thus, in a campaign for reelection, the president was saying that New Yorkers should vote for Dinkins not because he would be more effective than Giuliani, but because the white voters had to prove they weren't racists by reelecting him. It was, as one reporter noted, the exact "sort of identity politics that [Clinton] claimed to have repudiated during the presidential campaign and that he piously declared was the reason he withdrew his support for Lani Guinier."[18] Thus, the president stood for an old-line Democrat who happened to be black, who ruled on behalf of minority coalitions and public sector unions whose policies were bank-rupting the city's treasury. Four years earlier, Dinkins had won with 25 percent of the white vote. The fact that his support had dropped can hardly be placed at the door of racism.

The Clinton administration kept on supporting quotas. The president's Solicitor-General Drew Days argued that the Supreme Court should make retroactive the Civil Rights Act of 1991, which was based on use of quotas. And the president himself appeared before the Congressional Black Caucus and supported both quota-based black districts for Congress, and the nomination of black historian Mary Berry as chair of the Civil Rights Commission. Berry, because of her work on the commission, was regarded by some as a supporter of quotas.[19] Moreover, the Clinton administration reversed the position of the Bush administration in a case involving the layoff of a white teacher, Sharon Taxman, from a New Jersey school. The layoff was forced by dint of a budget shortfall. The school retained a black teacher, Debra Williams, though both teachers had been hired nine years earlier, and so, by union rules, had exactly the same seniority. Normally, in such a case, the decision would have been made by flipping a coin. The Bush administration had supported action to reinstate the white teacher, who, the school admitted, had been dismissed solely on grounds of her race. But acting with the full support of the President, the assistant attorney general for civil rights Deval Patrick brought legal action on behalf of the Justice Department to support the school board. The problem was that the teacher who got to keep her job was the only black in a nine-member business department. She was kept to promote diversity. Yet in New Jersey as a whole, and in Piscataway, where the case took place, the percentage of black teachers employed was twice that of the existing qualified labor pool. In other words, there was no existing pattern of discrimination within the local school board.

Moreover, as Nat Hentoff has explained, the Clinton policy was an attempt to reverse the Supreme Court's earlier decision that race preferences in teacher layoffs was unconstitutional. To hire someone through affirmative action is to keep its benefits concentrated and its harms diffuse. To *fire* a white, however, is to concentrate the harms intolerably. No wonder Hentoff concluded that once "on the campaign trail, the president will hear a lot about Piscataway."[20]

When he openly addressed the problem of race, the president struggled. That was clear in the speech he delivered on the sensitive topic of affirmative action, a program that had been a staple of the liberal agenda since the days of Lyndon Johnson, and which had, as *U.S. News and World Report* put it, become "a time bomb primed to detonate in the middle of the American political marketplace."[21]

Soon after he assumed the presidency, Clinton made it clear that he would be adopting the traditional Democratic pro-affirmative action position. Speaking to the Leadership Conference on Civil Rights in May of 1993, Clinton defended making appointments by race and gender by declaring that "I have been roundly attacked by people on the extreme right trying to make me look like some radical left-winger because I had this crazy notion that I ought to have an administration that would have some diversity and give women as well as men and people of color . . . the chance to serve if they could meet high standards of excellence." To Clinton, the issue was simply giving every American "a fair chance at the brass ring," and thus he rejected the charge that his administration was giving too much attention "to ethnicity and gender."[22]

But two years later, when the president returned to the theme, it was clear that it was more than the "extreme right wing" that was opposing the very concept of affirmative action. Clinton took a position that waffled between both sides, and satisfied neither. Arguing that affirmative action began as a means to gain "equal opportunity for all Americans," the President continued to list a litany of those discriminated against, including, as he put it, "Hispanics, Asian-Americans, Native Americans, [and] people with disabilities." It sounded like a politically correct list of those victimized who needed help. Clinton was still defining affirmative action as virtuous, a means, as he said, of addressing "the systemic exclusion of individuals of talent on the basis of their gender or race from opportunities to develop, perform, achieve and contribute."

But the president went on to say he was taking a "middle ground," that of keeping affirmative action but rejecting imposition of change by "leveling draconian penalties on employers who didn't meet certain imposed, ultimately arbitrary, and sometimes unachievable quotas." In other words, affirmative action was to be kept, and "done right." That meant a "flexible goal" was not to be viewed as a "quota," nor did it mean that unqualified people received the job of a qualified individual who deserved it. As Clinton put it: "I don't favor the unjustified preference of the unqualified over the qualified of any race or gender," or the use of "numerical quotas." Again, the president supported his hiring on the basis of "diversity," and he dismissed the claims of those who argued that affirmative action did little to help the situation of the black underclass. Acknowledging that some people genuinely felt that "affirmative action always amounts to group preferences over individual merit" and hence leads to reverse discrimination, the president argued that Americans had yet to decide how they felt about the argument. When push came to shove, the president rejected playing "politics with the issue of affirmative action," and decided that affirmative action "remains a useful tool for widening economic and educational opportunity." Hence the slogan that got to the television sound-bites, "Mend it, but don't end it."[23] Caught between the proverbial angry white males and liberal constituencies—polls showed that half of those voters who cast their ballot for Clinton opposed affirmative action—Clinton did what so many expected he would do, act as an arbiter between two hypothetical extremes. As the president's assistant attorney general for civil rights explained, "affirmative action is not always right. But neither is it always wrong."[24]

The problem, however, was in what the president's speech did not say—that the time had come when affirmative action programs were under sustained attack. The very week of his speech, the regents of the University of California voted to restrict racial preferences in admissions, and the Supreme Court's decision in the *Adarand* case a few weeks earlier clearly was going to make it harder to justify "set-aside" programs for minority contractors, a policy the president still said he supported. The question, columnist Joe Klein wrote, was whether Clinton "was simply throwing a pre-emptive bouquet to the Democratic Party's most loyal constituents . . . in order to cement them in place as affirmative action is whittled away in the months to come." Moreover, DLC supporters like Klein argued convincingly that throughout his administration, "competence was sacrificed for 'diversity.'" As Klein put it, "the entire Clinton administration—studded with mediocrities appointed because of *what* rather than *who* they are—is a compelling case study in the perils of affirmative action."[25]

Thus, on the race question, Clinton tried continually to have it both ways. Despite his sympathy with the DLC and the New Democrats, his liberal instincts, and perhaps his understanding that he could not afford to alienate the core liberal constituency groups, led him to endorse policies that were supported only by

Old Democrats. Clinton therefore regularly reached out to the black community and its most militant leadership, only to step back and rebuff them when he received criticism. Clinton, in rejecting his own nomination of Lani Guinier, provided a model for how he operated. He campaigned on the Right, sought to govern from the Left, and when it backfired, he retracted and moved once again toward the Center.

Clinton did succeed in getting Congress to pass a weak crime bill, a move that apparently indicates his push toward the center. But even on that issue, Clinton was pushed in two different directions, one suggested by Bruce Reed, a moderate who is a member of the president's Domestic Policy Council, and in the other direction by Gene Sperling, a traditional liberal who sits on Clinton's National Economic Council. Both men were described by the White House as "the guardians of the Clinton ideology." But these two "guardians" could not agree on what to guard. Reed stressed tough anticrime measures, while Sperling downplayed funds for police in favor of social-service programs. The result was a bill that created some funding for a slight increase nationwide in the police presence in local communities, along with a commitment to social programs widely derided by conservatives, such as sponsorship of "midnight basketball" programs in the inner cities.

The two also disagreed on the question of the budget. The president sided with Sperling, who wanted a stimulus package of government investments, without budget cuts to pay for them. Reed, on the other hand, argued for reduction in government programs before more spending was undertaken. When Clinton's resultant small stimulus investment program was killed in the Senate, he shifted and argued for deficit reduction—resulting in a budget bill that narrowly passed in the Congress. As Reed told the press, speaking of Sperling, "he looks for things that government can do. I look for things that government ought to stop doing." Commenting on their roles, one reporter wrote Clinton was "moving blithely from one end of the Democratic Party's spectrum to the other. Although he's almost invariably inclined at first toward the liberalism of Mr. Sperling, he's willing to move right toward Mr. Reed's moderate stance whenever he senses the political need."[26]

The President's most shining hour, one in which he firmly took the position of the New Democrats, was in the fight for the North American Free Trade Agreement, or NAFTA. As with the New Democrats' positions on race questions, this move required a frontal assault on one of the two core Democrat constituencies—organized labor. Indeed, the President won plaudits for his role in the fight from none other than one of Newt Gingrich's most prominent supporters, Vin Weber, the former conservative Republican congressman from Minnesota. "In fighting for NAFTA," Weber wrote, "he bucked the intense opposition of organized labor and the liberal establishment of his party, and succeeded in passing his first notable 'New Democrat' initiative. It was a major victory—and a major shift in direction for a president who had all but abandoned the New Democrat agenda he campaigned on a year ago."[27]

Weber was right. Not only had Clinton faced the opposition of the AFL-CIO, which made defeat of NAFTA a priority, but the fierce opposition on the Republican populist right coming from Pat Buchanan, who played to the insecurity felt by the white working class by arguing for protectionism. And, of course, Clinton faced the strong fight against NAFTA waged by Ross Perot, who argued that passage of the bill would mean the disappearance of thousands of the jobs of American workers. The bitter truth, however, was that Clinton was able to pass the NAFTA legislation only because he had molded together a coalition of centrist Democrats and centrist Republicans, who together bucked the left and right extremes of their own parties. For the party as a whole, therefore, the problem of the New Democrats is that they defined themselves in opposition to the only remaining Old Democrats. They needed to find an issue by which to define themselves as *Democrats*, not Republicans.

Perhaps because it avoided direct conflict with either blacks or labor, Clinton chose as the centerpiece of his first two years an ambitious new initiative on health care. Here, when all was said and done, was a litmus test of liberalism's fortunes. Would the instincts of those who wanted to expand government, and expand the safety net, be sound? Could they forge a mighty coalition to push the required legislative monstrosity?

No, they could not. The group that put together the White House proposals, led by Hillary Clinton and Ira Magaziner, created a massive and complicated structure that was doomed to defeat—one that would have forced citizens into HMOs, deprived them of free choice of doctors, and guaranteed universal coverage by decreasing the level of medical support. What Clinton and New Democrats might have supported, instead of standing behind a plan that was doomed to collapse, was a more limited program to create coverage for uninsured Americans, while allowing the market to function to protect medical quality and citizens' right of free choice. A plan introduced by Rep. Jim Cooper and backed by the DLC might have provided such an option. Cooper's managed competition plan relied on market incentives and rejected government mandates on employers. The president and his wife, however, opposed the Cooper-DLC plan, because it did not address true universal coverage, a definition that kept shifting, but in the end appeared to mean 95% or more of all citizens. Though Clinton rejected the so-called single-payer Canadian-style plan advocated by the far Left, he failed to pay attention to the great national dissatisfaction emerging from the critics. The Clinton-Magaziner plan, after hundreds of hours of planning and discussion, involving hundreds of people, died a painful death in Congress.[28]

In the midterm election of November 1994, the Republicans picked up seats in Congress, taking control of both houses for the first time since 1944. Some said the "Reagan realignment" had finally been accomplished. With Newt Gingrich as the new Speaker of the House, the leverage in Washington had shifted to the Congress, and for the time being, the executive branch was only capable of responding to Republican initiatives.

Scores of Democrats went down to defeat in November, including moderates like Rep. Dave McCurdy of Oklahoma, who then moved on to head the DLC. Even worse things were to follow. After the November election, nearly two hundred Democrats nationwide shifted to the Republican Party. And two of the Democrats' most prominent senators—Bill Bradley of New Jersey and Sam Nunn of Georgia, decided to leave the Senate as of 1996. In his August speech, Bradley, an independent Democrat who had even voted for support to the Nicaraguan *contras* during the Central American wars of the eighties, declared to his constituents his belief that "politics is broken," and that while Republicans were infatuated with the private sector, Democrats "distrust the market, preach government as the answer to our problems, and prefer the bureaucrat they know to the consumer they can't control." His own party had joined the Republicans, Bradley said, in moving away from a concept of service.[29]

Bradley's defection was important not just for residents of New Jersey, and, as Michael Wines of the *New York Times* explained, was not just a straw in the wind. "It foreshadows," Wines wrote, "the end of the Democratic Party as Americans know it today." Bradley, at that moment, was the sixth Senate

Democrat to announce his retirement in 1994, and he would be followed by others. Two Democrats had already left their party for the Republican side of the Senate, and the Democrats were four seats away from their lowest number in seventy years.[30]

When Sam Nunn announced his retirement, one commentator from his state wrote, "Georgia's political landscape must look to the Democrats like Hiroshima after the bomb." His seat would most likely go to any solid Republican candidate. The old solid (Democratic) South was no more. As the editorial columnist for the major Atlanta paper explained, if Nunn were running for the first time in 1995, "it is dead certain he would be a Republican." In 1972, when Nunn first ran for the Senate, he went about his state taking down "McGovern for President" signs. He was "the last true centrist left on the hill," at least among Democrats.[31]

His decision to leave the Senate and public service indicated a profound disappointment with the Clinton administration. Sam Nunn had been a key supporter of Bill Clinton. He worked to have Clinton replace him as chairman of the DLC, and he endorsed him for president in 1991, early in the game. His own hopes for revival of the Democratic Party rested on Clinton. At odds with the extreme right Congressional Republicans, and dismayed with Clinton's inability to create a new centrist model for the Democratic Party, Sam Nunn took the only honorable course he saw open—that of leaving the U.S. Senate.

Virtually all of the events in this book bode ill for the future of the Democratic Party. This is not to say that Clinton cannot win reelection. But decades of dominance since the New Deal in Washington and among voters generally, have long since ended. The party seems to have no principles, and no reason to attract followers except in opposition to excesses of Republicans. Not only is it likely to remain a minority party, the question has to be raised whether it can survive any longer as the second party in a two-party system. For a time, when Colin Powell was considering a run for the presidency, there loomed a real possibility of transforming the Republican Party into a new moderate centrist party, one that could hold the allegiance of people like Bill Bradley and Sam Nunn, as well as Republicans like Bill Bennett and William Kristol. Were that to happen, the extreme Right, led by Pat Buchanan, along with some on the Christian Right, might have defected to form their own political force—and these new entities would become the main contenders in a realignment not seen in our nation since the 1860s. With Powell on the sidelines, that sort of sudden shift is unlikely—but it still could happen in time.

Of great importance is the loss of the South to the Republicans, which means not only a loss of Democratic seats in the House and Senate, but a loss of moderate to conservative Democrats, as well as of the party's status as a national party. And as Democrats continue to support affirmative action, their support among the white middle classes is hurt. Furthermore, black conservatism has been increasing (albeit from minuscule levels). The Republicans' whites-only image is beginning to dissipate, as the Congress sees new members such as J.C. Watts, the representative from Oklahoma, and Gary Franks, the representative from Connecticut.

There is also the problem of funding. Corporate and trade association money flows to incumbents, who are now Republicans. More and more, the one constituency group with money for Democrats is the one they have been counting on since the FDR era: the AFL-CIO. In late October of 1995, the trade union federation entered a new era, as its membership elected John Sweeney as its new president. Pledging to use activist tactics not seen by labor since the 1930s, and to spend most of the organization's budget on massive membership drives, Sweeney noted that the union movement would begin to use civil disobedience and mass marches. His first day in office was begun with a mass march to New York's garment district. At the public rally, Sweeney was joined by Labor Secretary Robert Reich, who brought the AFL-CIO delegates the strongest pro-labor message to come from the administration since Clinton's assuming the presidency. Reich told the cheering throngs that the president would veto a list of bills that organized labor considers anti-union, and he told the assembled workers to "organize, mobilize, and energize to restore the American dream to all America."[32] As one perceptive news reporter wrote, the Sweeney election "will spell trouble for the Democrats in the form of a newly energized movement determined to settle accounts with an administration in Washington that left labor in the lurch, on, among other things, the North American Free Trade Agreement and the striker-replacement bill."[33]

Thus the Mine Workers leader Richard Trumka, who was to become secretary-treasurer of the AFL-CIO, castigated the DLC in a speech to the Americans for Democratic Action, calling their agenda "antiworker" as well as a "blueprint for Democratic disaster in 1996."[34] In 1996, the public employee unions and the Hollywood liberal elite will likely be the main backers of the Democratic Party—and it will be to these elements that any would-be candidate will have to turn for support.

Today, as the eminent political scientist Walter Dean Burnham told the press, "the Democratic Party has essentially run out of options." Predicting a new realignment of parties, Burnham thought that 1994's events entailed "a collapse of their credibility." The problem was clear. The heart of the old Democratic ideology was reliance on government to better the condition of the underdog. But with deficits growing, the public had come to understand that the continuing flow of money no longer was available. Moreover, the voters were turning against such a political stance. As Bill Daley of the Chicago Democratic Party put it, "whatever we thought the Democratic Party was, that's over. The only message we've got is the same one we had in November: The Republicans are going to cut Social Security and Medicare. People look at it and say, 'forget it. We don't buy that.'"[35]

For all these reasons, the Democratic Party finds itself at a crossroads. Bereft of ideas, its leaders seem only to be able to respond to unpopular Republican initiatives, or to try and rescue policies that were once poplar Democratic mainstays, but now have been revealed as problematic, if not altogether worthless. Some Democrats, especially those of the DLC, have tried in vain to formulate a vague kind of "third way," a potpourri of limited federal programs combined with a decisive effort to dismantle existing unnecessary agencies, government bureaucracies, and programs.

In the 1930s, when the issue was the Great Depression and the collapse of the market system, Democrats knew what to stand for. Since the 1920s, labor's rights had been suppressed, and a newly resurgent industrial unionism became the focus of the popular strength of the FDR New Deal Democrats. The New Deal, above all, gave organized labor its rights, and allowed working men and women to find their rightful place and representation in our political and economic system.

In the 1990s, America is no longer the blue-collar workplace it once had been. Smokestack industries have been replaced by high-tech firms. The remaining blue-collar workforce finds itself prone to insecurity and the threat of permanent unemployment. If jobs exist, they are to be found in the low-paying service industries. At the same time, membership in the union movement has declined tremendously, with most of the workforce now unorganized. Resentful over their plight, for understandable reasons, the remnants of the American working class are as likely to turn for support and understanding to a right-wing populist like Pat Buchanan as they are to the political Left and the ranks of Jesse Jackson's and John Sweeney's troops. Moreover, since a capitalist mixed economy is the only game in town, whatever the rhetoric of those trying to rebuild a labor-liberal coalition and to form a new Left, their efforts are bound to be in vain.

If the organized labor movement espouses some form of radicalism and gains the support of some intellectuals, its shift is hardly likely to gather mass popular support in the nation at large. Such a move would more likely further alienate middle American ethnics who supported the Democrats in the past as a way to enter the nation's mainstream. Like the middle class, working Americans seek to benefit from the creation of new wealth, and not to enter a movement that bases its policy on redistribution of existing wealth. As George McGovern so rudely found, calling for redistributionist schemes is more than likely to drive these groups right to the Republicans. Poll after poll has shown that the major recent losses of the Democrats came from the ranks of those white men who had only high school degrees and who were deeply worried about their economic well-being. And these men saw themselves as part of the suburban middle-class, a group that also looked askance at what they considered to be the cultural liberalism of the Democrats.

The Democrats hoped that somehow they would be able to regain the allegiance of their lost troops. But the problem for the party was that funding depended on the allegiance of just those old-line constituency groups whose policies the white ethnics hated most. And if a Democratic president moved to satisfy these interest groups, as well as the Congressional Democrats aligned with them, he would only further alienate precisely those people whose votes he needed to stay in power. Bill Clinton, for one, tried to be a president who showed the middle class that the Democratic Party had changed. But, despite his best intentions, he was subject to institutional pressures that were difficult to withstand. If he decides to back a good part of the Republican agenda and return to the kind of traditional Democratic policies that have middle-class appeal, he would endanger his Hollywood and union funding.

Whatever direction Bill Clinton or any other future Democratic candidate decides to adopt, the fact is that in America of the 1990s, the Democratic Party as a whole has shifted to the Left, precisely at the moment when the Republican Party has shifted toward the Right. That means that the old political Center has eroded once and for all—a fact that has led many Americans to hope for the creation of a new political party of the Center, the kind that might be led by the likes of Bill Bradley, Colin Powell, or Sam Nunn.

It has been the thesis of this book that the Democratic Party, ripped asunder by division and conflict, has collapsed beyond repair. Candidates may seek to rescue their own candidacy by carefully shifting between Left and Right, making their moves according to whatever direction their pollsters advise them to take. But while such strategic maneuvering may result occasionally in political victory, it is not the same thing as rebuilding a party whose base has eroded and whose basic constituency groups are permanently at odds with each other. That task, this writer believes, is insurmountable. The Democratic Party may continue to exist as a permanent minority party, or even as a sectarian small grouping whose remaining members have shifted far to the Left. But sooner or later, America faces a yet unknown political realignment, one that will create new political mechanisms that reflect the interests of the post–Cold War America, and that stands for fiscal and personal responsibility, cultural conservatism, and a more limited and constrained social safety net. The breakup of what once had been a proud majority party, the Democratic Party, shows that such a time is near at hand.

REFERENCES

Introduction

1. Adam Garfinkle, *Telltale Hearts: The Origins and Impact of the Vietnam Antiwar Movement* (New York: St. Martin's Press, 1995), p. 281.
2. Thomas Byrne Edsall and Mary D. Edsall, *Chain Reaction: The Impact of Race, Rights, and Taxes on American Politics* (New York: W. W. Norton and Co., 1991), p. 72.

Chapter 1. Atlantic City 1964

1. "Challenge of the Mississippi Freedom Democratic Party," cited in Herbert Parmet, *The Democrats: The Years After F.D.R.* (New York: Macmillan Publishing Co., 1976), p. 235.

2. Juan Williams, *Eyes on the Prize: America's Civil Rights Years: 1945–1965* (New York: The Viking Press, 1987), p. 208.

3. Interview with Jeane Kirkpatrick by Ben Wattenberg, June 2, 1988; transcript of outtakes from PBS-TV documentary, "The Democrats: A Quarter Century of Change," produced by Michael Pack and Ben Wattenberg for Manifold Productions, Inc. Used by permission of Ben Wattenberg and Michael Pack. All other interviews conducted by Ben Wattenberg come from these same outtakes.

4. Quoted in Clayborne Carson, *In Struggle: SNCC and the Black Awakening of the 1960s* (Cambridge, MA: Harvard University Press, 1981,) p. 125.

5. Interview with Joseph Rauh by Anne Cooke Romaine, June 16, 1967; Joseph Rauh MSS, box 86, Library of Congress, Washington, D.C.

6. See, for example, the discussion by historian Robert Weisbrot, *Freedom Bound: A History of America's Civil Rights Movement* (New York: W. W. Norton and Co., 1989), p. 118. Weisbrot charges that Rauh capitulated to Johnson because he did not want to jeopardize the support of Hubert Humphrey for the legislative goals of both the UAW and the ADA. "However sympathetic to the Freedom Party's cause," Weisbrot writes, "Rauh felt the stronger pull of Hubert Humphrey."

7. Joseph Rauh, "Memo on the Mississippi Freedom Democratic Party" 1972, Joseph Rauh MSS, box 36.

8. *Ibid.*

9. Quoted in Juan Williams, *op.cit.*, pp. 235; 241.

10. *Ibid.*, p. 242.

11. Quoted in Clayborne Carson, *op.cit.*, p. 125.

12. *Ibid.*, p. 126.

13. Joseph Rauh, Testimony to the Credentials Committee, Aug. 22, 1964; Joseph Rauh MSS, box 86.

14. Rauh, Interview with Anne Cooke Romaine, June 16, 1967; Joseph Rauh MSS, Box 86. Rauh, way after the events, wrote one correspondent that "Humphrey never once asked me for a single concession to help him win the high post he now holds." Rauh to Leslie McLemore, June 16, 1965, Joseph Rauh MSS, box 86.

15. *Ibid.*

16. Juan Williams, *op.cit.*, p. 243; Interview of Joe Rauh by Ann Cooke Romaine, June 16, 1967, Joseph Rauh MSS, box 86.

17. Robert Weisbrot, *op.cit.*, p. 121.

18. Quoted in Clayborne Carson, *op.cit.*, p. 127.

19. James Forman, *The Making of Black Revolutionaries* (New York: The Macmillan Co., 1972), p. 389. Others speaking for the administration compromise included the liberal activist Allard Lowenstein, Mississippi civil rights leader Aaron Henry, Jack Pratt and Robert Spike of the National Council of Churches, Senator Wayne Morse of Oregon, James Farmer of the Congress of Racial Equality (CORE), and Rauh.

20. *Ibid.*, p. 392; c.f., Weisbrot, *op.cit.*, p. 123; Rustin subsequently wrote up his comments as what became an influential article, "From Protest to Politics," *Commentary*, February 1965. The article is reprinted in Bayard Rustin, *Down the Line: The Collected Writings of Bayard Rustin* (Chicago: Quadrangle Books, 1971.)

21. James Forman, *op.cit.*, p. 392.

22. *Ibid.*, pp. 395–396.

23. *Ibid.*, p. 399.

24. *Ibid.*, pp. 405–406.

25. Charles Sherrod, "Mississippi at Atlantic City, *Grain of Salt* (Union Theological Seminary), Oct. 12, 1964; pp. 9–11.

26. Joe Rauh, "Memo on the Freedom Democratic Party," 1972, Joseph Rauh MSS, box 36.

27. Interview by Anne Cooke Romaine with Joe Rauh, June 16, 1967, Joseph Rauh MSS, box 86.

28. William Colmer to John McCormack, June 18, 1965; quoted in Herbert Parmet, *op.cit.*, p. 239.

29. See the discussion in Clayborne Carson, *op.cit.*, p. 125.

30. Evans and Novak, "Freedom Party Postscript," *Washington Post*, Sept. 3, 1964.

31. *Congressional Record*, U.S. Senate, Feb. 3, 1965, III, Part 2, pp. 1948–50.

32. *Newsweek*, April 12, 1965, p. 31.

33. See the columns by Evans and Novak, "Danger from the Left," the *Washington Post*, March 18, 1965; "A Long Look at SNICK," [sic] *Washington Post*, April 9, 1965; and "SNCC Head Denies Control by Reds," the *Washington Post*, March 28, 1965.

34. C. Vann Woodward, "After Watts—Where is The Negro Revolution Headed?" *New York Times Magazine*, Aug. 29, 1965, p. 82.

35. Joe Rauh, "Memo on the Mississippi Freedom Democratic Party," 1972, Joseph Rauh MSS, Box 36.

36. Joe Rauh, "*Memorandum for the Vice President Elect*," Dec. 24, 1964, Joseph Rauh MSS, box 86. Rauh was later to tell Vice President Humphrey that Baker "cut me to ribbons as an appeaser in terms I had not heard since our debates with the Wallace people back in 1948." Rauh, "*Memorandum for the Vice President Elect*," Dec. 24, 1964, Joseph Rauh MSS, box 86.

37. Arthur Waskow to Joe Rauh, Sept. 4, 1964, Joseph Rauh MSS, box 86.

38. Tristram Coffin to Joe Rauh, Aug. 31, 1964, Joseph Rauh MSS, box 86.

39. Marcus Raskin to Joe Rauh, Sept. 9, 1964, Joseph Rauh MSS, box 86.

40. Rauh to Leslie McLemore, June 16, 1965, Joseph Rauh MSS, box 86.

41. Stokely Carmichael and Charles V. Hamilton, *Black Power: The Politics of Liberation in America* (New York: Vintage Books, 1967), p. 96.

42. Lawrence Guyot and Mike Thelwell, "The Politics of Necessity and Survival in Mississippi," *Freedomways*, VI, no. 2 (Spring 1966), p. 132.

43. See, for example, Robert Gabriner, "The Deferred Moment," *Connections* (Madison, WI), March 16–31, 1967. Gabriner, a New Left activist and editor of a local movement paper, made just such a complaint.

44. See the discussion in Robert Weisbrot, *op.cit.*, pp. 222–261; quote on p. 253; c.f., Clayborne Carson, *op.cit*, pp. 175–190.

Chapter 2. The New Politics Convention

1. Jonathan Kaufman, *Broken Alliance: The Turbulent Times Between Blacks and Jews in America* (New York: Charles Scribner's Sons, 1988) p. 207.

2. Quoted in Kaufman, *op.cit.*, p. 202.

3. "Third World Round Up: The Palestine Problem: Test Your Knowledge," *SNCC Newsletter*, June–July 1967, pp. 4–5.; c.f., *New York Times*, Aug. 15, 1967; *Newsweek*, Aug. 28, 1967.

4. James Forman, "*The Making of Black Revolutionaries* (New York: Macmillan, 1972), p. 496.

5. Quoted in Jonathan Kaufman, *op.cit.*, pp. 208–209.

6. Martin Luther King, Jr., "Declaration of Independence from the War in Vietnam," in Banning Garrett and Katherine Barkley, eds., *Two, Three . . . Many Vietnams* (San Francisco: Canfield Press, 1971), pp. 206–215.

7. David Garrow, *Bearing the Cross: Martin Luther King, Jr., and the Southern Christian Leadership Conference* (New York: Morrow, 1986), pp. 546–547.

8. Quoted in *Ibid.*, p. 547.

9. The *New York Times*, April 2, 1967, p. 1.

10. See David Garrow, *op.cit.*, pp. 553–554.

11. "*Report on National Conference for New Politics Convention*, Chicago, August 29–September 4, 1967" by Sanford Gottlieb, Political Action Director, SANE; Allard Lowenstein MSS, Southern Historical Collection, Univ. of North Carolina Library, Chapel Hill, NC. All quotes from Gottlieb come from this document.

12. Arthur I. Waskow, "Notes on Chicago," Sept. 12, 1967; Lowenstein papers #4340. All citations from Waskow come from this report.

13. Richard Blumenthal, "New Politics at Chicago," *Nation*, Sept. 25, 1967; pp. 273–276.

14. Quoted in Kaufman, *op.cit.*, p. 210.

15. See Gottlieb, *op.cit.*, p. 6; Blumenthal, *op.cit.*, p. 274.

16. Gottlieb, *op.cit.*, p. 4; Kaufman, *op.cit.*, p. 210.

17. Waskow, *op.cit.*, p. 2.

18. Cited in Goodman, *op.cit.*, p. 124.

19. Gottlieb, *op.cit.*, p. 6

20. Goodman, *op.cit.*, p. 125.

21. *Ibid.*, p. 125.

22. Quoted in Kaufman, *op.cit.*, p. 209.
23. Gottlieb, *op.cit.*, p. 11.
24. Goodman, *op.cit.*, p. 127.
25. Gottlieb, *op.cit.*, p. 12–13.
26. Waskow, *op.cit.*, pp. 5–6.
27. *Ibid.*, p. 127–128.
28. Blumenthal, *op.cit.*, p. 276.

Chapter 3. Vietnam

1. Arthur M. Schlesinger, Jr., Keynote Speech to the 1965 ADA Convention, April 2, 1965; ADA MSS, unprocessed collection, ADA papers, ADA National Office, Washington, D.C.; cited in Steven M. Gillon, *Politics and Vision: The ADA and American Liberalism, 1947–1985* (New York: Oxford University Press, 1987), p. 169. Steven Gillon has written the definitive history of the postwar disputes surrounding American liberalism. I am deeply indebted to his pioneering work.
2. Godfrey Hodgson, *America In Our Time* (Garden City, NY: Doubleday and Co., 1976); p. 275.
3. Adam Garfinkle, *Telltale Hearts: The Origins and Impact of the Vietnam Antiwar Movement* (New York: St. Martin's Press, 1995), pp. 73–75.
4. Speech of Allard Lowenstein at Queens College, New York; 1965; Allard Lowenstein MSS, Series 7, Subseries 2–3, box 171; University of North Carolina at Chapel Hill.
5. *Ibid.*
6. Text of speech by Hubert Humphrey to the Americans for Democratic Action, *ADA World* (Vol. 21, no. 5) May 1966.
7. Charley Wiggins to Lowenstein, Sept. 21, 1966; Allard Lowenstein MSS, Series 1, subseries 1, box 10, Folder 357.

8. Margie (no second name) to Lowenstein, 1966; *Ibid.*

9. Text of draft for a speech, Jan. 19, 1967; *Ibid.*, Folder 365.

10. Text of article by Hubert Humphrey, *Pageant*, Oct. 1966, in *Ibid.*, Series 2, Subseries 2–3, box 171.

11. Draft Statement of ADA position on Vietnam, in Fraser to Lowenstein, Dec. 16, 1966; in *Ibid.*, Series 2, Subseries 21–22, Folder 448, box 34.

12. Steven M. Gillon, p. 191.

13. Quoted in *Ibid.*, p. 197. John P. Roche to Mavin Watson, April 1967.

14. Quoted in *Ibid.*, p. 197. "Notes on the Convention," Gus Tyler, April 1967, ADA Papers, State Historical Society of Wisconsin, Madison, WI.

15. Quoted in *Ibid.*, p. 193. Gillon cites several Tyler sources, including Tyler, "Johnson and the Intellectuals," *Midstream*, (Aug.–Sept. 1967), pp. 34–35, and Tyler to Galbraith, May 25, 1967; Tyler to Schlesinger, June 15, 1967; Tyler to Richard Goodwin, June 15, 1967; Tyler to Galbraith, May 23, 1967 and Tyler to Wechsler, July 6, 1967.

16. Gus Tyler to John Kenneth Galbraith, May 25, 1967; Allard Lowenstein MSS, Folder 448.

17. Quoted in Steven Gillon, p. 198. Gillon cites Tyler to Galbraith, May 25, 1967; Tyler to Schlesinger, June 15, 1967; and Tyler to Goodwin, June 15, 1967; Tyler to Galbraith, May 23, 1967; Tyler to Wechsler, July 7, 1967.

18. *Ibid.*, p. 198–199; Gillon cites Loeb to Tyler, June 16, 1967.

19. *Ibid.*, p. 199. Gillon cites Schlesinger to Tyler, June 13, 1967.

20. Galbraith to unnamed friend, June 1967, Joseph Rauh MSS, box 11, ADA folder 19.

21. Tyler to Schlesinger, July 6, 1967; Joseph Rauh MSS, box 11 June-Dec. 1967 Folder.

22. Douglas to Galbraith, June 13, 1967, Joseph Rauh MSS, box 11, June-Dec. 1967 Folder.

23. Roche to John Spiegel, June 26, 1967; *Ibid.*, p. 201.

24. Arthur M. Schlesinger, Jr., Memo to Subscribers of the ADA National Board, June 16, 1967; Allard Lowenstein MSS, Series 2, Subseries 21–22, box 34.

25. James Wechsler, "Fighting Issue," *New York Post*, July 6, 1967.

26. Tyler to Wechsler, July 7, 1967, Allard Lowenstein MSS, #4340.

27. Quoted in Steven Gillon, pp. 201–202.

28. Joe Rauh, *"A Proposal to Maximize Political Support for an End to the War in Vietnam*, July 28, 1967; Allard Lowenstein MSS, #4340.

29. *Ibid.*

30. Allard Lowenstein, "Comments on the Rauh Memorandum," Sept. 1967, Lowenstein MSS, #4340.

31. John P. Roche to Lyndon B. Johnson, Sept. 25, 1967, quoted in Steven Gillon, pp. 202–203.

32. Rauh to Gus Tyler, June 17, 1967, Joseph Rauh MSS, box 11.

33. Rauh to Mrs. Robert S. Benjamin, Dec. 21, 1967, Joseph Rauh MSS, Box 11. June-Dec. folder.

34. Rauh to Mrs. Paul G. Meyerson, Dec. 15, 1967; *Ibid.*

Chapter 4. McCarthy and the Quixotic Campaign

1. Carl Oglesby, "Trapped in the System," text of speech delivered at the October 1965 March on Washington, in Massimo Teodori, *The New Left: A Documentary History* (Indianapolis and New York: Bobbs-Merrill Co., 1969) pp. 182–188; c.f., Adam Garfinkle, *Telltale Hearts: The Origins*

and Impact of the Vietnam Antiwar Movement (New York: St. Martin's Press, 1995), pp. 80–81.

2. See, for example, Paul Breines, ed., *Critical Interruptions: New Left Perspectives on Herbert Marcuse* (New York: Herder and Herder, 1970).

3. Carl Oglesby, "An Open Letter to McCarthy Supporters," 1968; in Massimo Teodori, ed., *The New Left: A Documentary History*, pp. 445–450. All citations from Oglesby which follow are from this document. Oglesby's document was influential in New Left circles. This author recalls giving out the pamphlet on college campuses in the New York area, in the hope that it would deflect activists from working with the McCarthy campaign.

4. Herbert S. Parmet, *The Democrats: The Years After FDR* (New York: Macmillan, 1976), pp. 248–249.

5. *Wall Street Journal,* Nov. 1, 1967, p. 16.

6. Gerald N. Hill to General James Gavin, Aug. 9, 1967, Lowenstein MSS, Series 3, Subseries 6, box 54.

7. Cited in Charles Kaiser, *1968 in America* (New York: Weidenfeld and Nicolson, 1988), pp. 38–39.

8. *Ibid.,* p. 39.

9. Jack Newfield, "A Time of Plague," *The Village Voice,* Dec. 28, 1967.

10. Peter Mandler to Lowenstein, Nov. 16, 1967, Lowenstein MSS, box 89.

11. Albert Glotzer to Rauh, Oct. 30, 1967, Rauh MSS, box 29.

12. Rauh to Glotzer, Nov. 24, 1967, *Ibid.*

13. Rauh to Mrs. Paul G. Myerson, Dec. 15, 1967, *Ibid.,* box 11, June-Dec. 1967 folder.

14. Marilyn Gottlieb to Carl Auerbach, Sept. 28, 1967, Rauh MSS, box 30.

15. Interview with Allard Lowenstein, Eugene McCarthy Historical Project MSS, Georgetown Univ., Washington, D.C.
16. Martin Peretz, text of article for the March-April 1968 Dissent, Peretz files, Eugene McCarthy Historical Project MSS, box 43, Georgetown University Library, Washington, D.C.
17. Peretz to McCarthy, Dec. 22, 1967; *Ibid.*
18. *Ibid.*
19. Peretz to Eugene McCarthy, Feb. 8, 1968. Eugene McCarthy Historical Project MSS, box 43.
20. The best discussions of the McCarthy campaign and candidacy are to be found in Charles Kaiser, *1968 in America* (New York: Weidenfeld and Nicolson, 1988), and Irwin Unger and Debi Unger, *Turning Point: 1968* (New York: Scribners, 1988). My account is based on the narrative in both of these books.
21. Charles Kaiser, *op.cit.*, p. 83.
22. Interview with Allard Lowenstein, Eugene McCarthy Historical Project MSS, Georgetown University, Washington, D.C.
23. Eugene McCarthy, *Year of the People* (Garden City, NY: Doubleday and Co., 1969), pp. 58–59.
24. *Ibid.*, pp. 268–269.
25. Kaiser, *op.cit.*, p. 95.
26. Interview with Gerry Studds, McCarthy Historical Project MSS; c.f., Kaiser, *op.cit.*, pp. 103–105.
27. Interview with Allard Lowenstein, *Ibid.*
28. Cited in William H. Chafe, *Never Stop Running: Allard Lowenstein and the Struggle to Save American Liberalism* (New York: Basic Books, 1993), p. 270; c.f., Arthur M. Schlesinger, Jr., *Robert Kennedy and His Times* (Boston: Houghton Mifflin, 1978), pp. 824–825.

29. Chafe, *op.cit.*, p. 272.

30. Arnold S. Kaufman, *"Why Kennedy Candidacy is a Good Thing for McCarthy Supporters,"* Allard Lowenstein Papers, #4340.

31. Chafe, *op.cit.*, p. 282.

32. *Ibid.*, p. 284

33. Quoted in Kaiser, *op.cit.*, pp. 108–109.

34. The New York Post, March 26, 1968.

35. Irwin and Debi Unger, *op.cit.*, p. 341.

36. James Wechsler "Behind ADA's McCarthy Vote," *New York Post*, Feb. 12, 1968; c.f., Gillion, *op.cit.*, pp. 208–209.

37. Mike Armstrong to Lowenstein, March 27, 1968; Lowenstein MSS, Folder 388, box 11.

38. Eugene McCarthy interview with Ben Wattenberg, June 14, 1988; used by permission of Manifold Productions.

39. Richard M. Scammon and Ben J. Wattenberg, *The Real Majority: An Extraordinary Examination of the American Electorate* (New York: Coward-McCann, 1970), pp. 138–139. c.f.; Kaiser, *op.cit.*, pp. 180. Kaiser calls Kennedy's attack "a none-too-subtle appeal to white racism." It was, rather, as Scammon and Wattenberg pointed out, Kennedy's grabbing onto the social issue; i.e., "the awareness that the great majority of the electorate is unyoung, unpoor and unblack; the need to drive to the center. . . ."

40. Seymour Martin Lipset to Marty Peretz, March 20, 1968; Eugene McCarthy Historical Project, Peretz collection, box 43.

41. *Time*, April 12, 1968.

42. Schlesinger to David Ginsburg, July 9, 1968, Rauh MSS.

43. Humphrey to Schlesinger, July 19, 1968; *Ibid.*

44. Schlesinger to Humphrey, July 19, 1968; *Ibid.*

45. Marvin Rosenberg to Joseph Rauh, Aug. 6, 1968, Rauh MSS.

46. Rauh to Rosenberg, Aug. 6, 1968, *Ibid.*
47. Peretz memo, 10/17/68; in Eugene McCarthy Historical Project, Peretz collection, box 43.
48. Enclosed in *Ibid.*
49. Lawrence W. Levine to Schlesinger, June 10, 1968; National Files, box 50, *Ibid.*
50. Chafe, *op.cit.*, p. 273.
51. *Ibid.*, p. 275.

Chapter 5. The Chicago Convention

1. Stephen A. Mitchell, Memo to the Eugene McCarthy file, April 22, 1968, box 100, Stephen A. Mitchell MSS, Harry S Truman Library, Independence, MO.
2. Stephen A. Mitchell to Eugene McCarthy, March 29, 1968; Stephen A. Mitchell MSS, box 97.
3. "Introduction," Stephen A. Mitchell MSS, box 101.
4. Herbert Parmet, *op.cit.*, p. 277. I am indebted to the discussion of Stephen Mitchell's role at the 1968 convention, which was first discussed in Professor Parmet's book on the Democratic Party.
5. Donald O. Peterson to Michael V. DiSalle, Aug. 3, 1968, Mitchell MSS, box 98.
6. Stephen A. Mitchell, "Memo to: McCarthy file," July 9, 1968, Stephen A. Mitchell MSS, box 100, Harry S Truman Library, Independence, MO. Mitchell's reference to Coxey's army was an allusion to Jacob Coxey's 1898 March on Washington, in which Civil War veterans threatened to take arms against the federal government unless it met their demands.
7. *Ibid.*
8. Stephen A. Mitchell, Memorandum, June 18, 1968, Mitchell MSS.

References

9. Herbert S. Parmet, *The Democrats*, pp. 277–278.

10. *New York Times*, Aug. 28, 1968; cited in *Ibid.*, p. 280.

11. Mitchell to Donald C. McKinlay, Sept. 4, 1968, Mitchell MSS, box 97.

12. Jean S. Calhoun to Mitchell, Aug. 8, 1968, Mitchell MSS, box 100.

13. National Commission on the Causes and Prevention of Violence, *Rights in Conflict* (New York: Bantam Books, 1968), p. 4.

14. Abbie Hoffman, *Revolution for the Hell of It* (New York: The Dial Press, 1968), p. 102.

15. Henry Anderson, "The Case Against Drug Culture," *Liberation*, April 1967, p. 36.

16. Kirkpatrick Sale, *SDS* (New York: Random House, 1973), p. 474; c.f., interview with Tom Hayden, *Rolling Stone*, Oct. 21, 1972.

17. Tom Hayden, *Reunion: A Memoir* (New York: Random House, 1988), p. 309.

18. *Ibid.*, p. 324.

19. David Farber, *Chicago '68* (Chicago and London, Univ. of Chicago Press, 1988). Unless otherwise indicated, the following discussion is based upon material presented by Farber in his book.

20. Nigel Young, *An Infantile Disorder? Crisis and Decline of the New Left* (Boulder, CO: Westview Press, 1977), p. 208.

21. *Ibid.*, p. 221.

22. Quoted in Farber, p. 81.

23. Rennie Davis and Tom Hayden, "Movement Campaign 1968: An Election Year Offensive," March 1968; quoted in *Ibid.*, p. 90.

24. Tom Hayden, *Rebellion and Repression* (New York: Random

House, 1969), p. 182. Hayden quotes from a 1968 *Ramparts* article, titled "Two, Three, Many Columbias."

25. Tom Hayden, "The Cops and the Convention," and "Democracy is in the Streets," *Rat Convention Special,* July 1968, pp. 2–5. *Rat* was a counterculture radical newspaper published on the Lower East Side of New York City.

26. Quoted in Kaiser, *op.cit.*, p. 241. From Memorandum from Marie Ridder to Theodore H. White, "Wednesday night, [8/28/68] Theodore H. White Archive, Harvard University, Cambridge, Mass.

27. *Ibid,* p. 241. c.f., *New York Times,* Aug. 29, 1968, p. 1.

28. Tom Hayden, "The Reason Why," *Ramparts Wall Poster,* Aug. 24, 1968.

29. Jason Epstein, *The Great Conspiracy Trial* (New York: Random House, 1970), pp. 78–80.

30. Quoted in Farber, *op.cit.*, p. 173; c.f., David Lewis Stein, *Living the Revolution: The Yippies in Chicago* (Indianapolis: Bobbs-Merrill, 1969), p. 60.

31. *Ibid.*

32. Jack Mabley, *Chicago's American,* Aug. 25, 1968; pp. 1, 3.

33. Quoted in Farber, *op.cit.*, p. 193.

34. *Ibid.*, p. 193

35. *Ibid.*, p. 195.

36. Quoted in Epstein, *op.cit,* p. 294.

37. *Ibid.*, p. 296.

38. Farber, *op.cit.*, p. 200.

39. Robert Sam Anson, *McGovern,* (New York: Holt, Rinehart and Winston, 1972) p. 210.

40. Quoted in Farber, *op.cit.*, p. 204.

41. Arthur Waskow, *Running Riot* (New York: Herder and Herder, 1970), p. 154.

42. *Chicago Tribune*, Sept. 1, 1964, p. 4.

43. Norman Thomas letter to members of the Socialist Party. Aug. 2, 1968; Max Schachtman MSS, Tamiment Library of New York University, Microfilm reel #3375.

44. Martin Peretz to Eugene McCarthy, Oct. 3, 1968; Eugene McCarthy Historical Project, Peretz collection, box 43, Georgetown University Library.

45. Christopher Lasch, "The Revival of Political Controversy in the 60s," in Christopher Lasch, *The Agony of the American Left* (New York: Alfred A. Knopf, 1969), pp. 205–212.46.

46. Meeting of the Democratic National Committee, March 5, 1970, Washington, D.C. 16-10-A; typed transcripts of DNC Meetings; DNC Papers, National Archives of the United States, Washington, D.C. (Although the DNC is not a U.S. government agency, the Archives temporarily accepted their papers for storage and use by scholars).

Chapter 6, McGovernism and the Captured Party

1. David Broder, "The Election of 1968," in Arthur M. Schlesinger, Jr., and Fred Israel (eds.) *History of American Presidential Elections, 1789–1968* (4 vols.; NY: Chelsea House, 1971), vol. 4, p. 3750–51.

2. Herbert S. Parmet, *The Democrats: The Years After FDR*, p. 288.

3. Steve Denlinger and Jim Durham, "The New Democratic Coalition and the Revitalization of the Democratic Party: A Programmatic Approach (Discussion Draft), 11/15/68; Stephen A. Mitchell Papers, Harry S Truman Library.

4. Lawrence F. O'Brien, *No Final Victories* (Garden City, NY: Doubleday and Co., 1974), p. 289.

5. "Apportionment" by Richard M. Wade and "Fair Represen-

tation of Minority Political Views" by Alexander M. Bickel, Oct. 20, 1969; papers of the Democratic National Committee.

6. Statement of Joe Rauh to the Democratic National Committee, 1969, Rauh MSS, box 28.

7. Statement of Eugene J. McCarthy to the National Democratic Commtee's Commission on Party Structure and Delegate Selection, April 25, 1969; Papers of the Democratic National Committee.

8. McGovern to DNC meeting, March 5, 1970, Washington, D.C.; Papers of the Democratic National Committee, box 27.

9. *Mandate for Reform*, report of the McGovern Commission, reprinted in the *Congressional Record*, Sept. 22, 1971.

10. Cited in Herbert S. Parmet, *The Democrats: The Years after FDR*, pp. 294–295.

11. Quoted in *Ibid.*, p. 80.

12. Jeane Kirkpatrick, *The New Presidential Elite: Men and Women in American Politics* (New York: Russell Sage Foundation and The Twentieth Century Fund, 1976), p. 4.

13. *Ibid.*, p. 5.

14. Penn Kemble, "Who Needs the Liberals?" *Commentary* (Oct. 1970), pp. 58, 62.

15. Penn Kemble and Josh Muravchik, "The New Politics and the Democrats," *Commentary*, December 16, 1972, pp. 78–84.

16. Interview with George McGovern by Ben Wattenberg, June 15, 1988.

17. *Ibid.* 19

18. *Ibid.*, p. 81.

19. Ken Bode to Stanley Sheinbaum, Oct. 18, 1971, Joseph Rauh MSS, Library of Congress.

20. Jeane Kirkpatrick, *The New Presidential Elite*, p. 290.
21. The *New York Times*, June 29, 1972; c.f., Herbert Parmet, *The Democrats*, p. 296.
22. Stephan Lesher, *George Wallace: American Populist*, (Reading, MA: Addison-Wesley Publishing Co., 1993), p. xvi.
23. Dan T. Carter, *The Politics of Rage: George Wallace, The Origins of the New Conservatism, and the Transformation of American Politics* (New York: Simon and Schuster, 1995), p. 466.
24. Richard M. Scammon and Ben J. Wattenberg, *The Real Majority: An Extraordinary Examination of the American Electorate* (New York: Coward-McCann, Inc., 1970), pp. 185–199. The authors were even strangely prophetic when they wrote: "Suppose George Wallace, for all his youth, died or was disabled." One could predict a similar campaign by someone else, who "would be stronger than the perceived George Wallace: extremist, racist, Southern." They even predicted what happend to Wallace by the eighties—that he would "move to the center," and *support* "equal rights for all, and still maintain his basic constituency." Quote on p. 193.
25. Michael Kazin, *The Populist Persuasion: An American History*, (New York, Basic Books, 1995), p. 223.
26. Stephan Lesher, *George Wallace: American Populist*, p. 457.
27. *Ibid.*, p. 470–471; c.f., Stephan Lesher, "Who Knows What Evil Lurks in the Hearts of 'X' Million Americans? George Wallace Knows—and He's Off and Running" *New York Times Magazine*; Jan. 2, 1972.
28. Kenneth Auchincloss and Stephan Lesher, "They Have to Listen Now," *Newsweek*, March 27, 1972; c.f. Stephan Lesher, *George Wallace: American Populist*, pp. 471–472.
29. *Ibid.*, p. 475
30. *Time*, "A Jarring Message from George," March 27, 1972.
31. *Ibid.*

32. *Ibid.*
33. Michael Barone, *Our Country: The Shaping of America from Roosevelt to Reagan* (New York: The Free Press, 1990), p. 501.
34. Stephan Lesher, *George Wallace: American Populist*, p. 483.
35. George McGovern interview with Ben Wattenberg, June 15, 1988.
36. Robert Sam Anson, *McGovern: A Biography* (New York: Holt, Rinehart, and Winston, 1972), pp. 58–61. Anson points out that McGovern was involved in numerous left-wing causes, and also campaigned for the Progressive Party's Senate campaign for Northwestern University journalism professor Curtis McDougal, a man who later would write a three-volume history of Wallace's movement.
37. McGovern letter to *The Mitchell Daily Republic*, quoted in *Ibid.*
38. *Ibid.* However, McGovern told Anson that he "didn't vote at all." Somehow, as time passes, McGovern has moved his would-be disillusionment with Wallace to have prompted him to actually having voted for Truman.
39. George McGovern, "Peace and Politics," Aug. 26, 1956 television address; Stephen Mitchell Papers, General Political Files, Box 14; Harry S Truman Library, Independence, MO.
40. Mitchell to Sam Rayburn, Dec. 11, 1956; in *Ibid.*
41. Robert A. Low to Sterling Munro, Dec. 22, 1970; Henry M. Jackson Papers, #3650-12, box 31, Folder 11, University of Washington Library, Seattle, WA.
42. "*CONFIDENTIAL*" Memorandum for Sterling Munro from Ben Wattenberg, 1971; Henry M. Jackson Papers, #3560-12, box 36, Folder 24. Munro was Jackson's chief administrative assistant in his Senate office, and the aide who was closest to Jackson.

43. *Ibid.*

44. *Ibid.*

45. Steven Brill, "SENATOR HENRY M. JACKSON-LIB-ERAL?" Americans for Democratic Action, Aug. 14, 1975; in Henry M. Jackson Papers, #3560-12, box 40, Folder 8.

46. George McGovern, *Grassroots: The Autobiography of George McGovern* (New York: Random House, 1978). c.f., Arch Puddington, "Goldwater of the Left," *Commentary*, May 1978.

47. *Ibid.* McGovern also told the press that he was proud of his work for Wallace, and that had the United States listened to him, "we might have avoided the Korean War and the Vietnam War." c.f., the *Washington Daily News*, April 27, 1972; the *Washington Evening Star*, May 1, 1972.

48. Henry M. Jackson, "AMERICAN LIBERAL BLINDNESS ON SOVIET POWER AND POLICY," 1972; Henry M. Jackson Papers, #3560-6; box 9, Folder 9.

49. *Ibid.*

50. Jackson again proved more than prescient. c.f., John Lewis Gaddis, "The Tides of Cold War History: Reflections on Revisionism," *Foreign Affairs*, Jan.-Feb. 1994, pp. 142–154. Writing in *Foreign Affairs* in 1994, historian John L. Gaddis writes: "what is emerging from the archives are stories more horrifying than most of the images put forward, without the benefit of archives, by the Soviet Union's most strident critics while the Cold War was still going on" (p. 147). As for the propensity of many historians to argue that Stalin was not Hitler, and that the United States "should have undertaken a greater effort that it did at the beginning of the Cold War to 'get along' with the Soviet Union," Gaddis writes that the "similarities between Stalin and Hitler far outweigh

the differences," and that their visions of security "for themselves meant complete insecurity for everyone else." Thus, Gaddis concludes, "it is really quite difficult . . . to see how there could have been any long-term basis for co-existence . . . with either of these fundamentally evil dictators" (pp. 149–150).

51. Henry M. Jackson., speech of May 20, 1971; Henry M. Jackson Papers, 3560-6; box 9, Folder 22.

52. *Time*, "The Campaign: The Confrontation of the Two Americas," Oct. 2, 1972.

53. *Ibid.*

54. George McGovern interview with Ben Wattenberg, June 15, 1988.

55. *Ibid.*

56. *Ibid.*

57. "Meet the Press," NBC-TV, Feb. 21, 1971.

58. George McGovern, The *Playboy* interview, July 1971. This passage, while from the interview, did not appear in the version printed by *Playboy*. It is cited by Robert Sam Anson in his political biography of McGovern.

59. *Manchester Union Leader*, Aug. 10, 1971.

60. Mass mailing fund appeal from George McGovern to Democrats, 1971; in Henry M. Jackson Papers; #3560-12, Box 38, Folder 21.

61. 1968 speech by Henry M. Jackson, #3560-4, box 236, Folder 71.

62. Jackson speech, April 6, 1968; *Ibid.*, box 236, Folder 72.

63. Quoted in *Congressional Quarterly* Political Report, "Jackson Campaign: De-Emphasis of the Hard Line," July 16, 1971, p. 1524.

64. *Ibid.* p. 1524.

65. Henry M. Jackson to William P. Rogers, Dec. 17, 1970; Henry M. Jackson Papers, #3650-12, box 4, Folder 29.

66. Edward N. Costikyan to Henry M. Jackson, Oct. 21, 1971; Henry M. Jackson Papers, #3560-12; box 32, Folder 5.

67. Henry M. Jackson to Edward N. Costikyan, Nov. 29, 1971; *Ibid.*

68. "Memorandum on the McGovern-Hatfield Amendment," Henry M. Jackson Papers, #3560-6, box 9, Folder 22.

69. *Ibid.*, box 9, Folder 53; box 9, folder 60; text of Jackson's comments on ABC-TV's "Issues and Answers," Feb. 6, 1972.

70. Michael Barone, *Our Country: The Shaping of America from Roosevelt to Reagan* (New York: The Free Press, 1990), p. 496.

71. *Ibid.*, p. 501.

72. *New York Times*, June 30, July 10, 1972.

73. *Time*, "The Convention: Introducing the McGovern Machine," July 24, 1972.

74. Penn Kemble and Josh Muravchik, "The New Politics and the Democrats," *Commentary*, Dec. 1972, p. 82.

75. *Time*, July 24, 1972.

76. Michael Harrington recalled this to me during many different conversations.

77. Michael Barone, *Our Country*, p. 502.

78. Theodore White, *The Making of the President, 1972* (New York: Bantam, 1973), pp. 167–170.

79. Quoted in Kemble and Muravchik, "The New Politics and the Democrats," *Commentary*, Dec. 1972, p. 83.

80. Ben Wattenberg interview with George McGovern, June 15, 1988.

81. *Time*, July 24, 1972. I watched the live coverage of this

meeting, and remember vividly being stunned at McGovern's willingness to spend a great deal of time meeting and talking with this far Left protest group.

82. John G. Stewart, *One Last Chance* (New York: Praeger, 1974), p. 16.
83. #3560-12, Box 43, Folder 2; Henry M. Jackson Papers.
84. Jackson speech to Social Democrats, U.S.A., March 25, 1976, #3560-12, box 43, Folder 5, Henry M. Jackson papers.

Chapter 7. The Wilderness Years

1. Quoted in Frederick F. Siegel, *Troubled Journey: From Pearl Harbor to Ronald Reagan* (New York: Hill and Wang, 1984), p. 244. Thompson's words evoked the phrases made famous by poet Allen Ginsberg in his opus, "Howl."
2. Michael Barone, *Our Country: The Shaping of America from Roosevelt to Reagan*, pp. 533–534.
3. Jules Witcover, *Marathon* (New York: Viking, 1972), p. 92.
4. Quoted in Siegel, *Troubled Journey*, p. 263.
5. "Jimmy Carter's Big Breakthrough," *Time*, May 10, 1976.
6. *Ibid.*
7. E. J. Dionne, Jr., *Why Americans Hate Politics* (New York: Simon and Schuster, 1991), pp. 116–144. Quote on p. 125. c.f., Thomas Byrne Edsall and Mary D. Edsall, *Chain Reaction: The Impact of Race, Rights, and Taxes on American Politics* (New York: W.W. Norton and Co., 1991), pp. 99–115. The Edsalls comment in a chapter titled "The Conservative Ascendance" that contrary to the assertions of Carter's pollster Pat Cadell, who thought the Republicans were in a permanent downturn, that "in fact, it was the Democratic Party that was continuing to lose its class-based strength." Quote on p. 144.

8. *Ibid.*, pp. 104–105.

9. E. J. Dionne, *op.cit.*, p. 131.

10. This writer, then a member of the Democratic Socialist Organizing Committee, participated in the Washington meeting and the picket line at the Capitol.

11. Michael Barone, *op.cit.*, p. 596.

12. On this rally and the politics of the peace movement, see: Ronald Radosh, "The 'Peace Council' and Peace," *New Republic*, Jan. 31, 1983.

13. Jack W. Germond and Jules Witcover, *Wake Us When It's Over: Presidential Politics of 1984* (New York: Macmillan, 1985), p. 47.

14. Quoted in Joshua Muravchik, "Why the Democrats Lost Again," *Commentary*, Feb. 1989, p. 15.

15. *Time*, "Taking the Pledge," Sept. 5, 1988.

16. I am indebted to the analysis made after the election by Fred Siegel, "What Liberals Haven't Learned and Why," *Commonweal*, Jan. 13, 1989, pp. 16–20.

17. "Reaching Common Ground," *Time*, Aug. 1, 1988.

18. Max Lerner, "Behind Dukakis' plight: he's been unable to prevail over Jackson," *New York Post*, September 1988.

19. Ben Wattenberg, "Dems would be better off with a little less harmony," *New York Post*, July 1988.

20. A. M. Rosenthal, "What's Inside the Democratic Package?" *New York Times*, July 1988.

21. *New York Times*, July 20, 1988, p. 1.

22. Eric Breindel, "Can Dukakis Duck Leftist Embrace?," *New York Post*, July 21, 1988, p. 27.

23. Thomas B. Edsall, "Unlike 1984, Ticket Expected to Boost Other Democrats; But Liberal Leanings Worry Some in South," *Washington Post*, July 21, 1988, p. A1.

24. Eric Alterman, "Democrats: Split the Party?" *Washington Post*, Nov. 27, 1988, p. D5.
25. William Safire, "Hostage to Jackson," *New York Times*, July 4, 1988, p. 23.
26. Paul A. Gigot, "The Democrats' Teflon Platform," *Wall Street Journal*, July 19, 1988.
27. Quoted in *Ibid.*
28. Martin Peretz, "Why Dukakis Lost," *New Republic*, Nov. 28, 1988, pp. 14–18.
29. Andrew Kopkind, "What's Next for the Democrats," *Nation*, Nov. 28, 1988, p. 554.
30. Martin Peretz, *op.cit.*, pp. 14–18.
31. Polls cited in Barone, *op.cit.*, pp. 667–668.
32. Cited in Morton M. Kondracke, "Nunn's Story," *New Republic*, Dec. 5, 1988, p. 15.

Chapter 8. The Clinton Contradiction

1. Hedrik Hertzberg, "Hell, I Dunno," *New Republic*, Dec. 5, 1988-pp. 23–24.
2. William Rasberry, "There Is No Black Agenda," *Washington Post*, Nov. 18, 1988.
3. Joseph A. Califano, Jr., "Tough Talk for Democrats," *New York Times Magazine*, Jan. 8, 1989, pp. 28–29; 38; 43.
4. *The Nation*, Nov. 28, 1988, pp. 553–554.
5. Michael Kramer, Clinton's Troops Turn Away," *Time*, July 10, 1995.
6. Paul Bedard, "Pollster Tries to Reinvent Clinton," *Washington Times*, Sept. 18, 1995, p. 1.
7. David S. Broder and Dan Balz, "Democratic Group Finds No Champion," *Washington Post*, May 9, 1991, p. 3.

8. E. J. Dionne, Jr., "Anatomy of a Feud," *Washington Post*, Dec. 7, 1993.

9. Text of ad prepared by the Clinton campaign, Aug. 1992. I signed the ad, but my name was inadvertently left off the text that appeared in the *New York Times*.

10. Interview with Josh Muravchik, Oct. 7, 1995, Washington, D.C.

11. During the campaign, Shanker told me Clinton had asked him what issues he should emphasize. Shanker responded that the most important thing he could do was separate himself from Jesse Jackson. Conversation with Al Shanker in 1992, Washington, D.C. At that time, I was serving as Associate Director in the Office of the President, American Federation of Teachers.

12. Thomas B. Edsall, "Clinton Sues Rainbow Coalition," *Washington Post*, June 14, 1992, p. 1.

13. Dan Balz, "Clinton Says Jackson is Rewriting History," *Washington Post*, June 20, 1992, p. 11.

14. *Washington Post*, Nov. 4, 1992, p. 1.

15. I learned while working at the American Federation of Teachers that other prominent candidates for Secretary of Education were told they would not be appointed, since Cole was to get the position. In New York, Cole's chief supporters, Susan Thomases and Harold Ickes, Jr., were preparing to host a party in honor of her appointment.

16. The full story of the Cole incident can be found in David Twersky, "A New Kind of Democrat," *Commentary*, Feb. 1993, pp. 51–53.

17. Clint Bolick, "Quota Queen," *Wall Street Journal*, April 30, 1993. For a defense of Guinier's views, see Anthony Lewis, "Anatomy of a Smear," *New York Times*, June 4, 1993.

18. John Taylor, "What's at Stake," *New York Magazine*, Nov. 1, 1993, pp. 38–41.
19. Ben Wattenberg, "Grading Clinton After 'Gestation,'" *New York Post*, Oct. 10, 1995.
20. Nat Hentoff, "Laid Off Because of Affirmative Action," *Washington Post*, Sept. 10, 1995.
21. Steven B. Roberts, "Affirmative Action on the Edge," *U.S. News and World Report*, Feb. 13, 1995, p. 32.
22. "Remarks by the President to Leadership Conference on Civil Rights," May 11, 1993, Civil Rights Commission File, The White House, Office of the Press Secretary.
23. Remarks of president Bill Clinton at the National Archives and Records Administration, July 19, 1995; Weekly Compilation of Presidential Documents, July 24, 1995.
24. Remarks by Deval L. Patrick at the Anti-Defamation League Annual Convention, Feb. 10, 1995, U.S. Civil Rights Commission File.
25. Joe Klein, "Firm on Affirmative Action," *Newsweek*, July 31, 1995, p. 31.
26. Jeffrey H. Birnbaum, "Centrist Reed and Liberal Sperling Represent the Contradictory Blend of Clinton's Ideology," *The Wall Street Journal*, Dec. 10, 1993, p. 16.
27. Vin Weber, "Clinton's Winning Coalition," *Wall Street Journal*, Nov. 19, 1993.
28. E. J. Dionne, Jr., "Anatomy of a Feud," *Washington Post*, Dec. 7, 1993.
29. Remarks of U.S. Senator Bill Bradley, Aug. 16, 1995. Internet files of *U.S. News and World Report*.
30. Michael Wines, "Bradley's Exit is not Just the Democrats' Problem," *New York Times*, Aug. 20, 1995, Section 4, pp. 1,4.

31. Dick Williams, "The Last True Centrist on the Hill," *Atlanta Journal*, Oct. 10, 1995; p. 10. See also John B. Judis, "Nunn of the Above," *New Republic*, Oct. 30, 1995, pp. 16–18. Judis argues convincingly that Nunn was a moderate conservative who "provided a needed counterweight to both right-wing and left-wing reformers."
32. *Wall Street Journal*, Oct. 27, 1995, p. 2.
33. Jonathan Mahler, "Surge of Labor Sets Ill Omen for Bill Clinton," *Forward*, Oct. 27, 1995; pp. 1,5.
34. *Ibid.*, p. 5.
35. Michael Wines, "Bradley's Exit . . ." *New York Times*, Aug. 20, 1995, Section 4, p. 1.

BIBLIOGRAPHY

Manuscript Collections

The Allard Lowenstein papers, University of North Carolina, Chapel Hill.

Eugene McCarthy Historical Project Manuscripts, Georgetown University Library, Washington, D.C.

Stephen A. Mitchell Manuscripts, in the Harry S Truman Library, Presidential Papers, Independence, Missouri.

The Harry S Truman Papers, in the Harry S Truman Library, Presidential Papers, Independence, Missouri.

Democratic National Committee Papers, National Archives of the United States, Washington, D.C.

Henry M. Jackson Papers, University of Washington Library, Seattle, Washington.

The Papers of Max Shachtman, Tamiment Institute Library, New York University, New York City, New York.

The Papers of Students for a Democratic Society, Historical Society of Wisconsin, Madison, Wisconsin. Microfilm copy at the Tamiment Institute Library.

The Papers of Americans for Democratic Action, Historical Society of Wisconsin, Madison, Wisconsin. Microfilm copy at the Library of Congress, Washington, D.C.

The Papers of Joseph Rauh, Manuscript Division, The Library of Congress, Washington, D.C.

Text of interviews by Ben J. Wattenberg with George McGovern, Jeane Kirkpatrick, Walter Mondale, Gary Hart, Lane Kirkland, Tom Hayden, Eugene McCarthy, Bob Strauss, and Chuck Robb, conducted in June of 1988 for a PBS-TV production, "The Democrats: A Quarter Century of Change," produced by Ben Wattenberg and Michael Pack for Manifold Productions, Inc. Used by permission of Ben Wattenberg and Michael Pack. In possession of Ben Wattenberg, Washington, D.C.

Books

Robert Sam Anson, *McGovern: A Biography* (New York: Holt, Rinehart and Winston, 1972).

Michael Barone, *Our Country: The Shaping of America from Roosevelt to Reagan* (New York: The Free Press, 1990).

Paul Breines, ed., *Critical Interruptions: New Left Perspectives on Herbert Marcuse* (New York: Herder and Herder, 1970).

Peter Brown, *Minority Party: Why Democrats Face Defeat in 1992 and Beyond* (Washington, D.C., Regnery Gateway, 1991).

Clayborne Carson, *In Struggle: SNCC and the Black Awakening of the 1960s* (Cambridge, MA: Harvard University Press, 1981).

Dan T. Carter, *The Politics of Rage: George Wallace, the Origins of the New Conservatism, and the Transformation of American Politics* (New York: Simon and Schuster, 1995).

William H. Chafe, *Never Stop Running: Allard Lowenstein and the Struggle to Save American Liberalism* (New York: Basic Books, 1993).

Lewis Chester, Godfrey Hodgson and Bruce Page, *An American Melodrama: The Presidential Campaign of 1968* (New York: Viking, 1969).

E.J. Dionne, Jr., *Why Americans Hate Politics* (New York: Simon & Schuster, 1991).

————., *They Only Look Dead: Why Progressives Will Dominate the Next Political Era* (New York: Simon & Schuster, 1996).

Elizabeth Drew, *On the Edge: The Clinton Presidency* (New York: Simon & Schuster, 1994).

Thomas Byrne Edsall, *The New Politics of Inequality* (New York: W. W. Norton and Co., 1984).

———— and Mary D. Edsall, *Chain Reaction: The Impact of Race, Rights and Taxes on American Politics* (New York: W. W. Norton and Co., 1991).

John Ehrman, *The Rise of Neoconservatism: Intellectuals and Foreign Affairs 1945–1994* (New Haven and London: Yale University Press, 1995).

Albert Eisele, *Almost to the Presidency* (Blue Earth, MN.: The Piper Co., 1972).

Jason Epstein, *The Great Conspiracy Trial* (New York: Random House, 1969).

David Farber, *Chicago '68* (Chicago and London: Univ. of Chicago Press, 1988).

James Forman, *The Making of Black Revolutionaries* (New York: The Macmillan Co., 1972).

David Frum, *Dead Right* (New York: New Republic Books/Basic Books, 1994).

Adam Garfinkle, *Telltale Hearts: The Origins and Impact of the Vietnam Antiwar Movement* (New York: St. Martin's Press, 1995).

David Garrow, *Bearing the Cross: Martin Luther King, Jr. And the Southern Christian Leadership Conference* (New York: William Morrow and Co., 1986).

Jack W. Germond and Jules Witcover, *Wake Us When It's Over: Presidential Politics of 1984* (New York: Macmillan, 1985).

Stanley W. Greenberg, *Middle-Class Dreams: The Politics and Power of the New American Majority* (New York: Times Books, 1995).

Tom Hayden, *Rebellion and Repression* (New York: Random House, 1969).

———— *Reunion: A Memoir* (New York: Random House, 1988).

Godfrey Hodgson, *America in Our Time* (Garden City, NY: Doubleday and Co., 1976).

Abbie Hoffman, *Revolution for the Hell of It* (New York: The Dial Press, 1968).

Charles Kaiser, *1968 in America: Music, Politics, Chaos, Counterculture, and the Shaping of a Generation* (New York: Weidenfeld and Nicolson, 1988).

Michael Kazin, *The Populist Persuasion: An American History* (New York: Basic Books, 1995).

Jonathan Kaufman, *Broken Alliance: The Turbulent Times Between Blacks and Jews in America* (New York: Charles Scribner's Sons, 1988).

Jeane Kirkpatrick, *The New Presidential Elite: Men and Women in*

American Politics (New York: Russell Sage Foundation and the Twentieth Century Fund, 1976).

Jeremy Larner, *Nobody Knows: Reflections on the McCarthy Campaign of 1968* (New York: Macmillan, 1970).

Christopher Lasch, *The Agony of the American Left* (New York: Alfred A. Knopf, 1969).

Stephan Lesher, *George Wallace: American Populist* (Reading, MA: Addison-Wesley Publishing Co., 1993).

Norman Mailer, *Miami and the Siege of Chicago: An Informal History* (New York: World Publishing Co., 1968).

David Maraniss, *First in His Class: A Biography of Bill Clinton* (New York: Simon and Schuster, 1995).

Ernest R. May and Janet Fraser, eds., *Campaign '72: The Managers Speak* (Cambridge, MA: Harvard University Press, 1973).

Eugene McCarthy, *The Year of the People* (Garden City, NY: Doubleday, 1969).

Joe McGinniss, *The Selling of the President, 1968* (New York: Pocket Books, 1970).

George McGovern, *Grassroots: The Autobiography of George McGovern* (New York: Random House, 1978).

Lawrence F. O'Brien, *No Final Victories* (Garden City, NY: Doubleday and Co., 1974).

Herbert Parmet, *The Democrats: The Years After F.D.R.* (New York: Macmillan Publishing Co., 1976).

Kevin Phillips, *The Emerging Republican Majority* (New Rochelle, NY: Arlington House, 1969).

Thomas Powers, *The War at Home* (New York: Grossman Publishers, 1973).

Bayard Rustin, *Down the Line: The Collected Writings of Bayard Rustin* (Chicago: Quadrangle Books, 1971).

Kirkpatrick Sale, *SDS* (New York: Random House, 1973).

Richard W. Scammon and Ben J. Wattenberg, *The Real Majority: An Extraordinary Examination of the American Electorate* (New York: Coward-McCann, 1970).

Arthur M. Schlesinger Jr. and Fred Israel, eds., *History of American Presidential Elections, 1789–1968*, Vol. 4 (New York: Chelsea House, 1971).

Byron E. Shafer, *Quiet Revolution: The Struggle for the Democratic Party and the Shaping of Post-Reform Politics* (New York: Russell Sage Foundation, 1983).

Frederick F. Siegel, *Troubled Journey: From Pearl Harbor to Ronald Reagan* (New York: Hill and Wang, 1984).

Jim Sleeper, *The Closest of Strangers: Liberalism and the Politics of Race in New York* (New York: W. W. Norton and Co., 1990).

Carl Solberg, *Hubert Humphrey: A Biography* (New York: Norton, 1984).

Ben Stavis, *We Were the Campaign: New Hampshire to Chicago for McCarthy* (Boston: Beacon Press, 1969).

David Lewis Stein, *Living the Revolution: The Yippies in Chicago* (Indianapolis: Bobbs-Merrill, 1969).

John G. Stewart, *One Last Chance* (New York: Praeger, 1974).

James L. Sundquist, *Dynamics of the Party System: Alignment and Realignment of Political Parties in the United States* (Washington D.C., The Brookings Institution, 1973).

Massimo Teodori, *The New Left: A Documentary History* (Indianapolis and New York: Bobbs-Merrill Co., 1969).

Hunter S. Thompson, *Fear and Loathing on the Campaign Trail* (San Francisco: Straight Arrow Books, 1972).

Irwin Unger, *The Movement: A History of the American New Left, 1959–1972* (New York: Dodd-Mead, 1974).

———— and Debi Unger, *Turning Point: 1968* (New York: Charles Scribner's Son, 1988).

Arthur Waskow, *Running Riot* (New York: Herder and Herder, 1970).

Ben J. Wattenberg, *Values Matter Most: How Republicans or De-mocrats or a Third Party Can Win and Renew the American Way of Life*, (New York: The Free Press, 1995).

Robert Weisbrot, *Freedom Bound: A History of America's Civil Rights Movement* (New York: W. W. Norton and Co., 1989).

Theodore White, *The Making of the President, 1964* (New York: Atheneum, 1965).

—— *The Making of the President, 1968* (New York: Atheneum, 1969).

—— *The Making of the President, 1972* (New York: Atheneum, 1973).

Juan Williams, *Eyes on the Prize: America's Civil Rights Years: 1945–1965* (New York: The Viking Press, 1987).

Jules Witcover, *Marathon* (New York: Viking, 1972).

Bob Woodward, *The Agenda: Inside the Clinton White House* (New York: Simon & Schuster, 1994).

Nigel Young, *An Infantile Disorder? Crisis and Decline of the New Left* (Boulder, CO: Westview Press, 1977).

Newspapers:

Washington Post, Wall Street Journal, New York Post, Washington Times, Atlanta Journal, New York Times, Forward, Chicago's American, Chicago Tribune, Los Angeles Times

Magazines and Journals:

Commentary, New York Times Magazine, New Republic, Weekly Standard, U.S. News and World Report, Foreign Affairs, Con-gressional Quarterly, The American Prospect, Dissent, Public

Interest, Freedomways, Nation, ADA World, Midstream, Newsweek, Time, Atlantic Monthly, Harper's, New York Magazine, Commonweal, Studies on the Left, Liberation.

ACKNOWLEDGMENTS

This book had its start with a suggestion made by David Horowitz and Peter Collier, after their successful Second Thoughts Conference in 1988, at which former radicals and liberals looked back to reevaluate and reconsider their views and thoughts of the turbulent era of the sixties and seventies. They had the idea to edit a series of Second Thoughts Books that derived from the work of those at the conference. The late Erwin Glikes, the wonderful and serious editor who brought The Free Press to major prominence, liked their idea. Erwin had always wanted me to write something for him, and because of his prompting and enthusiasm, I signed on for the project.

I could not have written this book without consulting, studying, borrowing from, and learning from those who have labored in the vineyards of political history. The most important, to whom I am deeply indebted, include my friend and colleague

Herbert Parmet, who wrote one of the first interpretive histories of the Democratic Party; the journalists E. J. Dionne, Jr., and Thomas Byrne Edsall, both of the *Washington Post*, that indispensable newspaper for political junkies; the political journalist Joe Klein, whose articles in *New York Magazine* and now in *Newsweek* provide much food for thought; the political historians Steven M. Gillon and Adam Garfinkle, both of whom have written books that deal with the dilemmas and contradictions of American liberalism as it pertains to the Democratic Party, and my friends John B. Judis, senior editor of *New Republic* and one of the finest and most thoughtful students of the American political scene, and the historian and political analyst Fred Siegel, whose understanding of the pitfalls of American liberalism is second to none; and to Josh Muravchik, a good friend on whose work I have drawn, and with whom I have had numerous conversations about these events. I have learned and benefited from the work of all of them. Many of them will find judgments and views in my book with which they undoubtedly will most strongly disagree. That is to be expected. For whatever errors and faulty analysis appear in this book, of course I alone am responsible.

This book could not have been completed without the cooperation and support of the many archivists and librarians who helped me sort through many manuscript collections, at the National Archives, the Library of Congress, the University of Washington at Seattle, the Harry S Truman Library, Georgetown University, the Tamiment Institute of New York University, and the University of North Carolina at Chapel Hill. I thank them all. Ben J. Wattenberg and Michael Pack were kind enough to allow me to make full use of the transcripts of Wattenberg's 1988 interviews with leading Democrats, conducted for a television documentary they were preparing for PBS. I thank them both. As readers of this book will know, I have learned a lot from the observations and analysis of Ben Wattenberg. And as a scholar living in our postmodern world, I am deeply indebted to that marvelous creation known as the Net, with its invaluable newspaper databases that allow scholars and journalists to find newspaper and magazine articles and get them instantly at home, without having to run to major libraries.

At an early phase in this project, I received a most generous grant from the Lynde and Harry Bradley Foundation of Milwaukee, Wisconsin. Their support enabled me to take a year off in which to do the research and begin the writing. I thank Michael Joyce and Hilell Fradkin for their understanding and trust in my project. I hope that they think the outcome was worth their investment.

At the Free Press, after the untimely passing of Erwin Glikes, the editorial duties were taken over by Bruce Nichols. His fine craftsmanship and critical reading and editing of the manuscript was carried out with aplomb. I thank him immensely. I am also thankful to Adam Bellow, editorial director of the Free Press, who decided that the project was worthy of completion, and who gave me necessary extensions in order to complete it.

Finally, I am indebted to the support and love of my family. My wife Allis has encouraged me over the years to finish the work, and her understanding and support was essential to carrying out the job. The joy I get from sharing my life with her, and with our son Michael, a fine young man and budding musician, is unparalleled.

INDEX

Abel, I. W., 95, 140
Abrams, Elliott, 69, 80
Achtenberg, Roberta, 220
ACLU. *See* American Civil Liberties
    Union
ADA. *See* Americans for Democratic
    Action
Adarand case, 229
AFL-CIO, 177, 215
    activist tactics of the 1990s, 235-
        36
    McGovern Commission reforms
        and, 144
    NAFTA and, 231
    1972 presidential election and,
        150, 154, 158
    1980 presidential election and,
        191
    1984 presidential election and,
        196

report card on 94th Congress,
    180
Alterman, Eric, 205
American Civil Liberties Union
        (ACLU), 96
    Dukakis and, 201, 202, 208, 216
    1970s and 1980s change in, 202
Americans for Democratic Action
        (ADA), 51
    Humphrey endorsed by, 133
    labor movement and, 236
    McCarthy endorsed by, 95
    1964 presidential election and, 4
    1968 presidential election and,
        63-69, 71-73, 75, 80, 85,
        87, 95, 102, 133
    1972 presidential election and,
        158
    Vietnam War and, 52, 56-57, 60-
        69, 71-72

American Veteran's Committee, 153
Anderson, Clinton P., 110
Anderson, John, 192
Anson, Robert Sam, 152
Armies of the Night, The (Mailer), 119
Armstrong, Michael, 96
Atwater, Lee, 200, 201

Baez, Joan, 222
Bailey, Koffi, 31
Baker, Ella, 16, 19-20
Baldwin, James, 16
Barone, Michael, 170-71, 175, 185, 192
Bayh, Birch, 156
Beatty, Warren, 176
Bennett, Bill, 235
Bentsen, Lloyd, 186
Berger, Samuel, 223
Berkeley Free Speech Movement, 26
Berry, Mary, 226
Bickel, Alexander M., 137
Bierne, Joseph, 64-65, 95
Bilbo, Theodore, 25
Bishop, Maurice, 193, 223
Black Muslims (Nation of Islam), 31
Black Panther Party, 26, 117, 118, 122-23, 161, 176, 178
Blumenthal, Richard, 39, 48
Bode, Ken, 143, 176
Bolick, Clint, 224
Bond, Julian, 113-14
Booth, Paul, 44
Boston Globe, 128
Bradley, Bill, 233-35, 239
Breindel, Eric, 223
Bremer, Arthur, 150
Brill, Steven, 158

Brown, H. Rap, 30
Brown, Sam, 103
Buchanan, Pat, 231, 235, 238
Bundy, McGeorge, 80
Burnham, Walter Dean, 236-37
Bush, George, 145, 148, 181
    civil rights and, 226
    1988 presidential election and, 200-202, 205, 207-9, 211
    1992 presidential election and, 218, 220
    opinion poll ratings (1988), 208-9

Calhoun, Jean, 114
Califano, Joseph A., Jr., 143
    redefinition of Democratic Party liberalism proposed by, 212-13
California Democratic Council (CDC), 81, 92
Camus, Albert, 16-17
Carmichael, Stokely, 12, 28, 34-35
    "black power" and, 4, 17
    Communism and, 17
    Mississippi Freedom Democratic Party and, 24-25
    Vietnam War and, 26
Carter, Dan T., 146
Carter, Jimmy, 145, 212
    background of, 186
    domestic policy of, 189-91
    foreign policy of, 189, 191, 199
    Iranian hostage crisis and, 189, 191
    1976 presidential election and, 185-89
    1980 presidential election and, 191-92
    opinion poll ratings (1980), 191

Casady, Simon, 44
Castro, Fidel, 16, 18, 84, 222
CBS/*New York Times* poll. *See New York Times*/CBS poll
CCD (Conference of Concerned Democrats), 80, 85, 89
Chafe, William, 54-55, 92, 94, 105
Chapman, Michael, 217-18
Chicago Convention (1968 Democratic National Convention)
   political maneuvering, 107-14, 121, 131
   street demonstrations, 103, 114-29, 131, 137-38, 176
   Unit Rule reform, 109-12, 131
Child Development Group, 25
Children's Defense Fund, 224
Christie, Julie, 176
Church, Frank, 173
   Cooper-Church Amendment, 168
Churchill, Winston, 157, 161
CIA (Central Intelligence Agency), 56
CIO. *See* AFL-CIO; Congress of Industrial Organizations
Civil rights, 1, 28, 30, 136, 157, 158, 174, 178. *See also* individual leaders and organizations
   "black power," 4, 17, 67
   Civil Rights Act of 1964, 3, 4
   Civil Rights Act of 1991, 226
   Civil Rights Commission, 226
   Clinton and, 214-15, 218-19, 223-30
   Communism and, 6, 15-23, 35, 44
   Congressional Black Caucus, 226
   Freedom Summer (Mississippi, 1964), 3, 17, 27, 55
   Humphrey and, 5-8, 10-13, 16, 20-22, 102, 164-65
   Johnson and, 4-9, 11, 13, 23, 25, 33-35, 64-65, 164, 227
   Mississippi Freedom Democratic Party (MFDP), 2-3, 5-16, 18-20, 22, 24-25, 70, 102
   Mondale and, 196
   "New Politics" convention (Chicago, 1967), 26-29, 36-49
   Vietnam War and, 53, 64-67
   Voting Rights Act of 1965, 4, 14, 23, 24
Civil Rights Act of 1964, 3, 4
Civil Rights Act of 1991, 226
Civil Rights Commission, 226
Clark, Septima, 41
Cleaver, Eldridge, 26
Cleveland, Grover, 189
Clifford, Clark, 80
Clinton, Bill, 145, 190
   anti-Communist policy of, 217, 222-23
   appointees, controversial, 220-25, 230
   background of, 213
   civil rights and, 214-15, 218-19, 223-30
   Democratic Leadership Council and, 213-16, 229, 232, 234
   domestic policy of, 215-33
   foreign policy of, 217-20, 231-32
   health care reform and, 232-33
   Jackson (Jesse), differences with, 218-19, 223

Clinton, Bill, (*continued*)
  labor movement and, 214-15,
    231, 236
  NAFTA and, 231-32, 236
  1988 presidential election and,
    213, 215-16
  1992 presidential election and,
    103, 151, 210, 213, 216-
    20, 222, 229, 234
  Nunn's disappointment with, 234
  "Reagan Democrats" and, 215-17
  shifting positions and promises
    vs. performance, 220-21,
    230-31, 234, 239
  Vietnam War and, 222
Clinton, Hillary, 224
  health care reform and, 232
Coffin, Tristam, 24
Coffin, William Sloane, 28
COFO (Council of Federated Orga-
    nizations), 15, 20-22
Cogen, Charles, 64-65
Cole, Johnnetta, 221-24
Commentary, 141-42, 213
Commission on Party Structure and
    Delegate Selection (Mc-
    Govern Commission),
    136-45, 170-72, 174-75
Committee on Political Education,
    180
Communications Workers of Amer-
    ica, 64-65, 95
Communism, 69, 90
  civil rights and, 6, 15-23, 35, 44
  Clinton policy and, 217, 222-23
  Cold War/U.S.-Soviet relations,
    1972 campaign views on,
    158-63, 166-67
  House Committee on Un-Ameri-

    can Activities, 5, 153
  McCarran Internal Security Act
    and, 153
  McGovern and, 151-53, 158-60,
    166
  Mundt-Nixon Bill and, 153
  New Left and, 19, 38, 39, 44,
    47, 56-58, 78, 79, 84-85,
    102
  1964 presidential election and, 4-
    6, 15-23
  1968 presidential election and,
    102
  1972 presidential election and,
    158-63
  1984 presidential election and,
    195-96
  1988 presidential election and,
    212
  1992 presidential election and,
    217
  Reagan policy and, 194-96, 199,
    206, 212
  Vietnam War and, 53, 56-60,
    62, 66, 72, 78, 84-85,
    123, 158, 160-61, 167,
    222
  Wallace (Henry) in 1948 presi-
    dential election and, 151-
    52
Conference of Concerned Democ-
    rats (CCD), 80, 85, 89
Congressional Black Caucus, 226
Congressional Quarterly, 167
Congressional Record, 21
Congress of Industrial Organizations
    (CIO), 61. *See also* AFL-
    CIO
Congress of Racial Equality (CORE)

"New Politics" convention
(Chicago, 1967) and, 39
1964 presidential election and,
13, 14
Connally, John, 111, 112
Cooper, Jim, 232
Cooper-Church Amendment, 168
CORE. *See* Congress of Racial
Equality
Costikayan, Edward N., 168
Council of Federated Organizations
(COFO), 15, 20-22
Cox, Courtland, 12
Crockett, George, 18
Cuomo, Mario, 197, 199

Daily Worker, 20
Daley, Bill, 237
Daley, Richard J.
1968 presidential election and,
112, 114, 115, 119, 127,
129
1972 presidential election and,
174-75
1976 presidential election and,
187
Davis, Rennie, 116, 119, 127
Dayan, Moshe, 31
Days, Drew, 226
Debs, Eugene, 66
Decs, Morris, 147
Dellinger, Dave, 116, 120, 125, 126
Democratic Agenda group, 190-91
Democratic Leadership Council
(DLC), 209, 233, 237
Clinton and, 213-16, 229, 232,
234
health care reform and, 232
labor movement and, 236

Democratic Socialist Organizing
Committee, 190-91
DePuy, William, 32
Devine, Annie, 7, 9
Diem, Ngo Dinh, 56
Dinkins, David, 225-26
Dionne, E. J., Jr., 188, 216
Dissent, 87-88
DLC. *See* Democratic Leadership
Council
Dodd, Christopher, 206
Douglas, Paul, 66-67
Duarte, JosÇ Napoleon, 193
Dubinsky, David, 64-65
Dukakis, Michael
ACLU and, 201, 202, 208, 216
background of, 199-200
Jackson (Jesse), alliance with,
203-6, 209, 218
1988 presidential election
and,199-209, 211-13, 216,
218
opinion poll ratings (1988), 208-
9
Duke, David, 218

Eagleton, Thomas, 179
Eastland, James, 16, 18, 21, 25
Edelman, Marion Wright, 224
Edsall, Thomas Byrne, 188
Emergency Public Integration Com-
mittee, 28
Epstein, Jason, 125
Estrich, Susan, 201-2
Evans, Roland, 16-18, 223
"Eyes on the Prize" (TV series), 11-
12

Farber, David, 118, 125-27

Farmer, James, 13, 14
FBI (Federal Bureau of Investigation), 18
Ferraro, Geraldine, 197
Finney, Tom, 110, 111
Ford, Gerald R.
   1976 presidential election and, 187, 188
   Nixon pardoned by, 184-85
Forman, James, 28, 31
   Communism and, 17, 18, 21
   Mississippi Freedom Democratic Party and, 11-15
   "New Politics" convention (Chicago, 1967) and, 29, 42, 44
Forward, 221-22
Franks, Gary, 235
Fraser, Don, 60-62, 64
Freedom Democrats. *See* Mississippi Freedom Democratic Party
Freedom Summer (Mississippi, 1964), 3, 17, 27, 55
French, Eleanor Clark, 102
From, Al, 214
Fulbright, J. William, 54

Galbraith, John Kenneth
   McCarthy supported by, 82, 95
   Vietnam War and, 57, 62, 65, 66, 82
Gallup poll
   on 1972 presidential election, 171
   on 1980 presidential election, 191
   on 1988 presidential election, 208
Galston, William, 214, 217

Gans, Curtis, 103
Gans, Herbert, 90
Garrow, David, 34-36
Gaskoff, Bert, 41-42
Gavin, James, 81-82
Gephardt, Richard, 199, 215
Germond, Jack, 197
Gigot, Paul A., 206
Gingrich, Newt, 231, 233
Ginsburg, David, 100
Giuliani, Rudolph, 225
Glotzer, Al, 84-85
Goldwater, Barry, 3, 5, 71, 77, 99-100
Goodman, Walter, 40, 43, 44, 48
Goodwin, Richard, 110
Gorbachev, Mikhail, 199
Gore, Al, 219, 223
Gorman, Paul, 103
Gottlieb, Marilyn, 86
Gottlieb, Sanford, 38, 43-47
Gray, Jesse, 18
Gray, Victoria, 7
Green, Edith, 9
Greenberg, Jack, 14, 17
Greenberg, Stanley, 215
Guinier, Lani, 221, 224-25, 230
Guyout, Lawrence, 25

Hamer, Fannie Lou, 7-8, 11, 14
Harriman, Averell, 128
Harrington, Michael, 32, 175, 190
Harris, Fred, 142, 173
Harris poll on 1972 presidential election, 177
Hart, Gary, 172-73, 195, 199
Hatfield, Mark, 166
   McGovern-Hatfield Amendment, 169

Hayden, Tom, 26, 116-22, 124,
125, 127
Hays, Wayne, 144-45
Hellman, Lillian, 5
Henry, Aaron, 7, 8, 36
Hentoff, Nat, 227
Hertzberg, Hendrik, 211
Heschel, Abraham Joshua, 30
Hill, Gerald N., 81-82
Hitler, Adolf, 159
Ho Chi Minh, 56-57, 161, 165
Hodgson, Godfrey, 51-52
Hoffman, Abbie, 116, 123, 126,
176
Hoover, J. Edgar, 18, 22
Horton, Willie, 201
Howe, Irving, 53
Humphrey, Hubert H., 137, 142,
187, 195
Chicago Convention (1968)
street demonstrations,
comments on, 127, 131
civil rights and, 5-8, 10-13, 16,
20-22, 102, 164-65
Humphrey-Hawkins Full Em-
ployment bill, 190
labor movement and, 5-7, 10, 12,
99, 103, 131, 133, 149,
150, 171, 172
Mississippi Freedom Democratic
Party and, 5-8, 10-13, 16,
20, 22, 102
1964 presidential election and,
3,5-8, 10-13, 16, 20-22,
102, 108
1968 presidential election and,
90, 98-105, 107-13, 117,
120-22, 125-31, 133-34,
138

1972 presidential election and,
145, 148-51, 164-65, 171-
73, 175-77
1976 presidential election and,
186
1988 presidential election and,
199
Unit Rule reform and, 109-12,
131
Vietnam War and, 56-57, 60, 99-
101, 103, 107, 112-13,
120, 121, 126-28, 133

Ickes, Harold, Jr., 103
Institute for Justice, 224
Institute for Policy Studies (IPS), 18,
24, 38
International Ladies Garment Workers Union (ILGWU), 64-
65, 95

Jackson, Henry ("Scoop")
background of, 154
Cold War/U.S.-Soviet relations,
views on, 160-63, 167
labor movement and, 154, 158,
172, 180, 186
legacy of, 181-82
New Left, views on, 155, 158,
161-64
1972 presidential election and,
131, 148, 149, 151, 154-58,
160-72, 175-77, 181-83
1976 presidential election and,
180-81, 186
1988 presidential election and,
205-6
Vietnam War and, 154, 156-58,
160-61, 166-70

Jackson, Jesse, 214-15, 238
  Clinton, differences with, 218-
    19, 223
  Dukakis, alliance with, 203-6,
    209, 218
  1972 presidential election and,
    174
  1988 presidential election and,
    199, 201, 203-6, 209-10
  1992 presidential election and,
    207, 211-12, 218-19
  Rainbow Coalition and, 218, 219
Jeffrey, Milly, 16
Johnson, Lyndon B., 40
  civil rights and, 4-9, 11, 13, 23,
    25, 33-35, 64-65, 164, 227
  decision not to seek second term,
    98, 119-20
  "dump Johnson" movement, 49,
    55-58, 60-62, 67, 69-73,
    80-86, 89, 91-94, 104-5
  Great Society of, 32, 51, 54, 55,
    63
  labor movement and, 4, 7, 10,
    23-24, 62-65, 69, 71, 95,
    99
  Mississippi Freedom Democratic
    Party and, 3, 5-9, 11, 13,
    23, 25
  New Left and, 23-26, 32-34, 39,
    73, 75, 76
  1964 presidential election and, 3-
    9, 11, 13, 23, 25, 77, 108
  1968 presidential election and,
    45, 49, 55-58, 60-75, 80-
    86, 88-95, 97-99, 104-5,
    108, 110-12, 117, 119-20
  Vietnam War and, 27, 28, 32-35,
    39, 46, 51-58, 60-74, 76,

    80, 81, 86, 88-91, 93, 98-
    99, 103, 107, 117, 119-20,
    127, 166
Jones, Jeff, 127

Kaiser, Charles, 82-83, 89, 90
Kampelman, Max, 6, 173
Karynytcky, Adrian, 217-18
Kaufman, Arnold S., 92-93
Kazin, Michael, 146-47
Kemble, Penn, 141-43, 181, 217-18
Kempton, Murray, 94
Kennedy, Edward M. (Ted), 190
  1968 presidential election and,
    112
  1980 presidential election and,
    191
  Vietnam War and, 157
Kennedy, John F., 32, 100, 204
  1960 presidential election and,
    188, 191
  Vietnam War and, 166
Kennedy, Robert F.
  assassination of, 99, 101, 102,
    104, 107
  McCarthy feud with, 88, 91-92,
    94-100, 102, 104, 107,
    108
  New Democratic Coalition and
    supporters of, 134-35
  1968 presidential election and,
    49, 70, 72, 79, 81, 88, 91-
    102, 104, 107, 108, 121,
    129, 155
  presidential candidacy announced
    by, 91-93
  Vietnam War and, 35, 46, 52,
    79, 88, 93, 98
Keyserling, Leon, 64-65

King, Ed, 7, 8, 10
King, Martin Luther, Jr., 7, 22, 28,
    79
    Mississippi Freedom Democratic
        Party and, 10-15
    "New Politics" convention
        (Chicago, 1967) and, 36-
        38, 45
    1964 presidential election and,
        10-15
    1968 presidential election and,
        29, 36, 37, 45, 70, 81
    1972 presidential election and, 178
    Vietnam War and, 33-37
Kinoy, Arthur, 15
Kirk, Paul, 206-7
Kirkpatrick, Jeane, 3-4, 178
    McGovern Commission reforms
        and, 140-41, 144
Klein, Joe, 229
Kopkind, Andrew, 207
Kramer, Michael, 214
Kristol, William, 235
Kunstler, William, 15

Labor movement, 3, 42, 134, 158,
    177, 187, 191. *See also* in-
    dividual unions   and
    leaders
    Clinton and, 214-15, 231, 236
    Committee on Political Educa-
        tion, 180
    Humphrey and, 5-7, 10, 12, 99,
        103, 131, 133, 149, 150,
        171, 172
    Jackson (Scoop) and, 154, 158,
        172, 180, 186
    Johnson and, 4, 7, 10, 23-24, 62-
        65, 69, 71, 95, 99

McGovern Commission reforms
    and, 139-40, 144, 172
Mondale and, 196-97
NAFTA and, 231
New Democratic Coalition and,
    135
1980s changes in, 181-82, 198
1990s changes in, 235-38
Vietnam War and, 52, 53, 62-65,
    69, 71, 74
Lake, Anthony, 217
Lasch, Christopher, 128-30
Leadership Conference on Civil
    Rights, 227
Lens, Sid, 120
Lerner, Max, 203
Lesher, Stephan, 148, 151
Levison, Stanley, 35
Lewis, John, 19
Liberation, 116
Lindsay, John, 149, 164
Lipset, Seymour Martin, 97-98
Loeb, James, 65, 92
Loeb, William, 170
Low, Robert A., 154-55
Lowenstein, Allard
    background of, 54-55
    "dump Johnson" movement and,
        49, 55-58, 60-62, 67, 69,
        71-72, 80-86, 89, 91-92,
        94, 104-5
    Mississippi Freedom Democratic
        Party and, 14
    National Lawyers Guild and, 17
    1964 presidential election and,
        14, 15
    Vietnam War and, 52, 55-62, 66,
        67, 69, 71-72, 78, 81, 82,
        165

Lowndes County Freedom Organization, 25
Lucey, Pat, 173

McCarran Internal Security Act, 153
McCarthy, Eugene F., 156
   Humphrey endorsed by, 133
   Kennedy feud with, 88, 91-92, 94-100, 102, 104, 107, 108
   McGovern Commission reforms and, 137-38, 142
   New Democratic Coalition and supporters of, 134-35
   New Hampshire triumph, 88-91, 93, 96, 108
   1968 presidential election and, 49, 72-75, 77-80, 82-104, 107-14, 116-18, 121, 122, 124, 125, 128, 129, 133, 137-39, 155
   presidential candidacy announced by, 83, 92, 93
   Unit Rule reform and, 109-14
   Vietnam War and, 52, 77-80, 83, 84, 88-91, 93, 95, 98, 102-3, 109, 113, 114, 121, 128
McCarthy, Joseph, 153
McCormack, John, 16-17
McCoy, Tom, 111
McCurdy, Dave, 217, 233
McGovern, George, 188, 204, 209, 238
   background of, 151-53
   Cold War/U.S.-Soviet relations, views on, 158-60, 166
   Communism and, 151-53, 158-60, 166
   Eagleton withdraws as running mate, 179

McGovern Commission (Commission on Party Structure and Delegate Selection) reforms, 136-45, 170-72, 174-75
McGovern-Hatfield Amendment, 169
   New Democratic Coalition and supporters of, 134-35
   1968 presidential election and, 72, 81-83, 112, 113, 122, 126, 143
   1972 presidential election and, 49, 131, 143, 145, 149-52, 154, 158-60, 164-66, 169-80, 184, 212, 213, 234
   Vietnam War and, 52, 82, 113, 126, 131, 142, 151, 152, 165-66, 169-71, 179, 212
   as Wallace (Henry) supporter in 1948 presidential election, 151-52
McGrory, Mary, 94, 110
MacLaine, Shirley, 173, 176
McNamara, Robert, 33, 80
McNaughton, John, 33
Maddox, Lester, 113-14
Magaziner, Ira, 232, 233
Mailer, Norman, 119
Malcolm X, 79
Manchester Union Leader, 170
Mandler, Peter, 84
Maoist Progressive Labor Party group, 179
Mao Tse-tung, 16
Marcuse, Herbert, 76-78
Marx, Karl, 16, 77
Meany, George, 154
"Meet the Press," 165

Michigan Law Review, 224
Minor, Ethel, 31
Mississippi Freedom Democratic
      Party (MFDP), 2-3, 5-16,
      18-20, 22, 24-25, 70, 102
Mitchell, Stephen A., 108-14, 153-
      54
"Mobe, the" (National Mobilization
      to End the War in Viet-
      nam), 115-16, 120, 125
Moe, Richard, 197
Mondale, Walter, 90
   background of, 195
   civil rights and, 8, 11, 196
   labor movement and, 196-97
   Mississippi Freedom Democratic
      Party and, 8, 11
   1964 presidential election and, 8,
      11
   1976 presidential election and,
      186, 187
   1984 presidential election and,
      195-98
   1988 presidential election and,
      199
   women's movement and, 196
Montoya, Joseph M., 110
Morley, Jefferson, 213
Moses, Henry, 10
Moses, Robert, 4-5, 17-18, 20-22
   Mississippi Freedom Democratic
      Party and, 10-14
Moynihan, Daniel Patrick, 84
Muhammad, Elijah, 31
Mundt, Karl, 153
Mundt-Nixon Bill, 153
Munro, Sterling, 155
Muravchik, Joshua, 142, 143, 181,
      213, 217-18

Muskie, Edmund
   1972 presidential election and,
      145, 148-49, 154-55, 164,
      169, 170
   Vietnam War and, 169, 170
Muskie, Jane, 148
Myers, Dee Dee, 223

NAACP (National Association for
      the Advancement of Col-
      ored People), 20, 35
   Mississippi Freedom Democratic
      Party and, 14
   1964 presidential election and,
      14, 22
NAFTA (North American Free
      Trade Agreement), 231-32,
      236
Nasser, Gamel Abdul, 29-30
Nation, the, 39, 48, 207, 213
National Conference for New Poli-
      tics (NCNP). *See* "New
      Politics" convention
National Council of Churches, 14
National Education Association
National Guardian, 21
National Journal, 139
National Lawyers Guild, 6, 15, 17-
      20
National Mobilization to End the
      War in Vietnam ("the
      Mobe"), 115-16, 120, 125
National Organization for Women
      (NOW), 196
National Student Association, 55
Nation of Islam (Black Muslims), 31
NBC, 165
NBC/ *Wall Street Journal* poll on 1988
      presidential election, 208

Negotiation Now!, 36, 63, 71
Nelson, Gaylord, 173
Neuman, Tom, 125
New Democratic Coalition (NDC),
    134-36
Newfield, Jack, 83-84, 91, 92
New Left, 148, 180. *See also* individ-
    ual leaders and organizations
  birth of, 3
  Chicago Convention (1968)
      street demonstrations, 103,
      114-29, 131, 137-38, 176
  Communism and, 19, 38, 39, 44,
      47, 56-58, 78, 79, 84-85,
      102
  Jackson's (Scoop's) views on, 155,
      158, 161-64
  Johnson and, 23-26, 32-34, 39,
      73, 75, 76
  Marcuse's influence on, 76-78
  "New Politics" convention
      (Chicago, 1967), 26-29,
      36-49, 70
  1968 presidential election and,
      87-88, 102, 103, 107, 114-
      27
  1972 presidential election and,
      135, 155, 158, 161-64,
      179
  Vietnam War and, 26, 32-34, 39,
      45-47, 49, 53, 56-58, 61,
      76-79, 107, 114-27
Newman, Paul, 90
"New Politics" convention (Chicago,
    1967), 26-29, 70
  details of, 36-49
New Politics movement, 183
  McGovern Commission (Com-
      mission on Party Structure

and Delegate Selection) re-
    forms, 136-45, 170-72,
    174-75
New Democratic Coalition
    (NDC), 134-36
"New Politics" convention
    (Chicago, 1967), 26-29,
    36-49, 70
New Republic, 211
Newsweek, 16, 18-19
Newton, Huey, 26
New York Post, 68, 223
New York Review of Books, 128
New York Times, 35-36, 217, 222,
    233
New York Times/CBS poll
  on 1980 presidential election,
      191
  on 1988 presidential election,
      208-9
New York Times Magazine, 40
Nixon, Richard M., 145, 216
  Mundt-Nixon Bill and, 153
  1968 presidential election and,
      70, 96, 99-101, 104, 105,
      117, 126, 128-30, 133-34
  1972 presidential election and,
      167, 169-71, 178-80, 184
  pardoned by Ford, 184-85
  resignation of, 184
  Vietnam War and, 100, 128,
      167, 169-70
  Watergate scandal, 184-85, 187,
      188, 198
North, Oliver, 198
North American Free Trade Agree-
    ment (NAFTA), 231-32,
    236
Novak, Robert, 16-18, 165, 223

Index

NOW (National Organization for
    Women), 196
Nunn, Sam, 209, 210, 233-35, 239

O'Brien, Larry, 136, 143-44, 172,
    173
O'Donnell, Ken, 6-7
Oglesby, Carl, 53, 75-76
    anti-McCarthy speech of, 77-79
O'Hara, James, 136
O'Hara Commission, 136, 140

Pageant, 60
Parmet, Herbert, 79-80, 89, 109,
    111, 134, 139-40
Patrick, Deval, 226
Pepper, William F., 36
Peretz, Anne Farnsworth, 27-28, 87
Peretz, Martin, 31-32, 208
    background of, 27-28
    Jackson-Dukakis alliance, com-
        ments on,207
    McCarthy supported by, 79, 86-
        88, 103, 128
    "New Politics" convention 1967)
        and, 27-29, 36-37, 42, 44,
        46
Perle, Richard, 181
Perot, Ross, 220, 231
Peterson, Don, 109-10
Phillips, Kevin, 184, 185
Playboy, 159-60, 165-66
Podhoretz, Norman, 141
Populist Persuasion, The (Kazin),
    146-47
Potter, Paul, 76
Powell, Colin, 221, 235, 239
Progressive Policy Institute (PPI),
    209, 214

Rabinowitz, Joni, 18
Rabinowitz, Victor, 18
Rainbow Coalition, 218, 219
Ramparts, 35, 43
Randolph, A. Philip, 36
Raspberry, William, 212
Raskin, Marc, 24
Rauh, Joseph, 36
    anti-Communist stance of, 4-5
    McGovern Commission reforms
        and, 137
    Mississippi Freedom Democratic
        Party and, 5-7, 9-11, 14-
        16, 20, 22-24, 102
    1964 presidential election and, 4-
        7, 9-11, 14-17, 20-24,
        102, 137
    1968 presidential election amd,
        69-73, 84-85, 87, 90, 92,
        95
    Vietnam War and, 52, 62, 69-74,
        84-85, 95
Rayburn, Sam, 153
Reagan, Ronald, 80, 145, 148, 204,
    205
    anti-Communist policy of, 194-
        96, 199, 206, 212
    Central America and, 193-94,
        196, 198, 206, 222
    domestic policy of, 192, 194-98
    foreign policy of, 192-96, 198-
        99, 206, 212, 222
    Iran-Contra affair, 198-99
    1968 presidential election and,
        85
    1976 presidential election and,
        180, 185-88
    1980 presidential election and,
        189, 191-92

Reagan, Ronald, (*continued*)
  1984 presidential election and,
    134, 194-98
  1988 presidential election and,
    198, 200, 206, 207, 212
  "Reagan Democrats," 134, 181,
    189, 191, 196, 207, 215-
    17
  "Reaganomics," 192, 194-98
Real Majority, The (Scammon and
    Wattenberg), 146, 147,
    155
Reed, Bruce, 230-31
Reich, Robert, 236
Reno, Janet, 220
Reuther, Victor, 64-65
Reuther, Walter, 6, 10-12, 15, 142
Ribicoff, Abraham, 122, 173
Robb, Chuck, 209
Roche, John P.
  ADA, resigns from, 95
  Vietnam War and, 62, 64-65, 67-
    68, 71-72
Rockefeller, Nelson, 184
Rockwell, George Lincoln, 40
Rolling Stone, 183-84
Roosevelt, Franklin Delano, 3, 63,
    65, 141, 160, 204, 237
Roosevelt, Theodore, 220
Rosenberg, Marvin, 102
Rosenthal, A. M., 204
Rowe, Jim, 6
Rubin, Jerry, 116, 120, 123, 125,
    126, 176
Rubin, Samuel, 18
Russell, Carlos, 39, 44
Rustin, Bayard, 35, 36, 67
  Mississippi Freedom Democratic
    Party and, 7, 9-15

  Vietnam War and, 53, 64-65

Safire, William, 206
Samstein, Mendy, 13-15
Sanders, Ed, 123
SANE Nuclear Policy Committee,
    38, 53
Savimbi, Jonas, 206
Savio, Mario, 26
Scammon, Richard M., 146, 147,
    155
SCEF (Southern Conference Educa-
    tion Fund), 19-20
Scheer, Robert, 43, 44
Schlesinger, Arthur M., Jr., 87, 92,
    102
  Carter, comments on, 189
  Humphrey, comments on, 99-
    101
  Johnson, comments on, 51, 68
  McCarthy, comments on, 104
  Vietnam War and, 57, 65-66, 68,
    72, 73, 82
SCLC. *See* Southern Christian Lead-
    ership Conference
SDS. *See* Students for a Democratic
    Society
Seabury, Paul, 64-65
Seale, Bobby, 117, 122-23
Shah of Iran, 189
Shalala, Donna, 224
Shanker, Al, 218
Sheinbaum, Stanley, 143-44
Sherrod, Charles, 11-12, 15
Siegel, Fred, 202
Simon, Paul, 199
Sirhan, Sirhan, 99
Six-Day War (June 1967), 27, 29-31
Smith, Benjamin, 18

Smith, Roland, 36
SNCC. *See* Student Nonviolent Co-
    ordinating Committee
Socialist Workers Party, 39
Somoza Debayle, Anastasio, 189,
    194
Souljah, Sister, 218-19
Southern Christian Leadership Con-
    ference (SCLC), 28
    Mississippi Freedom Democratic
        Party and, 11
    "New Politics" convention
        (Chicago, 1967) and, 39
    1964 presidential election and,
        11
    Vietnam War and, 35, 36
Southern Conference Education
    Fund (SCEF), 19-20
Sperling, Gene, 230, 231
Spock, Benjamin, 28
    1968 presidential election and,
        29, 37, 45, 81
Stalin, Joseph, 161, 162
Stavis, Morty, 15
Stearns, Rick, 173
Stevenson, Adlai, 89, 108, 111
Stone, I. F., 89
Streicher, Julius, 31
Studds, Gerry, 91
Student Nonviolent Coordinating
    Committee (SNCC), 28,
    113
    "black power" and, 4
    Communism and, 6, 15-21, 44
    Mississippi Freedom Democratic
        Party and, 5-6, 10-16, 18
    "New Politics" convention
        (Chicago, 1967) and, 39,
        42, 44

1964 presidential election and, 4-
    6, 10-21
Six-Day War (June 1967) and,
    30-31
SNCC *Newsletter,* 31-32
Students for a Democratic Society
    (SDS), 75, 135, 138
    Chicago Convention (1968) street
        demonstrations and, 116-
        21, 123, 124, 126, 127
    Communism and, 19, 58
    importance of, 120-21
    1964 presidential election and,
        77
    1968 presidential election and,
        77-79, 87, 116-21, 123,
        124, 126, 127
    1972 presidential election and,
        179
    "Port Huron" statement, 26
    Vietnam War and, 26, 53, 58,
        76-79, 116-21, 123, 124,
        126, 127, 179
    "Weatherman" faction, 127
Studies on the Left, 54
Stulberg, Louis, 64-65, 95
Sweeney, John, 235-36, 238

Taxman, Sharon, 226-27
Thelwell, Mike, 25
Thomas, Marlo, 176
Thomas, Norman, 35, 66, 127-28,
    141
Thompson, Hunter, 183-84
Time, 148-49, 165, 174-75, 186,
    203, 214
Toynbee, Arnold, 89
"Triumph of Tokenism, The"
    (Guinier), 224

Truman, Harry, 61, 141, 153, 160,
162
1948 presidential election and,
151, 152
Trumka, Richard, 236
Tsongas, Paul, 215
Twersky, David, 222
Tyler, Gus, 62-69, 72, 73

Unger, Debi, 94-95
Unger, Irwin, 94-95
United Automobile Workers (UAW)
1964 presidential election and, 4-
6, 10, 11
1968 presidential election and,
64-65, 69, 133
1972 presidential election and,
178
Vietnam War and, 52, 64-65, 69
United Federation of Teachers, 64-
65
United Mine Workers of America,
236
U.S. Congress, 230, 238-39
AFL-CIO report card on 94th
Congress, 180
Bradley and Nunn retirements,
significance of, 233-35
Congressional Black Caucus, 226
Congressional Quarterly, 167
Congressional Record, 21
Cooper-Church Amendment,
168
Gulf of Tonkin Resolution, 54
House Committee on Un-Ameri-
can Activities, 5, 153
House Judiciary Committee, 185
Humphrey-Hawkins Full Em-
ployment bill, 190

Iran-Contra affair and, 198
McGovern-Hatfield Amendment,
169
NAFTA, passage of, 231-32
1994 congressional elections, 233
Senate Foreign Relations Com-
mittee, 54
U.S.-Grenada Friendship Society,
222-23
U.S. News and World Report, 227
U.S. Peace Council, 222
United Steelworkers of America, 95,
140
Unruh, Jesse, 112
Urban League, 35

Vanden Heuvel, Jean, 35
Vanden Heuvel, William, 35
Vietnam Day Committee, 76
Vietnam Mobilization Committee
(VMC), 34-35
Vietnam Moratorium Committee,
142
Vietnam War, 15, 183-84
amnesty for war-resisters proposed, 171
antiwar movement, 2, 22, 26-28,
32-37, 39, 45-47, 49, 52-
74, 76-86, 88-91, 93, 95,
98-103, 107, 109, 112-29,
131, 133, 134, 137-38,
142, 151, 152, 154, 157,
165-71, 176, 178, 179,
212, 222
bombing policy, 33, 53, 58, 60-
62, 88, 98, 113, 166
Cambodia, U.S. troops in, 167
ceasefire proposed, 56, 62, 167,
169

Chicago Convention (1968)
  street demonstrations, 103,
  114-29, 131, 137-38, 176
Communism and, 53, 56-60, 62,
  66, 72, 78, 84-85, 123,
  158, 160-61, 167, 222
Cooper-Church Amendment,
  168
cost of, 32
elections proposed, 56, 57, 59,
  61, 169
Gulf of Tonkin Resolution, 54
Johnson and, 27, 28, 32-35, 39,
  46, 51-58, 60-74, 76, 80,
  81, 86, 88-91, 93, 98-99,
  103, 107, 117, 119-20,
  127, 166
McGovern-Hatfield Amendment,
  169
march on the Pentagon (1967),
  119
National Liberation Front (NLF),
  56-57, 59, 61, 62, 79, 88,
  113, 118, 169
negotiations proposed, 56, 59-63,
  89, 156, 167, 169
origins of Democratic Party split
  over, 51-74
POWs, 169, 179
Tet offensive, 90, 95, 118
Vietcong, 33, 34, 37, 57-59, 78,
  79, 85, 118, 157
"Vietnam syndrome" legacy of
  the war, 193, 196, 198
withdrawal proposed, 58, 63,
  113, 166-69, 179
Viguerie, Richard, 147
Village Reform Democrats, 84
Viorst, Milton, 159-60, 165-66

Virginia Law Review, 224
VMC (Vietnam Mobilization Committee), 34-35
Voting Rights Act of 1965, 4, 14,
  23, 24

Wade, Richard, 137
Walker Commission, 115, 125-26
Wallace, George, 156, 158, 189
  attempted assassination of, 145,
  150-51, 170-71
  new populism espoused by, 145-
  49, 151
  1968 presidential election and,
  133-34, 145
  1972 presidential election and,
  145-51, 164, 165, 170-71,
  177
  1976 presidential election and,
  185-86
  Vietnam War and, 170
Wallace, Henry A., 5, 73, 84, 85,
  160, 204
  Communism and 1948 presidential election, 151-52
Wall Street Journal, 224
Wall Street Journal/NBC poll
  on 1988 presidential election, 208
Walzer, Michael, 28
Washington Post, 2, 36, 177, 205,
  215, 219
Waskow, Arthur I., 24, 124, 125,
  127
  "New Politics" convention
  (Chicago, 1967) and, 38-
  45, 47-48
Watergate scandal, 184-85, 187,
  188, 198

Wattenberg, Ben J., 96, 170, 203-4,
217
as Jackson's (Scoop's) campaign
manager, 155-58, 162,
181
Real Majority, The, 146, 147, 155
Watts, J. C., 235
Weber, Vin, 231
Wechsler, James A., 68, 95, 96
Weisbrot, Robert, 26
Weiss, Cora, 18
Weiss, Ted, 46
Westmoreland, William, 80
Wilkins, Roy, 22, 34-36
Mississippi Freedom Democratic
Party and, 14
Williams, Debra, 226-27
Williams, Juan, 2, 10
Williams, Robert F., 18
Wines, Michael, 233
Witcover, Jules, 197
Women for Peace, 123
Women's movement
Mondale and, 196

National Organization for
Women (NOW), 196
1972 presidential election and,
172-73
1984 presidential election and,
196
Women for Peace, 123
Woodcock, Leonard, 178
Woodward, C. Vann, 19

Yippies (Youth International Party)
1968 presidential election and,
114, 116, 118, 123
1972 presidential election and, 176
Young, Andrew, 14, 28, 35
Mississippi Freedom Democratic
Party and, 14
"New Politics" convention
(Chicago, 1967) and, 46
1964 presidential election and, 14
Vietnam War and, 35
Young, Nigel, 119
Young, Whitney, 35, 36
Young People's Socialist League, 142